Knowing Dil Das

Contemporary Ethnography

Series Editors
Dan Rose
Paul Stoller

A complete list of books in the series
is available from the publisher.

Knowing Dil Das

Stories of a Himalayan Hunter

Joseph S. Alter

दिल दास

PENN

University of Pennsylvania Press

Philadelphia

10 9 8 7 6 5 4 3 2 1

Published by
University of Pennsylvania Press
Philadelphia, Pennsylvania 19104-4011

Library of Congress Cataloging-in-Publication Data
Alter, Joseph S.
Knowing Dil Das : stories of a Himalayan hunter / Joseph S. Alter.
p.   cm. — (Contemporary ethnography)
Includes bibliographical references and index.
ISBN 0-8122-3524-X (cloth: alk. paper). — ISBN 0-8122-1712-8 (paper: alk. paper).
1. Ethnology—India—Garhwāl.   2. Das, Dil, d. 1986.   3. Garhwāl (India) Biography.
4. Culture conflict—India—Garhwāl.   5. Friendship—India—Garhwāl.   6. Hunters—
India—Garhwāl Biography.   I. Title.   II. Series.
GN635.I4A727   1999
305.8′00954—dc21   99-32283
                                                                        CIP

For Gerry
and
for Betsy

In other words, is there a mythology of the mythologist? No doubt, and the reader will easily see where I stand. But to tell the truth, I don't think that this is quite the right way of stating the problem. "Demystification"—to use a word which is beginning to show signs of wear—is not an Olympian operation. What I mean is that I cannot countenance the traditional belief which postulates a natural dichotomy between the objectivity of the scientist and the subjectivity of the writer, as if the former were endowed with a "freedom" and the latter with a "vocation" equally suitable for spiriting away or sublimating the actual limitations of their situation. What I claim is to live to the full the contradiction of my time, which may well make sarcasm the condition of truth.

—Roland Barthes, *Mythologies*, tr. Lavers, 1957 [1972], p. 12

No one will deny that in questions of historic authenticity *hearsay* does not equal *eye-witness*; for in the latter the eye of the observer apprehends the substance of that which is observed, both in time when and in the place where it exists, whilst hearsay has its peculiar drawbacks. But for these, it would even be preferable to eye-witness; for the object of eye-witness can only be *actual* momentary existence, whilst hearsay comprehends alike the present, the past, and the future, so as to apply in a certain sense both to that which *is* and to that which is *not* (i.e., which either has ceased to exist or has not yet come into existence). Written tradition is one of the species of hearsay—we might almost say, the most preferable. How could we know the history of nations but for the everlasting monuments of the pen?

—Alberuni, *Alberuni's India*, tr. Edward Sachau, 1030 [1964], p. 3

Contents

Preface

This book is about the life of Dil Das, a North Indian villager who was
born in the lower ranges of the Himalayas. Although Dil Das spent most
of his life as a peasant farmer raising buffaloes and selling their milk,
and was poor by almost any standard, most of the stories he told were
not about everyday life, but about great adventures. Shooting tigers
and leopards with kings, princes, and politicians; trekking into the high
Himalayas with missionary families; traveling to Nepal to join an American friend in building and running a luxury resort in a wildlife refuge;
and endless tales about friendship and hunting that seemed to have
nothing to do with culture as such, but a great deal to do with the history of colonialism. What I have set out to do in this book is make sense
of this very local, very personal history of colonialism and the relationship therein between culture and a biography of encounter. As such,
this book is about the problematic, intimate interface of difference in
the postcolonial world. It is about the meaning of friendship between
Anglo-Saxon Protestant missionary men and a low-caste Hindu peasant,
people who, if left to their own devices, would be regarded as coming
from worlds apart, even though they spent most of their lives together.

Since I am a son of a missionary, and a long time friend of a low-caste
peasant, as well as an anthropologist who has conducted field research in
the village where Dil Das was born, this book is also about the problematic interface of ethnography and colonial or postcolonial encounter. It
deals directly with the moral ambiguity of writing and living in a field of
power where, despite intimacy, self and other are not equal; where the
legacy of colonialism relentlessly undermines the praxis of friendship,
and where a condition of friendship makes anthropology, if not impossible, at least morally violent. This book is, therefore, about the limits
of friendship and knowledge; about the way in which missionary lives
defined a structure of power in which Dil Das lived, through which he
spoke, and, I think, as a consequence of which he died. This book is,

therefore, about both the heroics of representation and the tragedy of encounter.

As I recorded Dil Das's stories, and in subsequent reflections on his life, I came to realize that it was impossible to make sense of him, to write his story that is, in terms of any standard ethnographic categories. One could read his life in purely ethnographic terms, and extract from it pieces which, when fit together, would make sense in terms of peasant life in North India, caste hierarchy in North India, social change in North India, or some other phraseology of social science. But this is not the point. That some might blithely engage in such an endeavor is the point of my contention, for Dil Das simply did not clearly stand for any discrete social reality—regional, national, historical, or ethnographic. He defied classification, and my efforts at classification seemed to undermine precisely that which made him human. Moreover, as I experimented with various methods of representing his life, it became clear that I could not extricate myself from the text without doing a great deal of violence to his narrative. In telling stories about himself, Dil Das was telling stories in which I was directly implicated, not as an ethnographer but as a family friend.

Because Dil Das tells his story to, through, and with missionaries, a word is in order on this category of person. In North India in general, and the town of Mussoorie near Dil Das's village in particular—but also probably everywhere—there are missionaries and there are missionaries. Some are blinded by faith and preoccupied with their own spiritual convictions, but there are others who, while deeply motivated by their beliefs, are more concerned with resolving worldly problems. They have profound faith in the prospect that, in the end, the human spirit will prevail. Among missionaries such as these there is little talk of salvation, as such, and even less preaching per se, but there is a deep, undying faith in basic human goodness. Most of the missionaries Dil Das encountered and befriended were of this kind, some more radical than others, but all involved in social work and reform of some sort. And so there are few if any religious undertones to the stories he tells. There is no search for God. There are, however, very strong humanitarian overtones.

And it is here, despite the virtue of goodness and faith in human kindness, where I see a problem of moral ambiguity and political impropriety. I see a problem in the work of social reform, development work, and various kinds of community service that are predicated on the universality of human experience in a starkly differentiated, hierarchical world where inequality and injustice are constantly reproduced. I take it on faith, following Nietzsche and Foucault—as well as Marx—that we create our own history, but we do not live the history we create. And so the larger consequences of our actions are hardly ever manifest in the specific goals of our intent. As good-intentioned, liberal, often radical humanists, those of us implicated in the stories Dil Das told are fundamentally "nice people," if such a normal category is able to exist in a world whose postmodern logic makes self-definition virtually impossible. However, there is also something fundamentally wrong with the consequences of our actions.

Had Dil Das been the target of a successful evangelical project, it would be easy and perhaps reassuring to squarely lay the blame and clearly define the criteria of condemnation. Had he been obviously exploited by landlords or alienated through the interests of venture capitalism, one could voice any number of clearly articulated protests, and chart a clear course of action. Had he only been an outcast, and simply been made to suffer the stigma of oppressive untouchability, it would be easy to envision an alternative world of justice and equality. But when inequality and injustice are intertwined with friendship, and when extreme differences in wealth, power, and status are, in some sense, the criteria of intimacy, rather than its undoing, one is dealing with a very different animal. This animal appears tame and docile enough—even friendly—but is, in fact, more dangerous in spite of itself, and for that very reason. I can only ask those of this species who are explicitly implicated in this book to realize that my intention is not to blame or "bad name" anyone, but to in some way come to terms with a problem of moral justice for which I feel directly responsible; a beastly problem of justice which elides the civilizing rhetoric of human virtue.

What I have written is based on Dil Das's memory, Dil Das's imagination, and my own situated knowledge. Contrary to what anthropology requires, and what good judgment demands, I have made absolutely no attempt to corroborate anything Dil Das said about other people. I am sure that much of what he said is true. I am also sure that he fabricated a great many of the stories in which many of his friends figure prominently. While I make no apology for what I have written, I must apologize to those people in Dil Das's life—Ernie Campbell, Ray Smith, and John Coapman in particular, Dil Das's boyhood friends and fellow hunters; to Robert C. Alter and Ellen Alter, my parents, Stephen Alter and Andrew Alter, my brothers, and by extension my whole family; to Ratnu, Sheri, Rukam, and Tara, Dil Das's brothers; to Azad and Sunder, his nephews; to Abloo, Tulasi, and Jankhi, his uncles; and to his last wife Rani Devi and daughter, Gura. I have no doubt that John Coapman, Ray Smith and Ernie Campbell in particular would remember the things they did with Dil Das in very different ways.

With regard to my own situated knowledge, I fully concede that I have, in some sense, appropriated Dil Das's voice and have translated a heroic autobiography into a biography that seeks to communicate more

than just a life story. If Dil Das had had his way, for example, the title of
this book would be simply *Tiger*. But that would have led to entrapment
and capture, to a fiction of untamed freedom, or, worse still, to extinc-
tion. The story I have written is, therefore, a story of half-truths, partial
knowledge, and inevitable distortions. In this sense it is based on and
reproduces hearsay rather than eyewitness. As such, following the epi-
graphs from Alberuni and Barthes, it suggests a different way of seeing
more truly whole realities.

The structure I have imposed on Dil Das's narrative is completely
contrived from start to finish. Therefore, it is particularly important to
present, at the outset, the research method I designed to produce Dil
Das's narrative, a history of my analysis of the narrative text, and a brief
genealogy of my thinking on the subject as a whole.

During the summer of 1985 I spent three months at my family's estate
in the Himalayan town of Mussoorie, and at Dil Das's home seven kilometers away in the village of Pathreni, recording the stories Dil Das told
about himself. I told him that I was interested in recording his life, and
then captured everything he said on tape. I also kept a journal of what
else we did, which included going on hunting trips, attending weddings,
participating in ritual events, dropping in on friends, and walking to
town to pick up supplies.

Dil Das's style of narration was enigmatic to say the least. It was often
very difficult to know when he was telling a story—as opposed to just
talking—and virtually impossible, at times, to disentangle beginnings,
middles, and ends. He would often indicate when he wanted the tape
recorder on, and was always aware of the machine's presence. So it is
possible to say that Dil Das's discourse, no matter how rambling and disengaged, was always, or at least almost always, consciously and thematically structured. Nevertheless, I recorded long passages that, when tran-
scribed literally, read like a rambling collection of words, half sentences,
and exclamations and made little sense. Many of the more readily comprehensible tales are pithy, devoid of context, and frankly anecdotal.
And yet, at times, Dil Das told very coherent stories that are easier to
understand and locate within a biographical framework. Even so, these
biographical fragments are often so full of intimate (as opposed to local)
knowledge that they would be virtually incomprehensible to anyone unfamiliar with the larger context of our fused lives.

In response to my stated goals, Dil Das told me the story of his life,
but each story was clearly a unit unto itself—or else a meandering flow
of consciousness—and there was no discernable chronology or logical
progression to the tales he told. Significantly, however, the stories were
narrated while we were either sitting in his home or walking through
the mountains. It was, more often than not, the basic geography of the

forest around the village of Pathreni that gave the narrative a degree of coherence. It was our happenstance encounter with people, places, and things that triggered Dil Das's memory and thereby evoked a narrative structured by random nouns of the present rather than by history, life, or identity. When Dil Das told a story, I grunted, nodded, and otherwise showed that I was following the conversation, but I did not speak. Again, contrary to good ethnographic method, and perhaps even good manners, I did not ask questions or seek clarification. When he was not telling a story, we rarely if ever talked about the project.

Transcribing Dil Das's narrative was extremely difficult, and the exercise has contributed to my skepticism about the relationship between knowledge and truth. Although Dil Das was a master storyteller, it was difficult to produce a meaningful translation of stories that seemed caught halfway between memory and speech. To be sure, I could have sat down with Dil Das and clarified certain points. I could have asked him any number of things in order to start making sense of what he said while he spoke. But I wanted him to come as close as he possibly could to writing and that required a much higher degree of strategic silence than dialogic engagement; all of which may seem counterintuitive, but then again participant observation is precisely ambiguous on the critical point of communication.

I divided the 30 hours of narrative into 185 more or less cohesive tales. I translated each cassette tape, and then worked over each story numerous times in order to capture the meaning and flavor of the original telling. I then read through all the stories, in conjunction with my journal, in light of my memories, and experimented with various methods of classification. Early on I realized that chronology was not a very useful mode of organization. To follow the sequence of Dil Das, who told particular stories on the basis of what geography brought to mind—a rock here, a vista there, a *chan* (hamlet or cow shed) in the valley—was simply too enigmatic. In the end I organized the stories thematically. Then I went back to the original narrative text and merged the shortest, least coherent tales into congruent longer ones, and cut out a large number of redundancies. This left me with roughly one hundred stories, about 80 percent of which dealt with hunting.

My original goal in recording Dil Das's narrative had been to present Garhwali peasant culture through the eyes of one man, and so even in the early stages of translation, working in 1985 I was still not fully aware of the effect of Dil Das's commentary on my life and our shared past. I was, however, painfully aware of the fact that his story of hunting was not very useful, or noteworthy, as a document of culture. After Dil Das died in 1986, I had reached a point from which I could see no return, and not much future, so I put the project away.

I started rereading the stories again in 1992, this time from a completely new perspective. Rather than look for culture, I saw that Dil Das was talking against culture in order to produce what I am calling a hybrid history of encounter. From this viewpoint I could make sense of the narrative precisely in those terms which had earlier seemed to render it useless—his ambivalence toward dairying, his obsession with hunting, and above all his celebration of friendship. I have used these thematic categories to organize Dil Das's life story, but I have not selectively included stories in order to exaggerate the significance of certain themes.

Much as I would have liked to, it would be impractical to publish all the tales Dil Das told. I have therefore included about half the stories, primarily those which are least enigmatic and most coherent, while still keeping the basic thematic ratio of the original collection intact. The stories, therefore, are chosen on the basis of their own merit to provide a focused biographical synopsis. These are a representative sample of what I collected, and many of them are stories Dil Das told over and over again.

However, given the fact that my family and I figure in a significant number of the stories Dil Das told, I have chosen to include most of these and exclude those stories that refer to characters who appear far less often. This limits the number of personal names that come into play, and provides coherence, critical focus, and continuity to Dil Das's story of encounter. It should be abundantly clear that I have chosen to write about myself and my family for no other reason than because Dil Das chose to bring us into his narrative.

In translating Dil Das's life story into some kind of comprehensible, public knowledge I have strategically played with the context of meaning, played with what both Dil Das and I could take for granted. I have done this in order to entertain, to make sense, and also work out—in an autobiographical way—where exactly I stand in relation to the subject of this biography. On one level, though, I am just doing what Dil Das always did—spinning a good yarn in order to have some fun, make some sense of things, enjoy life, and pass the time. By extension I am fulfilling an obligation by writing a book I had promised to write. But it is a book that also, I hope, broadens the appeal of these stories, defines their context, and gives them permanent form—a kind of immortality about which I have ambivalent intimations. But as Dil Das often pointed out, "whatever else is said about anyone, good must be said about him. Something, anything good must be said on his behalf. Then, even when he dies he will stay alive."

*   *   *

This book is composed of four parts, whose titles are taken from the poet Tulsi Das's epic *Ramacaritmanas*. Part I, Bal Kand, the Book of Childhood, focuses on childhood memories of hunting in and around the American community of Landour, the village of Pathreni, and the hill station of Mussoorie. Part II, Aranya Kand, the Forest Book, deals with the time in Dil Das's life when he and John Coapman traveled and hunted together. Part III, Shram Kand, the Book of Labor, concerns the relationship between hunting, hard work, and the transactions of dairying in a petty-capitalist economy. Part IV, Uttarkhand, seeks the confluence of caste, class, colonialism, and friendship. Part I deals with boyhood adventures, Part II with a kind of forest exile, Part III with a return home to reality—if not Ayodhya per se—and Part IV simply with the perils of Himalayan life. Throughout it is a battle with demons and a search for something lost, as well as a devotional hymn of sorts. Parts I, II, and III each contain three chapters. The first chapter in each part is my reflections or background on some aspect of Dil Das's story. The second chapter in each part is a collection of stories told by Dil Das as I have translated them. Each part concludes with a short essay by me. In Part IV, Chapter 10 is in Dil Das's voice, and Chapter 11 is my reflections on the themes raised in Dil Das's life story.

Part I
Bal Kand

THE BOOK OF CHILDHOOD

Chapter 1
Dil Das—Enslaved Heart

Dil Das was a poor, low-caste, Himalayan peasant who defined himself, heroically, as a hunter of animals, and as a close friend of the missionary children he hunted with. I knew Dil Das progressively well from the time I was about ten as the son of American missionaries working in North India, until his death in 1986 when I was twenty-nine and he was about sixty.

Our families go way back, as they say—almost three generations. My grandparents and parents knew Dil Das and his father as *dudwallas*: men who delivered milk to our community. I knew Dil Das and his family first when I was growing up in North India between 1958 and 1977, and then, from 1980 on, as an anthropologist.

Dil Das was born in the Garhwali village of Pathreni about seven kilometers to the east of Mussoorie, a resort town or hill station, which gained prominence and jaded notoriety as a place for elite recreation and gay entertainment during the era of British imperialism. He was the son of an illiterate, untouchable basket-weaver who migrated south to the Himalayan foothills from a village near the source of the river Ganga. I was born in Mussoorie, in the Landour Community Hospital. My parents were among the American missionaries, who, for the past seventy years or so, have been, in various ways, associated with Woodstock, a Christian boarding school at the east end of town. Because Woodstock, and the people who went to Woodstock as teachers and students, came to play a central role in Dil Das's memory of himself, I must begin the story of a Garhwali villager by describing a rather strange permutation of Western lives.

I grew up in the curious, postcolonial environment of Landour where the culture was, until the late 1970s, equal parts North American midwestern Christian and British colonial. Woodstock, which largely defines this culture, was, for all practical purposes, an American prep school where one was far more likely to read Chaucer, Shakespeare, Whitman, and Poe than the great Indian poets like Valmiki, Mira, or Tulsi Das before being graduated to attend college in the United States—anything from Baptist bible college in the South to Ivy League university in the Northeast.

Academic conformity notwithstanding, it is hard to describe this environment exactly, because it was not what we thought it was. Imagine 350 predominantly white middle-class Protestant missionary children—and a large minority of elite, Westernized Indians—both groups born and raised in small out-of-the-way places and trying to be, in some way, and with various degrees of consciousness, American, while at the same time either unclear, critical, or simply confused about what being American meant. Who we were (and are, I suppose) is not so much people caught between two worlds, as people who are condemned to conceive of ourselves in terms of something that we are not; reluctant Americans who played basketball, joined the Boy Scouts and went trekking, listened to Elvis, Jimi Hendrix, and the Beatles, crowned May queens, and danced around the May Pole. We read Hemingway while taking Christian Endeavor retreats to a place called Satya Narayan, which means "God's Truth," and learned Christmas carols in languages our friends "at home" spoke in order to entertain grandparents who lived far away. We wore Levis and T-shirts, bell bottoms, tie-dyed *kurtas*, and Nehru jackets. And yet whenever I visited America (and even now after twenty years) it seems like a foreign country. It is all the more alien because it is supposed to be, in some fundamental way and despite extreme emotional ambivalence, home, that place that Woodstock sought to define but simply could not be because of where it was. Its location, 280 kilometers north of Delhi on the first range of the Himalayas, to be exact, was, less precisely, in a highly mythologized India. We imagined ourselves to be strangely yet concretely part of this India by virtue of birth and language on the one hand, and environment on the other—that which is born from the epic, utopian union of Father Land and Mother Tongue.

As an international school, Woodstock prided itself over the years on its multicultural environment. Growing up in this environment I took for granted that this pride was well founded. We did, after all, come into close, long-term contact with people whose "culture" put our own into critical perspective. For many of us English was not our first language. But looking back, it now seems that we had somehow convinced ourselves that our unique cross-cultural perspective on things was characteristic of an unbounded global world view when in fact it was simply a measure of our idiosyncratic modern insularity. Our "exposure" to different things was fairly complete. Along with the ritual priests at the Kedarnath temple, the lines of beggars at Rishikesh come to mind, as do the shepherds with their massive, barb-studded steel-collared *bho-*

tiya hounds, who herd flocks of sheep and goats down out of the alpine meadows into the lower valleys not far from the school. But "difference" as such was never really allowed to break down the fundamentals of a culture which, despite the input of people from all over the world, was strictly defined by a Christian world view and incipient First-World modernism.

Leaving aside, if I may judiciously employ Dil Das's profanity of choice, the narrow minded input of "sister-fucking evangelicals," perhaps there are some for whom Woodstock's liberal humanism has provided a global perspective, an international identity nervously compatible with the transnational nature of postmodernizing culture—and it is here where I would like to pay my debt. But it is also, and despite its best intentions, a provincial parochial place that has given birth to a form of shallow, sentimental Orientalism in which India, as a romantic ideal, fills a deep void left by our emotional ambivalence about being people without an identity. This Orientalism is not exactly the same as that which evolved in the purely imperial imagination and colonial experience of men like Sir Richard Burton or T. E. Lawrence. Our image of self and other was scaled down. It was less magically epic and more mystically intimate, but still implicated in the production of monumental difference.

Many of us who went to Woodstock enjoyed hiking, and the environment of the Himalayas is well suited to this form of recreation. Treks to particular mountains, springs, lakes, and rivers—Nag Tibba, Smith's Hole, Deodital, and the Aglar—would follow trails which, because they were meant for more practical and less leisure purposes, often led to and from villages. And so I suppose it is not surprising that these villages became, for us, part of a timeless, picturesque, natural landscape, named, to be sure, and populated by people whose names were often known, but experienced anonymously in purely aesthetic terms. In wood smoke and cow dung, carved wooden pillars and slate roofs, homemade water pipes and women's jewelry, even the wrinkles on an old man's face, or his calloused hands spinning wool into yarn, there was a curious melding of sensuality, knowledge, and intimate strangeness. In the 1970s we would have called it funky (which is, as one of my teachers rightly pointed out, a good "ethnographic" term). The everyday things of the people in these villages evoked, in those of us who lived in another world not far off, a sense of mystical intimacy with difference. There was also a sense in which this funky experience of the rustic, "grungy" character of the villagers came to represent, I think, some kind of basic Christian desire for that which was essentially good and uncorrupted in everyone. Not in so many words, of course, for that would break the spell, even for those of us who had critically secularized a faith we could not lose, but I think there was something about "camping out" in a humble cow shed—along with the ox and the ass, if you will—which, by bringing a search for self and God together in the imaginary, exotic space of village India, undermined the history of industrial progress—the spirit of capitalism, if you will—with a kind of passionate, discursive humanism, while giving to the obliquity of our Western, or Westernized lives, a certain meaningful significance.

On the surface Woodstock school and Pathreni village are worlds apart in every way, and yet it is in terms of Woodstock and his encounter with "alienated" Protestant missionary children that Dil Das tells his story. It is in this way that I, among others, am implicated in his narrative. And, symmetrically speaking, as an anthropologist with an incriminating past, I have implicated Dil Das in my own narrative by having chosen to tell my stories, both intellectual and personal, through an encounter with him and other Garhwali villagers.

But narratives are never whole realities, nor do stories always capture the truth. Sometimes narratives make reference to a reality about which nothing or very little is ever said, even though it is regarded, by all concerned, as being of fundamental importance. In Dil Das's case this unspoken fact of life—a cultural fact of immense importance, to be sure—was the absence of a son. He tried for many years to ensure that his name would be carried on. He only gave up hope for good when his third wife was diagnosed with cervical cancer, the same disease that had killed her two predecessors. But while holding on to hope, and then when giving it up, Dil Das did not speak about his failure. In fact, being without an heir was of so much significance that it did not need to be articulated. It simply was the single most important fact of life in an otherwise fictional domain of experience. It stands, therefore, in some sense, as the signified—the eyewitnessed but unspoken—of all the signifiers that follow. Much of what Dil Das did can be explained from this point of reference, for without a son he was both the object of pity and self-recrimination, but also more or less free to live for the moment, and for himself, rather than required by convention to invest in the future. However, the absence of a son also made Dil Das into a storyteller, a raconteur reflecting on the past rather than one looking to the future. And perhaps in telling stories to me he was talking to a son, of sorts, and also perhaps thereby constructing a legacy.

Dil Das knew, of course, that I was going to write a book about our conversations—his stories about me and mine about him. He had, I think, a great deal of fun telling these stories. And there is no denying the fact that he also derived—as have I—a great deal of satisfaction, and a feeling of enhanced self worth, from the project of writing as a whole. But he did not know, fully, how he would be written and read. And so, behind the heroic bravado and pure joy of "having lived a good life," as he put it, there is in Dil Das's voice, I think, a deep sense of self-doubt and pain—born of being poor and outcaste, of having not produced a son, of having been widowed three times, and of having wandered too far from home—that compelled him to spin a good yarn and take so much pride and pleasure in being something he was not quite. For my part I do not fully understand the implications of having written Dil Das out of a framework of pure friendship and into the ambiguous complicity of a text that promises more than simply a new perspective on us and them, me and him, being here and being there, by looking closely at the intimate questions of self-doubt that are born of encounter.

Dil Das was more than willing to narrate his life experiences since he prided himself on being a master raconteur. However, what gave him license to speak, as it were, was the fact that he was "unemployed" during the summer of 1985, and was not looking for work. His income came from a contract he had to deliver milk to the kitchen at Woodstock School, and he subcontracted this to his younger brother in exchange for a regular stipend. In any case, Dil Das was never too concerned with the routine of work and labor, and had, as we shall see, a rather ambivalent attitude toward his role in the peasant economy. All of which is to say that he had both the time and inclination to talk at great length with me about his past.

One of the reasons I originally wanted to record Dil Das's life was that he seemed to clearly represent a certain configuration of power. I have said that he was inherently impossible to classify, a point that I will explain momentarily, but he did, on the surface, appear to fit neatly into a network of labels generated by colonial and postcolonial discourses alike: intellectual, linguist, secular humanist reformer, Marxist, and post-structural cultural critic. These labels seemed to fix his identity in terms of the larger workings of the empire and its academic, administrative, national heirs. In these terms Dil Das was a Pahari, a person from the hills and mountains of northern Uttar Pradesh. By virtue of the language he spoke—among friends, family and neighbors—he was also a Garhwali. As an Auji or Baijgi, he belonged to a caste of drummers and musicians who also weave bamboo baskets. By virtue of this caste group's position in the hierarchy of other such groups, Dil Das was also an outcast; a stigmatized untouchable. Officially, therefore, he was a Harijan; a "child of god" in the apologetic nomenclature of modern, secular India and a Dalit in the Ambedkarite language of opposition to this nomenclature. Because of where he lived and what he did, as a tiller of the soil, he was a poor peasant who owned a small parcel of unproductive land. Consequently, he was a member of an exploited, disenfranchised underclass—a classic subaltern.

Given the weight and specificity of these myriad labels, one must legitimately ask what I mean by claiming that Dil Das defies classification. I mean that Dil Das resists these modes of classification. He tells a story that dismantles this configuration of power, a story of self against society while caught in a web of normative social facts. Ignoring the terms of caste and class, stigma and poverty, language and place, Dil Das called himself a *shikari*: a hunter. For him hunting was an obsession, an all-consuming passion that defined his identity. Significantly, he shared this obsession with a number of young men from the American missionary community in Landour, in particular Ernie Campbell and Ray Smith, but above all others John Coapman

I do not know when Dil Das first started hunting. It must have been when he was a young man, around 1947. However, it is very clear from the stories he tells that he soon began to identify closely with the young men from Woodstock School who came to the forest around his village to shoot pheasant, *kakar* (barking deer), *ghoral* (mountain goat), and leopard. To a degree in fact, but most significantly in Dil Das's memory, hunting merged his and the missionary boys' identities, and thereby superseded and rendered irrelevant all differences of class, caste, nationality, religion, and language. The intimate experience of hunting together radically decentered the prevailing structure of power and provided a means by which Dil Das could redefine himself outside the framework of normal classification.

The curious thing about hunting is that it seems strikingly incongruous to the encounter of missionaries and peasants, neither of whom are, in any sense, typical hunters. The political economy of hunting does not seem to make sense in terms either of an agrarian mode of production or a calling to save souls. Quite apart from blood sport as such, as a vocation, as a mode of production, and as a way of life, hunting is not particularly loaded with cultural meaning in twentieth-century North India. That is, it does not so much define a specific category of person as an arena of passion and infatuation. Precisely because of this, however, it does provide an alternative framework for self-perception and the construction of identity. Which means that when the sons of missionaries hunted with the son of a peasant in the lower Himalayas between 1940 and 1984 they were able to merge their self-images through hunting on neutral ground.

It is important to keep in mind that both peasants and missionaries were marginal actors—albeit to different degrees, and with different allegiances—in the drama of empire building, and that their encounter, as hunters in the jungles of northern India, was categorically different from the epic drama of colonial and precolonial blood sport: "the sport of kings." Hunting of this sort among the imperial elite was an activity conducted on a massive scale with scores of elephants, beaters, gun-bearers, scouts, cooks, porters, and valets. In pre-independence India, hunting was transformed into a fine art of excess in which the size of the bag—four tigers, five swamp deer, twelve boar, fifteen pheasant, eight peafowl, and two dozen rock pigeons, for example—had to keep pace with the scale of the expedition in a kind of frenetic leisure parody of subsistence. Along these lines, blood sport may be understood as a direct extension of imperial conquest, a kind of overt enactment of covert intentions, a ritualized and often dramatic penetration of the jungle to "bag a trophy"—to possess in that most final of all ways, by killing. Whatever else blood sport may be, it is, essentially, heroic to the point of self-parody; a leisure activity that underscores, and allegorically engenders, the moral economy of colonialism.

Despite what might be called the innocence of encounter in Dil Das's memory, it is, ultimately, the power-saturated significance of "the sport of kings" with which he must come to terms in his own narrative. He and his missionary compatriots hunted in the shadow of an imperial allegory that, in part, defined colonial identity at large. The freedom from structure and class while hunting in and around Mussoorie and Pathreni was meaningful, in the context of postindependence India, precisely because of the legacy of the colonial allegory. And the mutable space Dil Das and his friends had created always ran the risk of being subverted by the terms of this more literal metaphor of power. Moreover, as an adult, Dil Das hunted with rajas, maharajahs, and various members of the colonial and postcolonial elite. He became enamored of blood sport, and his own story is—ironically and tragically—constructed in terms of this imperial allegory of power. He tells his story within the rubric of "the sport of kings," and this raises the problematic question of where, in the end, does Dil Das—the hero of his own narrative—stand in relation to the colonial drama that inspired him. The missionaries with whom he hunted on the fringes of the empire were able, for the most part, to make their escape into nostalgia by leaving India and going "back home" to the United States. There they were able to retell—or strategically forget—the myth of complicity from a perspective that could ignore the implications of what they had done. Dil Das, in contrast, had no choice but to stay, and the complicity that had animated his narrative as it fused with theirs, became a half-story of tragic heroism and enslaved imagination. Until his death in 1986 he remained caught between memory, allegory, and the harsh reality of peasant life. He ended up telling a story about himself that promised escape, encoded enslavement, and bespoke, consequently, the tragedy of encounter.

Chapter 2
Woodstock School

Protestants, Peasants, and Ethics

"School had just reopened, and all of the children had come back up to Mussoorie from the plains where they had been for the winter holidays. Back then there were many *sahib*s* who came hunting in our jungle, but Ray Smith was different. He was a hunter; a real hunter."

"In those days I was young and did not know very much. As I have told you, [Ernie] Campbell was my guru. When I went hunting, it was with his gun, his ammunition, and his planning. I didn't even know which gun was which. I would just go and pick one out of the cupboard and hunt. These are great things I am telling you; things to think about. But anyway, Ray Smith and I hunted together and he wanted me to tell him if I ever heard of a chance to shoot a leopard."

"It is the village children who know where leopards are. They tend the cattle and the sheep and goats and come across leopards in the jungle. We were waiting for news of a fresh kill so that we could make plans. And we needed to get word in the morning so that we could be at the site by evening of the same day."

"One morning, on my way into town, one of the village children who knew that I was interested in these things gave me the word that a cow had been killed by a leopard over near Kimoi. I had to deliver milk, so I went on into Landour. But after quickly finishing my work I came back to Ray Smith's house in order to tell him and make plans. He wasn't there, but the *memsahib* [madam], his mother, showed me a place to rest, and I slept until noon."

*The term *sahib* can be translated as an honorific title such as "sir" or "Mr.," but it also suggests a hierarchical relationship marking relative class status. Although used casually in everyday speech, when used by someone like Dil Das to refer to someone like Ray Smith, who was at the time a senior in high school, it evokes a colonial relationship in spite of what may or may not have been intended.

"Finally, after school had finished, Ray Smith came and we began to talk and make plans for the hunt. It was getting late, so we took the carbine apart and put it in a bag to hide it from the forest guard and then headed out for Jaunpur. I dropped off my milk containers at home, and then we set off again toward Jhak and Panch Ram's *chan* [hamlet or cow shed] by way of Masrana. I guess it must have been one of his cows that was killed. Anyway, we set out from there in search of the kill wondering what would happen if we actually shot the leopard."

"Down in the valley below Jhak there is a cremation ground, and nearby we found where the leopard, or what we thought was a leopard, had pissed. The piss was warm, so the leopard must have been just in front of us. It must have gotten scared when it heard us approaching. We went on slowly, up the slope of the mountain to a ridge where there was an oak tree and some bushes. I saw something moving in the bushes and could just make out half of a body and what I thought must have been a leopard's tail. Ray Smith could see it too, but said to me that he thought it was a *barasingha* [a "twelve-horned" deer]. I said, 'I don't know; I'm not sure; barasingha aren't usually found in these mountain jungles; they aren't usually found in my jungle. But, in any case, shoot the damn thing and we'll find out!' So we went on up slowly and reached the ridge. The bushes in which we had seen the animal were not very far away; maybe as far away as that chan over there, about fifteen meters. From the top of the ridge we could see down below where a buffalo was grazing across the stream, and where a ravine ran up the opposite slope past some chans. Had we not approached very slowly and quietly the leopard—or what we thought was a leopard—would have heard us and run off. We were very careful."

"Now, what we thought was a barasingha in the bushes turned out to be what we thought was a leopard! Whatever it was, it had now turned in our direction and was moving slightly. It was dusk now, about 6:30 or 7:00, and getting dark, but there was still just enough light to shoot. Taking aim, Ray Smith fired, and the carbine went 'Phutt!' And then right away he fired again, and hit the leopard—or what we thought was a leopard—in the chest. Much to our relief it fell down. We were thrilled!"

"Now, in those days I didn't know what I now know. It was on that day that I first learned the English word 'tiger,' for a leopard is a leopard, but this thing we had shot had stripes! I said to Ray Smith, 'OK, let's lift it up and carry it home.' So I bent down and tried to lift one end, but it wouldn't budge. I didn't have enough strength to even move it an inch. 'OK,' I said, 'let's hide it over there behind those bushes, and then we'll go home for help.' So that is what we did, and we left the gun behind too and ran back toward the school."

"At Bhataghat we met a forest guard, but we said nothing and just ran on until we got back to the school. Then we went to Palisades, down below Taftan, and told the sahib—Ray Smith's father—what we had done. After telling everyone what had happened, we returned by way of the Tehri road to retrieve the tiger. We brought some coolies with us, and a *dandi* (a sedan chair) to carry the tiger in. John sahib, Campbell sahib, and Smith sahib, Ray Smith's father—all the important men—also came along. They brought torches and their big rifles."

"Now, what I had done was to place leaves along the path so that we would not forget our way back to the place where the tiger-we-had-thought-was-a-leopard was. We got as far as Masrana when Campbell sahib asked if we really knew where we were going. I told him that we were following the leaves. When we got close to the spot I said that we should be careful in case the tiger had a mate. I told Campbell sahib to take the lead since it was a very narrow path and we could not go side by side. He said, 'Hey, what are you doing, trying to get me killed? You go first. This is your doing, after all!' "

"When we got within range, I took a shotgun and fired a round of bird shot into the tiger to make sure it was dead. I shot twice. It was then that I told them that I did not know what it was that we had shot. It was not an animal from our jungle. Campbell sahib and the others said it was a tiger. They told us that we should not have shot it, but then they said it would be all right; that they would take care of any problem with the forest department. Campbell sahib said that we should learn our lesson well. It was only because of the carbine that we were alive. 'Otherwise,' he said, 'they would be there collecting our bones and not those of the tiger!' "

"That day there was such a commotion about our having shot a tiger that the whole school was shut down. Everyone from Mussoorie came to see the tiger and take our picture. Then we began to skin it. But what was to be done with the skin since it was illegal to kill a tiger? We tried to take it down to Buddhoo Moochi's house in Dehra Dun and get him to do the tanning, but all he could say was, 'What is this? Where did you shoot it?' "

"Now, there were two officials from the forest department there as well, and they began to ask the same questions. I said, straight out, 'We shot it in my village, where else!' But we had no permit, no license, you see, and so we got into trouble. In the end the case was taken all the way to the chief conservator of forests in Naini Tal. I don't know exactly what happened, but I am told that it was only the person who owned the rifle who was held accountable, no one else."

"It was all out in the open. It was a public issue and we did not try to hide. Our pictures were taken with the skin, and everyone knew who had shot the tiger. Something must have been done to resolve the case, however. A fine had to be paid, but it was all out in the open. We did not try to hide anything."

"The skin of the tiger was kept at the old skating rink for some time. I saw it there. One day my friends came to see it, too, one of whom was a *sardar*, a Sikh gentleman. We had a drink together and got to talking about the tiger. He said he knew about these things and wanted to see where the shot had gone into the body. He started looking in the stomach area, but I told him the bullet went into the head. But he kept on saying that he knew all about tiger shooting and where the bullet must have gone. I told him not to talk as though he knew more than he did."

"Now, my friend, the skin was rightfully ours—Ray Smith's and mine— and I told everyone who wanted it that they could not have it. It was ours. We had shot it. Many big men came to try and get their hands on it, but I told them that I was the one they would have to talk to. They offered ten thousand rupees. They wanted to buy it as a trophy to decorate their homes. In the end it was sold; sold by the forest department to someone who knew the conservator, I guess. It was rightfully ours, but they sold it for ten thousand rupees. And then when they came to carry it away, I told them they would need four men to lift the skin, but they didn't listen. I said they had better listen to me. I said I would just keep talking until they listened. They could not ignore me. In the end they lost; all the big sardars I mean. Vinod from Hamer and Company [a local shop] was also there. He understood what I was saying. He was with me. He understood that I was a hunter and that the skin was ours."

"Now, from that day onward I was a hunter. From that very day, mind you. Campbell sahib instructed me; he taught me what I know, and he told me that hunting was a dangerous business. But from that day I have become addicted to hunting. It is my life."

*   *   *

"Ray Smith and I had walked and walked and got all the way to Jaunpur; you know the place north of Landour, across the Aglar River around Nag Tibba. We pitched our 'camp' in some long, flat fields. Then we went down below the lowest field about thirty or forty meters and I saw a *kakar* [a "barking" deer]. But we had been walking all day, and I was tired, so we sat down and I had a smoke before saying anything. When I was finished I said, as though I had just seen it, 'There, a kakar has come out of the bushes.' Ray had a .22 rifle with him. He fired and hit the deer, but it was only wounded and still moving. He always kept one cartridge in the chamber and another held between his teeth. He did this so that no time would be wasted in reloading. That was his style; our style. You can tell people this when you write my story. If you see Ray you can remind him. Anyway, he reloaded and killed the deer with the second shot."

"After shooting the kakar, we came back up and visited an old man whose acquaintance we had made. We had stayed with him and he had fed us. We had nothing with us except one old sleeping bag; no food. We said, thanking him: 'You have fed us and we have hunted in front of you.' Then I took the deer and presented it to the old man. He said, 'What am I supposed to do with this?' I said, 'Eat it. We cannot take it back to Mussoorie with us.' The old man was all alone, poor fellow."

"Well, the old man was pleased, so he took out some *sur* [a fermented beerlike drink] and gave it to us to drink. We sat through the night and cooked the kakar and drank sur. In the morning we left and walked up along the ridges as far as Kyari village. When we got to the village we told the people we were hungry. So what did they do? They got out sur for us to drink. They also brought out food, so we ate and drank. . . . You see, all along the way we got food and liquor. We didn't have to worry."

*   *   *

"When I was young, probably about my nephew Beeji's age, seven, maybe eight years old, or possibly younger, I went with my mother to her natal village up beyond Uttarkashi. I remember the road even now. There was a rope bridge across the river.

"Once, many years later, Ray Smith and I went up to a village near there where it was reported that a leopard had killed a cow. We were going to try and shoot the leopard. However, when we got to the village we discovered that the cow had already been eaten, and it was too late to sit up over the kill."

"Since I knew the road, and it was not far, I went on up to my mother's village; up where my mamu lives above Uttarkashi. Later on Ray Smith and I went up to the fish hatcheries, past the forest office on the road to Agora. As we had stopped there to make our camp, the forest officer came out and asked us to provide him with some meat. I told the officer that the sahib was sleeping. I could not wake him and ask, but that since we did have a license we would most likely be able to do as he requested."

"The next morning we went up to the steep slopes above the forest office. There we saw three very big *ghoral* [mountain goats]. We had Campbell's old carbine—who has it now? Mark sahib, I think. Yes, that is right. Anyway, Ray Smith fired and the goats fell right at our feet! We did not have to move an inch or do a thing!"

"It was getting around the time we had planned to leave. We had decided that since the people there at the hatcheries had been so helpful we would shoot some ghoral and provide them with meat. Just as we were packing up our things and getting ready to go, however, the forest guard came and started acting very official. He asked us what we thought we were doing shooting ghoral without his permission. I said, sarcastically: 'OK, friend, so this is your game. Yesterday everything was fine, but now you have developed an attitude. So what's up?'"

"Now, in those days everything was cheap, even bribes, so I offered him a ten-rupee note. But what did he do; he grabbed the gun and took it into his house! So I went up to his door and once again offered him ten rupees, and also said he could have the ghoral we had shot. He would not listen."

"He was inside making *khichari* [a mixture of lentils and rice], and the rifle was leaning up against the wall in the corner. I was standing at his door, you see, and tried to slowly sneak in to where I could grab the gun. But then he got upset because I had shoes on in his house. Then again I offered him ten rupees, and ten more in addition to that, but he would not listen. Finally he leaned over to poke the fire and blow on the coals, and while he was not looking I jumped, picked up the gun, and whipped around. Then I said, while he was still standing there surprised, 'See here, one shot was fired at the ghoral and there are still fourteen left in the clip. Don't move or I'll shoot you in the chest!' I fired a warning shot just to emphasize the point."

"Well, the sahib heard all of this and got worried. He said that we had better get back to Uttarkashi. But then we decided not to since the forest guard was not about to try anything. He was left speechless! Even so, he was bold enough to ask us for the inside organs and the head of the goat. I told him to forget about it; we were going to take the ghoral up to Deodital and eat it there."

"We divided up the load between us and started out. I was strong. We walked up to those chans just below the bridge where there are people from Agora and Kasur. We wanted to cut up the goat to make it easier to carry. I tried to get help from a woman who was inside one of the chans, but she was afraid and would not come out to help us. Then a boy came by and I told him not to be afraid. I told him we needed help skinning and butchering the ghoral. So the boy helped us and we took three legs on up into the mountains with us, leaving the rest for the people in the chans to divide among themselves."

"After walking for hours we arrived at Deodital. We arrived at the lake and cooked and ate the three legs. We also met a number of other people from the school up there. I guess they had come hiking to enjoy the view. Later we went hunting again—in those days I did not even know the meaning of the word tired!"

"It was very cold up there. We were hunting *kastura* [musk deer]. We managed to kill one, but kastura are very small, and there were twenty of us altogether and not enough meat to go around. So this is what we did, we decided to tell everyone in the camp that we had shot a *langur* [monkey]! We butchered the musk deer out of sight and then brought the meat back to camp. We cooked it and ate, and told everyone that we had decided to eat monkey meat because we were hungry. The coolies who were with us would not touch the stuff! There was an old man, however, who said to himself, 'Now I know that Dil Das would never eat a monkey.' He knew what was going on. But when he took me aside and asked, I insisted that we were eating langur. I said it was a monkey and that he was welcome to help himself. When he asked how it was that I was able to eat the meat, I told him that it was just a matter of necessity, and that you have to do what you have to do. We bantered on like this for some time, and then he finally said, 'No matter, I too will eat some monkey.' He figured it out, you see."

"Bahadur was our cook. His uncle lives there at the toll gate now, and he used to work at the school with Fleming. Well, Bahadur had hung the butchered musk deer up in a tree and I told the men that they were all fools; if they would only go and smell the meat they would realize that it was not monkey. I told them to go and sniff the meat and judge for themselves, but no one would tell them outright that it was not a monkey we had shot!"

"In those days there was nothing but a small temple up at Deodital; nothing else. . . . No bungalow near the lake. . . . The fun we had back then is not to be had now. What a forest. But cars go right up there, you see; almost right to the lake."

* * *

"One time the Smith boys, my uncle Abloo, and I went on a hiking trip. The boys were all very young then, probably not much older than Beeji; about twelve or thirteen. We were going up toward Kathling, the glacier behind Tehri, and Smith sahib and memsahib had asked me to look after their children."

"Along the way we stopped and Abloo bought a basket of *cholu* fruit [small sour plums] from some kids for a couple of rupees. I told him not to, but he did anyway. He ate the whole thing and, just as I suspected, he got sick with cholera. We were on our way up to Gansali and stopped in a rest house at Ghanti along the way. We got as far as Ghanti by car, and planned to walk on from there. So the next day we started out. Up at Gansali now there is a bridge and a town, but back then there was nothing. We had to go all the way down the mountain to Ganga ji [the Ganga River], to find a place to make some tea."

"Well, we were walking up to Gansali and got as far as Sankhari when Abloo started to get very sick. I stayed back with him and told the Smith boys I would meet them on ahead at the pilgrim rest house. After I got

Abloo settled down I went on. What else could I do? I gave him a tin of fruit to eat in case he got hungry. I tell you, that day was a bad one for me. I was supposed to look after the children but had to take care of my uncle. So I went on up the trail to catch up with the children. When we got up to Gansali we found that there was just a pilgrim's guest house, a mill, and a few tea shops—nothing else. Even so, we got settled in. I made some *khichari*, fed the kids, and then told them that I had to go back down and take care of Abloo. I told them not to move until I got back. I had to travel at night and the distance and terrain was like from here to Rajpur, about ten kilometers up and down. Twenty, round trip."

"Now, I thought to myself that the place was very strange and unfamiliar, but that if I wanted to make it safely I would. I could. So I kept going and going until I came near to Sankhari. Near the village I saw that my uncle was coming along the path toward me and said to myself, 'Ah, he is not dead!' I was relieved. I had thought to myself on the way down that if he had died I would have just thrown his body into the Ganga and that would have been that. It took us a long time to reach one another, but when finally we met along the path I saw that he was crying. I told him not to worry; everything would be all right. I picked up his bags and started to carry them back up the path to Gansali, back to where I had left the boys."

"When we got there I asked some people to provide us with a coolie to carry our things on up to Gangi. I had friends up there and we could leave our loads with them and then go on up to Kathling, to the glacier. Well, a coolie was found, and I told him that I would give him food and tea as payment. He agreed, and we went on up. As we got higher and higher it began to get cold. All along I kept giving Abloo medicine and he improved somewhat. We got as far as Dhokari, where I found a friend of mine. I told him we would be going hunting further up, so he decided to come along. He had a muzzle loader and kept everything he needed in the collar of his woolen jacket; his powder, shot, and cotton—everything."

"As we got further up, Abloo's health got worse again. Then my friend from Dhokari took out some medicine he kept in his collar and gave it to uncle. Soon he felt better. That night we found an overhanging rock and all of us climbed under it and fell asleep. In the morning we got up and made some tea. Then there was the question of food. What were we going to do? I told everyone to wait and that we would be able to get some where we were going. Now, the trail from there was all covered with snow but was marked by a path of stones which had been placed on top of the snow to show the way. We walked and walked until finally we got to the glacier. We tried to make some food there, but there was no wood to start a fire. All we had were some paraffin pellets, and with these we made some coffee. We ate some cookies, a little popcorn, and puffed oats and this served as our meal."

"After a short time we started back down to Gangi, but along the way Abloo's knees gave out and he could not walk. Even though I was carrying a load I had to carry him as well. There was nothing else to do. I put him on my shoulders and carried him. Now, if Ghanti had been as far away as Landour from here, about five kilometers, it would not have been a problem. But it was a long way. Ghanti was two or three days' walk away. I had my load and I had to carry my uncle. So we walked and walked. But then I realized that the children's school was going to re-open soon and that we had to hurry back. I told them we would have to walk at night as well. Finally we got back to where the bridge is now and I told everyone that I would go on and make arrangements for a car. This was after the second day and Abloo was feeling a little better. He was able to walk slowly. Even so, I told them all to wait for me there."

"I walked on to Ghanti and made arrangements for a bus. There were no cars. I bought six tickets and told the driver to wait for us, but that if we were late to wait only ten minutes before leaving. I went back quickly and we all made it back down to Ghanti in time."

"Now, I was very tired and when we got into the bus I told the Smith boys and Abloo to take the seats but to leave me the aisle. I had a bag with me which I put down as a pillow. I said, 'You may put your feet on me. I don't care. Just let me go to sleep!' I lay down and went to sleep and didn't wake up until Agrakhala, on the road to Mussoorie beyond Tehri, but below Chamba, where there is a police station. I got off to buy some food and saw a policeman standing nearby. He turned out to be a friend of mine. He asked where I was coming from and I told him the whole story—the children, the cold, the lack of food, and my uncle's sickness. He invited me in to have some tea. I said, 'Never mind the tea, but if you have anything which will relieve my tiredness I will take it.' I asked him for some liquor, you see. It was not easily available, and there was nobody else there who would be able to provide it. No sir! Now, had I been in Mussoorie or Dehra Dun I could have made arrangements, but not there. But I told my friend the policeman I was dead tired. So he said, 'Sit, sit,' and gave the others tea. Then he took me aside and brought me into the police station. He brought out a bottle of kacchi, and he, another policeman, and I drank it together. I thanked him and then we went on our way."

"When we got to Dehra Dun I bought a quarter bottle of liquor but didn't drink it. I didn't eat anything right away, either. There was one man on the bus with us then who wouldn't eat any meat or drink any liquor. I told him he would die of hunger and of weakness if he did not.

But all he ate were some *jalebi*s (sweets). That was all. So I drank the liquor and ate some meat and rice. Then we started off on the road to Mussoorie, and by the time we got to Kulukhet, to the municipal toll gate, I was feeling very strong again. At Kulukhet I had many friends; they are our people there, you know, people from the hills. There are villages nearby and kacchi is easily available, you see. The Munsi there gave me a shot of liquor; you know him, the toll collector. Well, by the time we got back up to Mussoorie everything was fine. I was feeling good. So I took the children back home. I could have stayed, but I told the memsahib, Mrs. Smith, that I was very tired and would go straight back to the village."

"Three days later I came back up to the school and told both sahib and memsahib the whole story. They agreed that I had suffered greatly. It was only because I went along that the memsahib had agreed to let the children go, you see. If I had not gone along they would not have been allowed to go. And the children were all behind me as well. They were the ones who wanted me to go with them."

*　*　*

"I had gone to Kulu, over in the mountains beyond Simla in Himachal, with Taylor sahib, his wife, and their children. They were on vacation from school. At that time there were military people in the valley, and so there were restaurants and places to buy meat. We, of course, wanted to go hunting, so we asked around about guns and ammunition. Now, back then I didn't know very much, but I was worried. You see, there were Buddhist lamas in the area, and I was worried about what might happen if they found out we were hunting. After all, the children were with us."

"Anyway, when I returned from Kulu I fell ill with a fever. At home my mother had made *dehi* [yogurt]. I was eager to eat some, but she told me not to as it would make my fever worse. Dehi is a cold thing, you see. I did not get better for a long time. I still had a fever, so I came up to the Landour Community Hospital to get a diagnosis. There was a doctor back then named Chapman, and I went to the hospital to be examined by him."

"I remember that he gave me as much tomato salad and dehi to eat as I wanted, as much as I wanted! This was in October and November. Then he told me I had tuberculosis and sent me off with a letter of explanation to the hospital in Ludhiana where I could receive intensive treatment. Dr. Fisch and Dr. Garst were there. I went with my father, but then told him to leave me and go on back as the expense of staying would be too great. I had to have injections and many other things. So I went to Ludhiana and stayed a long time. I stayed a long time in the Punjab."

"Now, in the village here in the hills I have many friends, so it was only natural that I would befriend many people in Ludhiana. I even made friends with the doctor. I said to myself, 'Now I have friends so I know I am not going to die.' I made friends with people in all the villages around there. They gave me milk, food, and liquor. I took my regular meals with the doctor, though. His house was just behind the hospital. As soon as it was light I would go over there to his place. Dr. Fisch covered some of my expenses. He and the other doctors fixed me up but told me that I should take medicine for a whole year. They said that only then would I recover. So I didn't work or even move for a full year. I just sat there and took medicine."

"When I came back from Ludhiana, the principal of Woodstock, Burgoyen sahib's wife—Breni's mother—told me that I was well enough to go back to the village. I did not feel fully recovered and was still weak. But with a stick in my hand I made my way home. . . . You know, Mrs. Burgoyen had asked me to take her son and show him around the hills when he was going to come back here from America. I told her not to worry about anything; that I would show Breni around. I was waiting for him to come back when they got the letter saying that he had died; that he had been killed. . . . And then, you know, there was also Dean Fasnath who went blind in the war in Viet Nam. . . . They couldn't come back after that . . ."

*   *   *

"I had gone with Taylor to Rhotang, up above Manali, to hunt *tangnor*. What do you call them? Ibex. That's right. They live up high in the mountains. We went down from Rhotang to Lahul and stopped for two days as the guest of a lama, a Tibetan monk. Then we went on across a river where a road to Baramas was being built. There is a ravine there, a valley called Situ Nalla, or something like that, and we came back up that way. Along the road shepherds have built houses into the rocks and we stayed in one of these for two days. The houses are built to protect the young lambs. They are way up in the high country."

"Now up at that altitude the distance between here and Chamasari would take us two days to travel rather than two hours. We had been hunting like this, slowly, for a long time when finally we saw some ibex a long way away. We followed them, but when we got close enough sahib said that the horns were not the right size; they were too small! Well, I heard this and said, 'Listen, I have practically died up here on the ridges in the snow. Go ahead and shoot it, regardless of how small it may seem.'"

"So we tried to get closer, but one of them, which we had not seen above us, saw us and warned the others. They all ran off. They have a very good sense of smell and a 'guard' is always posted to warn the herd if there is any sign of danger. That is what John sahib [Coapman] told me anyway. You have the horns of one up at Oakville you know. The one John sahib used to have in his house down here."

"So we left that place and came down. On the way we found two *ram chakor* ["king" partridge], and killed them both. They were as big as chickens and we shot them with bird shot."

"It was after I returned from this trip that I got T.B. and went to Ludhiana for treatment. After a year had passed, and I had recovered, I heard that Dr. Taylor was planing another trip up to Rhotang to hunt ibex. He wanted me to come, but I said I could not. He went anyway and on the way back fell ill at Chandigarh. He too went to Ludhiana for treatment. You see, it is our mutual story. Our stories are the same!"

"The first time we went up into the high mountains, we were sitting together taking a rest. The rifle was on one side and sahib was on the other. When we tried to get up and go on, however, we could not move. Both of us needed help, but neither of us could so much as move! I don't know what happened to us, but we both got very weak. Finally a Tibetan horse trader came along the road and helped us up. He told us we would have to cross the pass before noon or else it would be impossible. There was a storm coming and snow would block the way. He told us there was a 'hotel' on the other side where we could stay. Forsgren sahib, from the school, along with Taylor and I, had gone all the way up to the Rhotang pass from the Manali side. But from there Taylor and I had gone hunting on higher up while Forsgren turned back down to the Kulu valley to join his family in Manali."

"We didn't shoot a thing up there! Not a thing! I went once, and sahib went twice. The whole problem was finding an ibex which was the right size. Taylor would always check his rifle to make sure it was working properly, but in the end he never got to use it. When we got back down to the valley I told him that I was upset. We should have shot at least one regardless of the size. Later he told me that I was right."

*   *   *

"One day Nasirudeen Shah's father—a Nawab [aristocrat]—came hunting up here. He wanted to shoot a bear and came with a full entourage: servants, bearers, a cook, and a valet—the works. He had a sedan chair and was being carried from Mussoorie over toward Motidhar where those fields lead off down the ridge. We were going to hunt on the slopes below the road."

"It was this time of year, the monsoon, and a bear, unlike a kakar or ghoral, is not easily visible. You can't see the ears wiggle or anything like that. Anyway, I was looking and saw a bear sleeping in a narrow ravine. It was asleep. I had a gun and some cartridges, and since the Nawab sahib had not yet arrived, it came into my mind that I ought to shoot the bear myself. But then I thought that the Nawab sahib might get angry."

"Well sir, it took a full four hours for him to arrive! And then, even though the shot was only a matter of a short distance, of 120 meters, the Nawab sahib had to get himself ready. First he had to undo and then retie his leggings. Then his servants got out the *pan* [beetle-nut, lime paste, tobacco and spice concoction] making paraphernalia and made him a pan to chew on. All the while I was thinking to myself, what sort of hunting is this? I have hunted with big men before, but none have ever chewed pan like this! Then, finally, his servants took out the rifle and placed it in his hands. But you know what, then he took out a cloth and carefully wiped it clean. From top to bottom. And all this time the bear was laying there asleep! Finally he fired and wounded the bear, which went off into a thicket."

"Now, who was going to go in after it? All of the Nawab sahib's men were from the plains and had no experience. So I said I would go into the narrow ravine, where the bear was hiding, from the ridge road. The Nawab came down half way. I told him to hurry otherwise the bear would run off. Did he walk? No! Believe it or not, four men brought him down into the jungle in the sedan chair!"

"Well, we managed to find the bear, and with the second shot he killed it. He took pictures and his servants brought it back up in the sedan chair. He was happy."

"Now, the bear had been sleeping from about three or four in the afternoon until six o'clock, and as I watched the bear waiting for the Nawab to arrive it had rolled over once and then went back to sleep. I kept on watching. . . . Have you seen this kind of hunting? Have you ever heard of such a thing. I guess the bear's time was simply up. Even with the waiting, the leggings, the pan, and the cleaning off of the rifle it had not got away. Its time was up!"

*   *   *

"When I was very young, Regi sahib, who lived over in Barlowganj, would come and hunt in our forest. Whenever he came he would bring a box of *gul gulla* [sweets] for me. They were only eleven rupees in those days. We would go down into the lower fields below the *chan*s and wait for the pheasants to come up out of the jungle. We would sit there and eat gul gullas. This was the business of hunting."

"Later, when I grew up, Regi sahib fell sick and I went to see him. I asked him what the matter was, why he was sick. But he wouldn't say, he just gave me advice. He told me to go ahead and hunt, but to hunt well: to do good work. 'If you are hunting with an inexperienced hunter always be cautious,' he told me. Those who don't know any better will shout out 'shoot!! shoot!!' without even waiting to see what it is they are aiming at. You have to know what it is first. Even if you just have an old muzzle loader, you have to know how to load and fire."

"Regi sahib was a military man. Every year he would take a two- or three-month vacation and would come over to Pathreni to stay. Regi was from the Hershey family, from the family for whom Harsil up in the high Himalayas is named. It was Hershey who started an apple orchard up there, and they still call them "Hershial" apples. You must go and see it some time. I have never been. It is his orchard though. It goes by his name. They are his apples."

"It is like that house up there on the ridge; Miss Campbell's house we call it. Jain sahib had a court case in which he won the land between here and Chamasari, the whole ridge on which Miss Campbell's house is built. But no one can say that house up there is Mr. Jain's. He owns it, that is true, but we call it Miss Campbell's house even now. My whole family does. Even Gura, my daughter. Yes, it was sold to Jain, but the name is still hers. Isn't that right?"

"The jungle all around us is being cut down. Where are the guards? They stay up above on the road and do not come down. Yes, Jain sahib is our *malik* [landlord or master], but many people come and go through the forest, not only those of us who live here. We do not want anything to happen to the forest. If a fire starts, we are not the ones to blame. We are the ones who put it out! Even when I was sick I went and helped put out a forest fire. Otherwise everything would get burned up."

"After all, I am a hunter and know that the *kalij* pheasants are sitting on their eggs. In a fire they will not fly away and leave their eggs. They will sit and be burned. They cannot run. There is nowhere for them to run. Nothing survives. The fire burns very fast."

"Everything and everyone must have food to eat and water to drink. That is basic and necessary. One must not let anyone beat you. One must not let anyone put you down or put any one else down. One should not cheat or be a thief. . . ."

"I saw a man at the courts once. Who knows what he had done, but the police had brought him to the courts. I was just sitting by. The police were cursing him, you see. They had made a fool out of the poor fellow; they had put him down. I guess he got what he deserved. But what is the point. One should eat, drink, and be merry. Enjoy life! They say that a hunter like me is a sinner, you know. Sure I have killed. But in fact everyone is a hunter; everyone kills. Some do it more than others, but everyone does it. Is that not true?"

*   *   *

"A cow had been killed here near the village, and we were all distraught. The cow was a good one. At today's price it would not cost less than two or three thousand rupees. It was a big loss for us, and Mr. Pickett came from the school to see if he could shoot it. He said to me, 'This gun will shoot half a foot to the left, so we must aim to the right.' I said, 'I will hold the light so that you may take aim. You will be the one to shoot. I will simply hold the spot light and stop the leopard in its tracks.' "

"We did not build a *machan* [a seat or platform in a tree], but instead gathered together some brush and hid ourselves behind it. We sat this way waiting for the leopard to come. The kill was down below about as far away from us as the other end of the chan here, about ten meters. However, instead of coming from below, as we had thought, the leopard came from above and behind us, and when he was about as far away from us as we were from the kill . . . he pissed! He pissed right on top of us! 'Now,' I said to myself, 'what will happen? The kill is over there, and here we are stuck in the middle, not even able to stand up!' Anyway, the leopard pissed on us and then ran off, so we just sat there quietly."

"It was the cold season. October, I think . . . no, it was November . . . no, it was October not November. So we just sat like this all crouched down and curled up to keep warm. I told Mr. Pickett that he could go to sleep, and that I would stay awake since I was not tired. He slept. He was tired."

"The ground was very dry, and later I heard the rustling of leaves and thought to myself, here he comes. The leopard came up from below and started to eat the cow. Let him eat, I thought to myself. There is no point in hurrying and scaring him away. There would have been no point in hurrying and ruining our chances. Now, you remember that he had told me that it was a matter of this much, a matter of six inches. The gun would shoot half a foot to the left. It was a matter of guess-work and judgment . . . of just this much, just six inches."

"I woke Mr. Pickett quietly and said, 'Take your time. Give the leopard fifteen minutes to eat its fill and settle down.' Fifteen minutes was plenty of time for the leopard to get comfortable. So we waited. And then Mr. Pickett made sure, took careful aim, and fired. The leopard let out a terrific roar . . . and then there was silence. Mr. Pickett turned to me and said, 'Friend, what has happened? Did the bullet hit or not?' I told him that if the bullet did not hit, then the leopard would have run away, but instead it roared. The bullet must have gone true."

"By now it was dusk and getting late, but we searched and searched. I took the twelve-gauge and went down one way and he took the rifle and went down another. We searched and searched, and finally found it. Yes, we found it . . . but then what were we to do? Mr. Pickett had duty back at school, so what were we supposed to do with the leopard? I told him not to worry, that I would take care of everything. I skinned the leopard, cleaned the skin, and brought it up to Mr. Pickett the following day."

"When I got to the school everyone was sitting around and they asked me, in amazement, how I had done this all by myself. I had no experience. Mrs. Pickett was there too. She was very knowledgeable, not like some, you know. She sat me down and offered me some tea."

"Now, we had the skin and had to go down to Dehra Dun. We drove down, ate and drank, and then went to the taxidermist who is a friend of Buddhoo Moochi on Mullangar, in Landour. Well, actually the taxidermist is a friend of mine as well. I gave him the leopard skin to tan and then returned home. After all, I am a milkman and had to get back to work."

"In the morning I came up to where my buffaloes were at Salarni. You know where, those chans just below Jain's place. It is really only a matter of two or three furlongs from here. So I brought my milk up to the school, did my work, and then went home. It was still early, and Mr. Pickett came down to see how things were going. I told him that everything was fine and that he should keep the skin just properly."

*   *   *

"One day I got word that a leopard had killed an ox over in one of the *chan*s at Kimoi village. They were in the middle of the plowing season, so they called me to hunt the leopard. I went, of course. It was during some festival or the other, and they had liquor. When I arrived to hunt, they offered me some. I said I would drink only one glass so as not to be afraid. I drank the glass and went into the jungle. There was also a young boy along with me to hold the light by which I was to shoot."

"As it was getting on toward dusk the leopard called from above the village. It called very loudly and I thought that there might be two. Anyway, the boy who was with me started to shake with fright. I told him to stop shaking unless he wanted to ruin things. There was still time for him to leave and go back to the village. 'Go and dance with the rest of them in the *cholai* [a kind of grain],' I said. 'Sing and dance and have fun.'"

"The celebration was going on in the village. The wheat was about elbow high. I don't know what sort of festival it was, but the wheat was still green in the fields."

"After I had been sitting for some time, I heard some rustling in the fields. I waited and watched, but then it stopped. I figured that the leopard had come up quietly and then gone away. It was being very cautious. Then it came back again after about half an hour. By this time night had fallen and the moon was out. I could not see clearly, but I thought I would be able to shoot when I saw the wheat moving. If I couldn't see the leopard itself, I would wait until I was absolutely sure."

"But then it went away again! Finally it came back a third time and jumped straight on top of the dead ox. It tried to drag the carcass away, but I had tied one of the ox's legs to a tree with some wire so it could not be moved. Presently the leopard gave up and simply bit off a big chunk of meat and took it some distance away to eat."

"The leopard seemed unconcerned and must have thought that no one was around. It could hear the singing and dancing in the village below and must have thought that whatever human scent there was, was coming from there. Soon it lay down next to the ox and ate the whole lower half."

"Now, the problem was that it was dark and I could not be sure where, exactly, the leopard was. I could not get a clear shot. I had to wait. Often hunters will make a mistake by thinking that a leopard is standing up when it is really laying down. This is how many shots are missed."

"About half an hour must have passed when the leopard finally stood up. I thought my chance had finally come. The moon was out and there was plenty of light. I was only as far away as the top of the chan is from that rock on the path down there, about eight meters. Now, Dr. Allison had given me two L.G.s [large-game cartridges] to shoot ghoral with; really powerful stuff. Well sir, I fired one shot, just one shot, and the leopard fell down dead. I hit it right on the side of its head. Not a sound! In fact, it was so quiet I thought I had missed. It was just laying there. I sat and waited. Then I saw its tail twitch, and it died."

"By this time Matbar Singh and many of the other villagers had come up to see what had happened. I told them to be careful and not go down to the kill as I was not absolutely certain it was dead. Well, sir, on account of the festival they were all drunk and had come up armed with spears, axes, and sickles, shouting to one another that they would kill the sister-fucking leopard on the spot! One of the men, who was particularly strong, took a *saletu* [a thick stick used for tying up loads of fodder] and struck the leopard just to see if it was dead. It was."

"Well now, they brought liquor for me right to that spot. Could they have not brought it? Look what I had done! Everyone was happy. So they put on a five-rupee *putai* [reward] and danced all night right there above the fields. I skinned the leopard by the light of the moon and took the skin to Dr. Allison in the morning. After all, it was his gun, and I had used his cartridges. It was his skin. He was very pleased."

"You know, Dr. Allison sent me a letter not long ago, from Tennessee, saying he remembered me. . . . I tell you, that sister-fucking leopard had killed an ox in the middle of the plowing season!"

* * *

"I was the hunter. I had the carbine. I even had the license for the rifle. I do not know what sort of arrangements Campbell sahib made, but he gave me the carbine and five hundred rounds of ammunition. He just gave these to me; and I was just a boy! What was I supposed to do? I had both the muzzle loader and the rifle. Then the carbine went to Matbar sahib. It was mine you understand, my carbine! First it was Smith sahib's, then Campbell sahib's. It was passed along to everyone. I had two thousand rounds of ammunition in a box!"

"When Campbell sahib gave me the carbine, I said, 'What is the meaning of this?' I could not understand. He was my guru. I was his *chela* [disciple], you understand. What! What am I saying? He is still my guru; even now!"

"This hunting business, is it important or not; is it a big thing or just a small matter? I think it is important. Big men go into the jungle and do it. And why is that? It is fun, of course! You see, if someone lives in town and cannot even find a place to walk, he will come into the jungle and find peace and relaxation. He will become earnest and reflective. These are ideas which come into my heart. I think about them."

Chapter 3
A Tiger's Tale

There was an old glass-doored bookcase which, at one time, sat on the stairway landing between the first and second floor of our house in Mussoorie. This is around the time when I was fifteen or so; after we had returned to Landour from a year's furlough in Princeton, after Martin Luther King, Jr., was shot and my teacher cried; after I failed fourth grade and, with one giant step for mankind, the eagle landed. It is during the time when my father was principal of Woodstock (1968–1978) and we, as a family, were living in the cottage below the school's main office; down below the terraced rose gardens and the lyre tree—the school symbol—an old Himalayan long-needle pine which lightning must have struck, scarred and stunted to give it an instrumental shape compatible with romantic poetry and, since classical images are here appropriate to the production of prep school emblems, a measure of nostalgic power. We lived, I guess, at the end of the stairs below a tree of classical, delineating knowledge—between narrative and dramatic modes in the Greek tradition, if memory serves—which was taken to represent the school, and reflexively position the lyrical emotions of its alumni.

The bookcase was in a place where faded dust-jacket titles caught the eye more by chance than by design while running up and down between kitchen and bathroom, bedroom and study; down and out to soccer practice, drama dress-rehearsals, Sunday morning church, and Wednesday night dances, and then back in and up again after school, after cricket matches, after weekend treks back into the hills, and quietly after late-night liaisons. This is a story of the books on those shelves; the dusty, monsoon-mold stained, silverfish-pitted, sun-baked books on the landing beside a window which looked out, on a clear day at least, onto the Doon and the plains of North India beyond; the fertile *doab* (two-river) plains bounded, with lyrate brackets—at least in the range of my romantic vision—by the two great sacred rivers, the Ganga flowing out through Haridwar to the east, and the Jammuna to the west.

Tightly packed, of various shapes and sizes, the books were a random collection, an indiscriminate reading list of family background—books on the sociology of rural development and church history for example, alongside a slim volume on the aerobic exercise routine of the Canadian air force; the *Aeneid* and Eliade side by side with *The Naked Ape* by Desmond Morris, Joseph Conrad's *Heart of Darkness*, and John Webster's sermons; works of liberal theology by Hans Kung and Roland Bainton next to James Michener's *The Source*; Alistair MacLean's *Ice Station Zebra* squeezed in between *Love and the Facts of Life* and the *Kamasutra* on one side and the Narnia series by C. S. Lewis on the other. Throughout, predominantly—and with somewhat more organization—there were the classics of English literature, my mother's field, and the standards of American sociology, my father's. There was an even mix of Shakespeare, Spenser, Shelley and Keats, with Mills, Mead, Parsons, and Dewey, along with a motley collection of books on India—the usual ones, to be sure, by Kipling and Forster, but also others less well known but closer to home. It is a pair of these books, placed randomly together—by me and my brothers, no doubt, while hunting for something else—to which I would like to draw biographical attention: Jim Corbett's *Man-Eaters of Kumaon* (1946) and Max Weber's *The Protestant Ethic and the Spirit of Capitalism* (1958). These two books have everything to do with one another, and also, I think, have everything to do with a sociology of postcolonial development, that is, with Dil Das's narrative.

Both books are about the desperate inevitability of progress, and they are also, nervously and ambivalently, about the moral imperative of modernity; about the ideological trajectory of industrial history on the one hand and colonialism on the other. As such, both texts are enigmatically rational. Corbett's book is about the intimate science of nature, the systematic structure of jungle lore, and the way in which one can learn to read the forest of symbols—the alarm call of a kakar, the stance of a langur monkey, and the distance between pug marks—in order to first understand, and then deeply empathize with, the natural order of things. It is also, therefore, about the devastating expansion of civilization. Weber's book is about the politics of faith, the structure of capitalist history—predestination, the fetish of salvation, the morality of work, and eternal damnation—along with the ironic confluence therein of ethics and economy. It is also, therefore, about how one can read between the lines of religion and ideology to discover the devastating logic of rational power. Although about man-eating tigers, Corbett's book is really about colonial expansion. Although about the spirit of capitalism, Weber's book is really about the irrationality of progress. They are both, in one way or another, ironic commentaries on the nature of change, the structure of modernity.

I grew up reading Corbett, and was enthralled by his vivid descriptions of tiger hunting, his almost uncanny ability to read the jungle and track a wounded animal, step by step, by following seemingly imperceptible signs—drops of blood, a broken twig here, there a crushed blade of grass, and on ahead, around the shoulder of a hill, the alarm "sneeze" of a ghoral. As a third-generation colonial, Corbett learned how to hunt while growing up at the turn of the century in the Himalayan foothills near Nainital, a colonial hill station to the east of Mussoorie. As a boy, and as a self-consciously ethical young man, Corbett hunted both for sport and in order to fill the pot, and spent most of his life in the terai, the band of forest land between the cultivated plains to the south and the high mountains to the north. It was here, as petty landlords, that his family had made its winter home near the small village of Kaladungi, from which they were entitled to rent.

As Corbett grew up he kept on hunting but also bid, somewhat halfheartedly in order to make a living rather than find a career, for railway transport contracts. Later he got involved in building railway lines and then in cutting timber: hard, slowly hot-burning sal wood from the terai to fuel the locomotives which ran in ever increasing numbers beside the Ganga, up to the Punjab and down again to Calcutta along one of the Empire's key economic lifelines. While working as a private railway contractor, Corbett's reputation as a hunter's hunter brought him into closer and closer contact with the elite sportsmen of the Empire, and the business of big *shikar* (hunting). In this context his perspective on hunting began to change. As a man who defined his morals by the law of the jungle, rather than a code of ethics, Corbett became critical of blood sport. Gradually his uncanny skill as a naturalist, his firsthand exposure to massive deforestation, and his increasing dislike for the dramatic pretense of imperial *shikar* turned him into an outspoken conservationist. He became a pacifist, that is—and, in as much as possible for an Anglo-Indian landlord and one-time station master—a socialist of sorts who identified himself, paternalistically at least, with the peasants and proletarian men and women under his control.

It was probably not until I was much older, twenty or so perhaps—and had, in my own way, grown at least ambivalent about if not yet critical of blood sport—that I came to realize that *Man-Eaters of Kumaon* is about capitalist ethics and the spirit of colonialism as much as it is about the brute, anethmatic terror of living near and hunting down tigers and leopards that eat people. Corbett was not explicit about this point; he was implicated too deeply. But the fact of the matter remains that, far from being natural born killers, man-eating tigers and leopards are the unique product of modernity, of the encroachment of civilization, the wholesale destruction of forests, and the crippling wounds inflicted, not only by men who are bad shots, but also by those who lack, in the language of the day, the courage to finish what they have started.

Corbett was known throughout British India as a man who knew the jungle intimately. And so, during the first half of the twentieth century, he was called upon by the district authorities to kill a large number of tigers and leopards that were terrifying the local population, and also disrupting the economy, communication, and work of government in and around Kumaun and Garhwal. *Man-Eaters of Kumaon* is the story of how he did this: how he tracked down and shot dangerous tigers and leopards by getting inside their heads, following their every step, and placing bullets into their hearts and minds. But, given its perspective, the book is also a natural history of terror, and a rational study of irrational acts of violence. The story is not so much a timeless tale of the tiger's beastly nature, as it is about what makes animals wild and species endangered.

Reading story after story of old, lame, wounded, and hungry tigers who, of necessity rather than by choice, resort to killing humans—a child herding cattle, a woman cutting fodder, a man walking into town—one is left with a bad taste in the mouth, for the pattern is clear. Beginning quite clearly around the turn of the century, and escalating to fever pitch in the interwar years—with the growth of the railway, the cutting of timber, and the expansion of fields and grazing land—leopards and tigers, more so than other animals, were squeezed out of *terai* forests and into competition with Himalayan peasants for space, resources, survival, development, and growth.

Reading Corbett on the subject of these leopards and tigers—and on rereading him more than a dozen times between the ages of fifteen and thirty—I found that an odd thing happened as a story of heroic adventure gradually translated into an elegy, at first, and then a eulogy. It was an ambiguous allegory of sorts in which I could not tell exactly who the victims of progress really were, but it was perfectly clear what was going on. What happened was that terror—the bite to the neck as you sleep, the claws tearing at your legs as you climb, throats ripped open, arms bitten off, and the hellish, pitch-black, total-silence of deep shadows as you walk through the night and think of these things—lost a clear point of reference for me as I began to see things in a new light. I began to see things, as I believe Corbett did, from the perspective of the hunted hunter.

You see, there is really no way around the fact that hunting is violent and destructive, and that, as such, it defines a moral space at the interstices of nature and culture. There might even be something pathetically farcical—if only such a high degree of skill and reason were not involved, and barbaric horror not quite so profound—in hunting down, with civilizing precision, "rural" leopards and tigers that have gone mad, that are acting "irrational"—that is, in a predictable sort of way, if not exactly wild. In any case, even where the lines are not so clearly blurred, the fact remains that killing encodes a myth of radical difference at the violent point of encounter, and what Corbett saw, in the eye of the tiger, so to speak, was that heart of darkness, that dimension of the colonial project (the steam engine of the capitalist spirit) in which he had implicated himself. His response, at once powerful, muted, and destined to fail, was to champion the cause of wildlife conservation in what was left, by 1940 or so, of the Indian forests around his home.

I grew up hunting. Not in these forests, of course, since most of them were long gone by the early 1970s, but in and around mountain villages to the west of Corbett's home, "further up and further in," as Reepicheep, a heroic character in one of C. S. Lewis's books, once put it. It could just as well be Conrad's Kurtz I am thinking of again. In any case, when all is said and done (confessions made, I guess) I was a post-colonial rural hunter. I was a rather poor shot, at first by aim and later by design.

It is hard to say exactly when I stopped hunting and began writing, but there are places in my memory at least where I can locate the horror of what I have done—the blood trails, the painful wounds, the shattered bones—if not quite target the practice of a post-Protestant ethic. If pushed, however, I would have to say that it was not until Dil Das died that I really stopped hunting, that we all stopped hunting, for by then my father had, as if to bring the point firmly home, sold the old rifle and taken up the work of development. I guess this is all that is left of conservation—ethically speaking, of course—when even the man-eaters have been squeezed out.

What was thought to be the last of the man-eaters was killed in the late 1940s; about the time Corbett quit India and moved to Kenya; about the time Dil Das started hunting. (Another, until it was captured and humanely taken to the Lucknow zoo, reportedly terrorized a team of loggers in the early 1980s.) Dil Das never hunted man-eaters, but there is deep irony—or, depending on your perspective, lyrate symmetry—in the fact that, as an Himalayan peasant, he hunted and killed some leopards, and, more by accident than by design, at least one tiger that encroached on his turf.

For my part, I have never killed a leopard. And the only tigers I have ever seen, aside from those in zoos and circuses, were a mother and two of the biggest sister-fucking cubs you have ever seen, as Dil Das would have said, three of several thousand left, walking through a sal forest in Corbett Park, a game sanctuary on the banks of the Ram Ganga in the terai just south of Nainital. As a family we went there often: to camp in forest bungalows, to fish and swim, to commune with nature and take our leisure from the hard work that we, as something more than nominal Protestants, were predestined to do. It is a nice place, or at least it was until 1978 or so, when the government flooded half the park to generate hydroelectric power to promote industrial growth and capital investment in the district of Moradabad. It would still be a nice place if I had not read, back to back, *Man-Eaters of Kumaon* and *The Protestant Ethic and the Spirit of Capitalism.* But having done so there is no turning back, no salvation from progress and no escape from modernity, that is—except, perhaps obliquely, by tracking down nostalgia and refusing, with conviction, to blithely let the last of India's inbred tigers masquerade, for our pleasure, as wild animals in a small-growing-smaller sanctuary, a contrived sanctuary, a place to passionately seek, if not forgiveness, at least the contingent absolution of sins in a jungle which seems, with every passing year, more and more out of place.

In the park which bears his name, Corbett would, of course, have seen the irony. But I also like to think that he, above others, would be able to appreciate the tragic confluence, in the forest near his home, of destruction, conservation, and the lyrically emblematic structure therein of a jungle book and a tiger's tale: a man-eating myth of progress and eternal damnation.

Part II
Aranya Kand

THE FOREST BOOK

Chapter 4
Coapman's Fall

It was late July 1982, and no time to be hunting, but I had set out from my house in the old cantonment at the edge of town for Pathreni, Dil Das's village, some five kilometers away. Dil Das and I had made arrangements two days earlier to meet at dawn, to be joined later by John Coapman, a local adventurer and businessman, and the night before I had loaded up twenty rounds of ammunition and cleaned my father's 30/06 Springfield rifle in preparation for the hunt.

Many years ago, before we sold most of them—a single shot .22, a hammer lock twenty-gauge, and Dr. Peterson's sixteen-bore—I can remember pulling out all the guns and coating them with heavy layers of grease both inside and out. The smell of oiled wood, gun grease, and burned powder still lingers in my nose, and I can feel, upon reflecting, the hard, smooth barrel in my hands, and the comfortable, balanced weight cradled in my arms.

The fog was thick as I walked out on the road from Mussoorie to Tehri, making my way up to the pass above Jabbarkhet from where I would cut down into the valley below Bhataghat. Even though I had walked this road a hundred times before and knew it well, the fog enveloped me in a caul of gray tendrils which added an extra weight to my shoulders and made it seem as though I was walking but going nowhere. As a young boy my friends and I would take advantage of the fast-blowing monsoon fog and stand on the edge of the hillside facing down toward the invisible doon, wet wind in our faces, and imagine ourselves into the blind terror of a ship's captain lost at sea in a full-blown gale. Tall deodars were our broken masts and gray wisps of fog their shredded sails. Any moment the hulking bow of another ship would break out of the gray valley below and smash our own crippled vessel into pieces. It was a curious thing about the fog that by obliterating all points of reference it made it possible to imagine just about any adventure or lapse into the momentary vertigo of manic disorientation—a slippage from anywhere to nowhere at all.

As I stood by a parapet wall on the side of the road just beyond the pass, I looked down in the direction of Pathreni, but could see nothing. My cigarettes were damp, as were the matches I had bought, along with a cup of tea, at the municipal toll gate below my house. Try as I might, I succeeded only in shredding the striking paper on the side of the matchbox. It was always that way in the monsoon; you needed two boxes of matches for every pack of cigarettes. I began to look forward to the fire that Dil Das would surely have burning; I was getting cold as well as damp.

For lack of a better word—although hamlet would do if it didn't evoke romantic images of the English countryside—Pathreni must be called a village. It is really just a loose cluster of homes belonging to the descendants of one Garib Das who migrated down from the higher Himalayas near Uttarkashi and settled in the area some one hundred years ago. The houses are very simple. For the most part they are one-room chans made of earth, stone, and thatch, dispersed across the hillside. There are roughly six of them in all—roughly, that is, because they come and go from year to year, and sometimes divide—three clustered around the goddess's oak tree, which might be called the village center, and three others further up on the low saddle of a north-south running ridge covered with pine trees. The slope is steep, and each chan is cut into the hillside such that in May and June, before the monsoon turns everything golden green, it is hard to distinguish the brown and golds of thatch and earthen walls from those of trees, grass, and scrub. Looking at a chan one gets a clear sense that it is part of the landscape aesthetically as well as architecturally, built as though someone had taken the raw material of a mountain and simply reconfigured it into a house.

I walked quickly along the narrow path which led out of the thick forest of scrub oak, across a grassy slope and up to the base of the big oak tree at the village center. I had left the fog higher up, and looking back I could see it sagging, as though under the soggy weight of some great load, taking support on the shoulders of steep grassy slopes which rose sharply out of view. It was only a matter of time, and the play of wind, until it would slide down the steep ravines, or until another bank, pushed from below by the hot, humid air of the plains, crept up and around the lower ridges like the rising tide of some great ocean whose rolling, silent waves always seemed about to crest and break.

Unlike many, Dil Das's chan was decrepit. It seemed to sag and bend at every point, and the one room where he, his wife, and his daughter Gura lived, was like the last defense of a losing battle against the elements. One end of the chan was completely broken down, the old beams having been scavenged long ago for some other building. *Kala ghas* and other weeds grew lush and tall on what had been the fertile floor of the cattle stalls, drawing strength from soil saturated with dung and urine for more than twenty years. Bits of plastic, ancient soleless shoes, broken pots, and odd pieces of metal stuck out here and there from the old rotting thatch which lay in a heap toward the back. What had once been sturdy, thick walls of earth and stone now lay in a crumbled ruin.

Technically speaking, a chan is not a permanent home. It is a temporary, seasonal residence whose primary function is to house cows and buffaloes, and "simply" accommodate those who take care of them. Chans are constructed for very pragmatic reasons: so that draft animals can be kept near fields, so that buffaloes are near water, so that manure can be easily transported to nearby fields, so that someone can stay near the fields and protect them from browsing deer, monkeys and porcupines, and so that milk buffaloes are either "up" at an altitude where it is cool in the summer or "down" in a warm valley when it is cold during the winter. Families ideally live in their *pakka makan*, their "solid house," which is usually located in a village comprised of other such houses in more or less tight configuration. Family members, along with cows, oxen, and buffaloes, move back and forth between the village base of operations and their various chans which are located anywhere from a few hundred meters to several kilometers away, and often as much as five hundred meters above or below the village proper. Chans are intrinsically *kaccha*, or unrefined, in relation to the more refined or pakka family home, where walls are made of cement or stone and roofs of tin or slate. Many of the "solid houses" in the villages near Pathreni have two stories, slate or cement floors, many rooms, and wide balconies with ornately carved wooden columns.

Despite their unrefined character, however, chans are not simply poorly constructed cow shed versions of what might otherwise be a comfortable family home. They are strategically unrefined to the extent that those who live in them on a seasonal basis do not try to make them any more "solid" than is required. The only way to maintain a chan is to move out and periodically rebuild from the floor up during that time of the year when it is not being used. To live in a chan permanently is to impose a solid veneer on an unrefined frame—to confuse pakka and kaccha—and it is not surprising that chans inhabited year round, like thrice-used paper cups, or shotgun shells which have been reloaded once too often, soon start to fall apart.

When Gur Das first settled in Pathreni he built himself a solid house in the shallow saddle above the ridge called Bandar Chowki (literally, monkey's post), on account of the monkeys who congregate there. Dil Das and his brothers were all born in this home. However, over the course of time the family's stock of cattle increased and chans were needed for the growing number of buffaloes. As Dil Das and his brothers grew up and married they also needed more space, and so the chans, which were all within a short distance of one another, gradually came to be used as more permanent dwellings which were connected, with variable degrees of socioeconomic adhesion, to the main family home. When Gur Das died, after three of his five sons had married, the significance of the solid house diminished and the chans, for all their unrefined contingency and both figurative and literal "insignificance," came to constitute—with a high degree of accidental irony and dubious permanence— the "village" of Pathreni.

Over the course of twenty-five years or so, from the time his father died until 1984, Dil Das's stock of buffaloes dwindled from nine or ten to none at all. His cows soon followed suit. Rustic utility had quickly degenerated into a condition of ironic poverty by drawing attention to the tragic fact—with ever-increasing visibility—that there were no "cows" in the cow shed. Dil Das and his family lived in a home whose significance, in the scheme of things, was a constant reminder of what and who, by virtue of where and how they lived, they should but could not be. The window which led into the broken part of the chan where the animals had once been tethered, and where I distinctly remember hearing his last cow ruminate, had been filled in so that the one room that remained was more intact, but, I suppose, also that much less of what it was designed to be.

The day we had planned to go hunting I turned up the narrow path from the big oak tree, coughed loudly to announce my presence, and then walked on, stepping carefully from one old flagstone to another to avoid the mud which made up most of the narrow flat space in front of the chan. Gray smoke oozed up through the pine needle thatch roof and clung to the edges, uncertain where to go, creeping down over the eaves as though intent on staying.

Everything was wet and heavy. Raindrops from the night before still clung to the ends of the long pine needles. The pungent smell of damp cows and buffaloes filled the air, and I could hear their heavy, restless movements from the chan below: their sighs and snorts, long, liquid, gushing urination, the soft, muffled ringing of the bells around their necks, and, most clearly, the synchronized sound, surprisingly loud, of rhythmic, moist rumination.

It took my eyes some time to grow accustomed to the dark interior of the chan. Dil Das was squatting inside, poking sticks into the fire and blowing on a small bed of sizzling coals trying to get a flame to catch the wad of damp pine needles he held in one hand. Finally the fire caught and the pine needles sputtered, sparked, and then briefly blazed into life, casting bright light and deep shadows onto the thick earthen walls.

The small room was crowded. A big cot near the door was piled high with old blankets and quilts. Above it, two wires suspended from one side of the ceiling to the other functioned as a storage space for clothes, baskets, and a few tools. An old shovel and a broken pick leaned up behind the door, and next to them was an old kerosene tin used for hauling water. A broken-down wooden chest of drawers against the back wall was supported, where one leg had been, by a pile of broken bricks. Next to the cupboard was a dented, rusty tin trunk and various pots and pans. The floor was damp, and, in places, almost slimy where the earth and cow dung was turning to mud. For the past few weeks Dil Das had been saying he would get some fresh pine needles and repair the leak in the back over the chest of drawers, but now that it had been raining off and on for two weeks, the back wall of the chan was beaded with seeping water, and it seemed impossible to do anything about the dampness. The fire helped, though, and despite the bad weather, simple furnishings, and state of impending decay it was, all in all, a comfortable home.

"Did you stop at John sahib's place?" Dil Das asked, rubbing smoke out of his eyes with one hand as he reached for the cigarette I offered with the other.

"No," I said. "I thought we were going to meet here. Anyway, I got a late start." Dil Das nodded and shrugged. It was well past dawn, but still very gray outside. The fog had settled in again, and there was no particular rush. We would not be able to see anything anyway. I put the rifle in the corner beside the cot, hung my shoulder bag on a hook above my head, and sat down next to the fire. "Where's Gura?" I asked.

"She spent the night down with the other girls in Sheri's [one of Dil Das's brothers] house. She gets lonely up here," Dil Das said.

I nodded. Dil Das's wife was often sick, and although Gura was able to cook and generally take care of the house, she was only twelve or thirteen, and hardly old enough to look after herself and her father. She was old enough to play with the other girls, Sheri's daughter and the daughters of the man from Jaunpur who rented part of the *chan* below Dil Das's place. But she was not old enough to take the ultimate step from carefree childhood into the routine drudgery of adult responsibility, and Dil Das was in no hurry to push her. "Let her play," he would say. "I can look after myself well enough."

But in looking after himself, he had let the rough edges of the house encroach closer toward the center. Things were not hung up. The corners were not swept. You could lie on the bed and hear white ants eating away the timbers of the roof sending down a ceaseless shower of light, soft, white dust as they burrowed deeper and deeper. But there was not much one could do about them. They were just part of the woodwork. Dil Das had been married twice before, and both wives had died. His third wife was sick with cervical cancer, and he still did not have a son.

He had no children by his first wife, one daughter by his second, and Gura by his third wife. But a son had not been forthcoming, and so the "natural order of things" was brought up short.

If Dil Das's life had to be reduced to one point, which by virtue of its fundamental significance defined the trajectory of both events and emotions, hopes, and fears, it would be that empty space which would have been taken up by the birth of a son. Even so, it was not as though Dil Das dwelt on the subject, or even lamented his ill fate. It was just that without a son his life began to lose its future tense. There was nothing to look forward to, quite literally. Like his first daughter, Gura would eventually get married and move out of the house, leaving Dil Das and his wife that much older and all alone. So underneath the chan's crumbling walls and the leaky roof, and listening to the slow but steady progress of the white ants, behind the death of a cow and the sale, year by year, of another buffalo, was Dil Das's unborn son. He was there, too, perhaps more so, in the heart of the hunter.

I don't know when I first met Dil Das. I must have been very young, probably only twelve or thirteen when my father took me and my two brothers hunting near Pathreni. It would have been fall or early winter—the proper time to hunt—when we were on vacation and the school was out. My father had an old twelve-gauge shotgun that had belonged to his father, and his father's mother's father before him—a sheriff from Ohio—who had bought it, not to enforce the law, as I had often imagined, but to shoot squirrels. It was a beautiful old gun with a richly oiled oak stock and an intricately carved undergrip—diamond shapes, if I remember right—on the sides below each of the tapered damascus steel barrels. You could see the outlines of the swirling, contorted wires which had been hand hammered into the brownish blue gun metal to give it texture, strength, and, I suppose, a certain aesthetic appeal. I remember being fascinated by the name of steel which seemed to come straight out of one of my Sunday school books—Damascus: an exotic place where Christ had walked and talked and healed. It seemed somehow appropriate then, an ironic conjunction of place, possessions, and purpose—to say nothing of history—for my grandfather came to India as a missionary, and I was certain, in an adolescent sort of way, that fate had somehow inscribed my great-grandfather's squirrel gun with an oblique intimation of his son-in-law's holy calling. It was a heavy gun, and my brothers and I would often struggle under its cold, heavy weight at the end of a long day, having walked many kilometers and climbed hundreds of meters. We would laugh, though, and shake our heads in admiration, at how Dil Das, having taken our burden, would carry it in one hand by the barrel, seemingly oblivious of its awkward, unbalanced weight.

He was still strong, and age had done nothing but gray a few hairs, knock out half his teeth, and stiffen a joint here and there. At six feet, he was taller than all of his brothers, and his broad shoulders and long arms and legs gave him a stalwart and dignified appearance. In particular, though, I remember his wrists and hands. They were big and thick with calloused palms and fingers. They were hands that had been shaped by hard work. As a hunter, though, it was Dil Das's eyes that mattered most, and for which he was best known. In fact his ability to see was legendary. It was said that he could spot the twitching ears of a sleeping ghoral at three hundred meters, and even with my father's Sears and Roebuck field glasses it was often hard to see what Dil Das was able to pick out with his naked eye. What made his reputation all the more legendary was his infamous notoriety as a "drinker" of raw homebrew, and, in conjunction with that, the popular belief (promulgated by horror stories in the local press) that drinkers of illicit liquor, among other things, go blind. But no matter how much he drank, Dil Das never succumbed to this fate. And he scoffed at the idea that drinking might blur his vision. What he made, he said, was *pyur mal*, "the real thing," and not the kind of bootleg liquor sold in the bazaar that was adulterated with chemicals. That stuff, he said, was poison. It would not only cloud your vision, but kill you outright as well.

As my eyes grew more accustomed to the darkness in the chan, I watched Dil Das prepare his still. It was a makeshift device, a temporary configuration of otherwise typical household items that could be easily disassembled in the event of a police raid. The most permanent feature of the still was an old, rectangular, fifteen-liter cooking oil tin with one end cut off. Washed, peeled, and slightly pounded wild blackberry roots were placed in the bottom of this and soaked in water and molasses until fermentation was well under way. To facilitate this process, which could take upward of four days, Dil Das always kept the tin near the back of the fireplace where it was warm. The degree of fermentation was always a matter of considerable interest and a topic of casual conversation upon which everyone was ready to comment and demonstrate their expertise. Once the fermentation was far enough along—a fact which could be determined by both listening carefully to the frothing bubbles and smelling the yeasty concoction—the tin was transferred to the fireplace and the mixture brought to a boil. A big brass container with a broad, convex bottom was then filled with cold water and placed on top of the tin. A small funnel was positioned such that it formed a narrow, graded trough running directly from under the lowest point on the rounded bottom of the water container out through a hole in one side of the tin and into an opaque plastic pipe which led into an old ketchup bottle. A long, stained rag, soaked in water, was then wrapped, turban-like, around the point at which the water container came in con-

tact with the tin. This made an effective seal, keeping the vapors from
the boiling concoction trapped inside the tin. When these vapors came
in contact with the bottom of the cold water container they would con-
dense and flow down the curved sides inside the tin until they dripped
down onto the trough and then out into the bottle.

Although simple, the process required careful management to ensure
that the fermented blackberry root concoction did not boil over into
the trough and drip into the bottle along with the liquor. One also had
to make sure that the water remained cold enough to facilitate conden-
sation, and that the rag seal did not dry out and catch fire. The distilled
liquor also needed to be tested occasionally to ensure that its alcohol
content remained sufficiently high and that the potency of the molasses and blackberry root mixture had not been significantly depleted. In
other words, brewing liquor is something of a fine art, and Dil was well
known as an artist. With panache and not a little drama he would test
the final product by first sticking one of his thick fingers into the fresh
liquor in the ketchup bottle, and then into the fire to see if it would ig-
nite. Usually it would, and to the horrified delight of Gura and the other
children, Dil Das's finger would be enveloped, momentarily, by a ghostly
blue flame.

Over time the concoction would lose its potency and the old molasses
had to be poured off and replaced with new stock. The blackberry roots
tended to last much longer, but they too would lose their flavor and
have to be thrown out before they gave the brew a harsh, bitter taste.
As Dil Das wrapped the damp rag around the tin and tucked one end
under the seal we began to talk about what to do. The weather did not
seem to be getting any worse, and with a little imagination it was even
possible to see that the fog was getting lighter.

"Chattarmani's son keeps telling me that he sees ghoral on the slopes
on this side of Bari Dhang," Dil Das said rather distractedly as he
crouched down to look through the plastic tube and see if anything was
yet flowing into the bottle.

"You mean over below the pine forest across from his house?" I asked,
trying to get a more specific fix on the exact spot.

"Yes, there always used to be lots over there. Perhaps that is where we
should start as soon as we are finished here," Dil Das said, having ad-
justed the still to his liking and now sitting back with a sigh and lighting
another cigarette.

There was no question that we would have to wait now that the still
was in full operation. It would take about two hours, and I lay back on
the cot to get comfortable. The fog had lifted again and the long sloping
ridge across from Pathreni was visible out the small window. There had
been times when ghoral and kakar could be seen right from the chan

door, but in general they tended to prefer the lower slopes—or other ridges altogether—where the noise from the village did not reach.

"Why don't we go down to Bandar Chowki? It's close by. Then we can work our way around to Bari Khet and back again by way of Donk and Chattarmani's house," I said.

"Yes. That sounds good," replied Dil Das. But both of us knew that it really didn't matter where we went. In the end it was all the same, and simply a matter of luck and timing rather than a question of finding the right place.

We settled back again and watched the sappy pine wood snarl, snap, and pop under the still. A spider, which must have found a dry hole in one of the sticks, had been forced out and now clung, stranded, on the tip of a burning branch. It kept running back and forth, frantically, between the tip and the encroaching flame until, at last, boiling bits of sap forced it to jump onto the sizzling hot coals below, all eight legs tucked in close as though to try, when all else had failed, to hide within itself. It seemed to vaporize, leaving behind a ghostly gray ash impression of itself until the heat from the flames scattered that too among the red coals.

Dil Das's bed was comfortable, although I always hesitated to lay in it. He used an old, home-cured kakar skin as a pillow, and once while rearranging things we had disturbed scores of tiny cockroaches which had made their home, or a meal—I am not sure which—inside the deerskin folds. This morning, however, I put the cockroaches out of my mind, lay back, closed my eyes and dozed while listening to the boiling still, the crackling fire, and the sound of buffaloes and muffled voices from the chan down below. Presently there was the sound of footsteps outside, a polite cough, and Dil Das's younger brother, Rukam, came in shivering.

"Hello, Hello, Hello. What have we here?" He asked, kicking off his shoes and removing a big, wet plastic bag from around his shoulders while looking at the still. It was a rhetorical question since the schedule of brewing and distilling in Dil Das's chan was one of the worst kept secrets in Pathreni. Before long others would arrive as well, and unless Dil Das was able to secret some kacchi away, the morning would quickly degenerate into what was known as a *parti*. Dil Das always complained that there was not enough for everyone, but inevitably everyone would get some. As a last resort I had a bottle of "Old Monk" rum in my bag, but Dil Das had said that we should keep that for later. So I had given it over to him for safe keeping.

Rukam Das was in his mid-forties and well known for his debonair style, melodious voice, and general good looks. He was the envy of his young nephews, Sundar and Azad, who exaggerated his amorous exploits and sought to emulate a heroic image of him which they had created. Rukam Das preferred the more martial, high-caste name of Lal

Singh, nominally exchanging, as it were, the stigma of "enslaved gold" for the stature of a "red lion." However, Rukam did not have any sanskritized pretensions, and I think he was more enamored of the name's poetic significance than with the change in rank it seemed to bespeak in other registers.

Rukam lived near the top of the ridge above Pathreni just below the Tehri road at a place called Tibri. It was about a kilometer away from Dil Das's chan, but almost straight up four hundred meters in altitude, and therefore a slow, long, difficult, back-and-forth walk up the mountain. Rukam worked as a watchman-cum-manager for an ex-military man known as Chowdhri Sahib who had bought most of the land on the ridge in order to start a fruit orchard. Chowdhri Sahib was an absentee landlord with considerable holdings elsewhere—mostly in the Doon valley forty kilometers away—and so Rukam was, for the most part, left to his own devices. He had to make sure that cattle—usually those of his brothers and uncles—as well as troops of marauding langur and rhesus monkeys, deer, and porcupine, did not cross into the orchard and browse on the young peach and apple trees. He also had to report weather damage and other problems.

Rukam lived in a one-room house constructed of loose brick and tin which was provided by Chowdhri Sahib. It was a curious place set off by itself just below the road, neither solid house nor chan, but one of those modern shed-like constructions which seem to be made from the bits and pieces of larger, more industrial projects. He lived there with his nine-year-old son Beeji, and one of his young nieces who helped with the cooking and cleaning. She came and went between Tibri and her parents home in the village below. In spite of the climb, and his duties, Rukam spent much of his time down in the village, either with Dil Das or his other two brothers, Sheri and Ratnu.

Despite his almost constant good humor, Rukam always struck me as passively disconsolate. He seemed to be oddly disengaged from the world around him; not so much alienated or embittered as self-consciously bemused in a way I can describe only as somewhere between irony and depression. There was a kind of tragic emptiness, and perhaps nervous distraction, to his constant laughter, even when he seemed to be enjoying himself, as though he was living simply for the pleasure of a moment which did not quite belie the more somber reality of yesterday, the larger monotony of today, or the uncertainty of tomorrow. I would guess that he was the kind of person who was most himself, and most comfortable with himself, when he was alone.

Rukam had a marvelous voice and enjoyed singing folk songs. His reputation as a ladies' man was clearly associated with his musical virtuosity. One style of singing in and around Garhwal is done almost exclusively in the context of cutting grass and leaves for fodder. Young boys and girls cut most of the fodder, and it is one of the few occasions when they can establish relatively private liaisons away from villages and chans. While cutting grass on the mountain slopes they sing a call-and-response type of song which is almost always romantic if not also sexually suggestive. The trick, or art, in singing these songs is to establish a dialogue wherein the sexual or romantic codes are at once clear enough to evoke the desired response, yet oblique enough to escape impropriety. The pitch, volume, and vocal style of the songs—usually short, pithy phrases where the last syllable of the last word is held for a long time and then cut abruptly short—seems well suited to the mountains. The songs are punctuated, when the sexual symbolism gets too direct, by long, high-pitched khikots, or yodel laughs. Sound carries well in the mountains, and couples can often communicate across great distances in this way, particularly when the wind is blowing in the right direction. The mix of wind, song, and space produces a kind of displaced, unbounded reverberation of sound across deep, wide, wooded valleys where vowels seem to ride the up drafts and whole phrases get spoken before they are ever heard. In his youth, Rukam was apparently skilled enough in this sort of verbal play to have gained quite a reputation, and it seemed somehow fitting that he should be identified, long after the music had stopped, in these oblique free-floating terms which laughter always seemed to bring up short. Dil Das, on the other hand, could not sing to save his life, but that is another story altogether.

Rukam had been married, but in the late 1970s, about the time I was graduated from Woodstock, his wife died in childbirth leaving him with a two-year-old son named Beeji and a newborn daughter. I remember going down to Pathreni not long after this had happened. It was late at night and the liquor was flowing freely. I had expected to find Rukam despondent and depressed, but he was in a curiously agitated state, laughing at virtually anything anyone said and telling stories almost before they came to mind, interrupting everyone and stumbling over his own memory. It was in the middle of some story he was telling that he broke down in tears of deep sorrow and grief which the shallow humor of our jokes and stories had only been able to briefly hide. It was not just that his wife had died, or that he was left with a young family to care for. He had, through no fault of his own, been forced to define the limits of his world and to measure himself in terms which he did not understand. He had been persuaded by any number of well-meaning folk that his newborn daughter would be better off if she was adopted into an American family.

I do not know whose idea this was, or what trajectory of values it followed back and forth between Landour and Pathreni until Rukam was forced to make a decision about the relative worth and wealth of nations. It was an idea, however, which must have got its start—was conceived, you might say—on the white sheets and under the bright neon lights of the birthing ward of the Landour Community Hospital where a motherless child seemed desperately out of place. Filling this accidental void of love and maternal symmetry, a Christian ethic, waiting patiently in the wings, got quickly to work as doctors, nurses, missionaries, and friends felt compelled to intercede on behalf of innocence; to save at least one soul—figuratively, of course, and with deep humanistic passion—from a life of suffering. Somehow everyone in Pathreni and Landour alike was convinced that sending her to America was the right thing to do, and that sending her back to Pathreni would be wrong; that it would condemn her to a life of marginal, insignificant suffering. At the time it seemed to make sense, but in retrospect I think it was simply unconscionable to have defined the fate of Rukam's daughter in terms of some global, First-World moral ethic. The final decision was Rukam's, and I can only imagine what must have been going through his head as he was forced to measure the harsh, parochial reality of Pathreni against a utopian American dream. But it is not even right to speak magnanimously of choice in a situation such as this when "options" are only seen as "alternatives" from a single "objective" point of view. We had, after all, defined a problem of human equality in terms of free will, the moral imperative of which belied its illegitimate assumptions. In the end it was decided, and Rukam was heartbroken, not only because his wife had died away from home as strange doctors tried to work their miracles, but because of his forced complicity in events that her death and his daughter's birth had set in to motion. In the end it was his call, his responsibility, and he simply did not know, and could not know, if what he had done was right or wrong. He was left without the burden of child care, but with a gnawing sense of doubt about himself and his world, a kind of heartbreaking burden of self-doubt born of other people's faith, their good intentions, and the kind of paternalism which inequality seems to breed.

That night in Dil Das's chan we were able to comfort Rukam. We told him that it was not his fault, and that everything would turn out right in the end. But although he calmed down, I do not think he ever absolved himself of the guilt he felt for sending her away. There was always a tinge of sadness in his giddy, distracted laughter which to me at least belied the deeper sorrow of his personal pain. As the years went by Rukam rarely talked about his daughter, just as Dil Das did not often speak of his unborn son. But during one of my last visits with Rukam, before I left to go back to graduate school and he died of asthma, he took my arm while we sat on his bed smoking and asked if I had ever seen his daughter in America. It was a question which, unlike most everything else he said, seemed to come straight from the heart. I was caught off guard. The question of his daughter had not crossed my mind for many years, but from the way he asked the question—out of the blue, in the middle of some other conversation—it was clear that she was always on his mind. I told him I had not. And yet, by the way he asked it was as though he was half afraid I might say yes, and begin to describe to him a daughter he might have known and loved but could not even begin to understand. He asked me to go and see her, to come back and tell him how she was doing, and to say hello from everyone at Pathreni. I said I would, but I have not. It was my responsibility, my call. But I did not know then, nor do I know now, if I should or should not. It is a situation in which the odd confluence of lives and friendships, of religion and civilization, has completely taken away any freedom of choice by confounding, in the name of some kind of universal human justice, the moral difference between right and wrong.

Rukam came into the *chan*, made himself comfortable by the fire, and looked around to see what was going on. We talked a while about the brew, and how it was coming along. The water was starting to get warm, and consequently very little liquor was dripping into the bottle. It was decided that we needed fresh, cold water before distilling more liquor, and so Dil Das told Rukam to go off to the spring and fetch a canister full. I stepped outside with him to check on the weather.

The fog had lifted. Looking up the steep ridge behind the *chan* I could see where Mussoorie proper ends at the municipal boundary which was marked, until road taxes were eliminated and the visibility of city limits didn't matter anymore, by a broken, rusted sign on the Tehri road. The boundary runs down a steep ravine to the west of which is a thick, scrub jungle owned by Mr. Jain the landlord, a respected and wealthy pillar of Mussoorie society, a Rotarian who now grows for commercial sale in "large urban markets"—but with an almost apologetic anticapitalist aesthetic—decorative off-season flowers, mostly pink and orange gladioli, in fields where others might grow wheat or potatoes. On the other side of the ravine is forest department land and a few of the oldest Pathreni fields which fan out as the steep ridge levels off slightly into a shallow saddle. The road I had walked on cuts through the scrub forest, across the ravine, and above the fields.

For all practical purposes, however, Mussoorie ends at Jabbarkhet, the old municipal toll gate, located at the easternmost point of the Landour cantonment estate. To the west of Jabbarkhet, away from Pathreni and back toward Mussoorie, there are houses which bear distinctly British and American names such as Oakville, Ashton Court, Sun Cliff, South Hill, Red Burn, Elcot Lodge and so forth, almost endlessly, until you arrive at Clouds End and Everest House at the other end of town some twelve kilometers away. Beyond Jabbarkhet, to the east toward Pathreni, there are no bungalows except for old Miss Campbell's house which sits vacant, for lack of water, atop the short spur of a ridge overlooking the Chamasari valley and the Doon beyond.

Miss Campbell owned the property up until the mid-1940s, at which time she quit India and sold it to Mr. Jain. In addition to Miss Campbell's "haunted house," as the dark, dilapidated bungalow is popularly known, Mr. Jain owns virtually all of the land from Jabbarkhet to Pathreni, a distance of three kilometers. Except for the two large fields located below the haunted house on the way down to the village, most of this land is forested.

Near the ravine which marks the municipal boundary, and just above the path which leads through Mr. Jain's land, is a small spring to which have been connected, over the years, various pieces of cast-iron, plastic, and rubber tubing in order to bring the water somewhat closer to Pathreni. Rukam was making his way along the path toward the end of this pipe.

It was below the spring, however, on a piece of land leased from Mr. Jain, across the valley from the Pathreni fields, that John Coapman— one-time manager of Hilton Hotels in Kenya, founder of Tiger Tops resort in Nepal, CEO of Coca-Cola India, son of missionaries, graduate of Woodstock School class of 1946, and Dil Das's closest friend for almost forty years—decided to build his house in the late 1970s. John Coapman is also the younger brother of my aunt by marriage, I should add, but this avuncular in-law status is beside the point, for I knew him less as an extended family member than as a friend of a friend.

By any estimation John Coapman is a unique character. At three hundred plus pounds and something over six feet four inches tall, his physical size is almost on par with his reputation as a maverick entrepreneur and renegade adventurer. Had he been born a century earlier, he would have fit right into the mold of a colonial soldier of fortune. But, as it happened, he was born too late—and of the wrong parents, I suppose— and ended up as a frustrated capitalist in postcolonial India.

During the 1960s and 1970s Coapman was in the business of selling exotic experiences, a sense of the "real thing" to those who could afford the luxury of a little first-class entertainment. He was a master of many things, but he was a genius at marketing the East to those in the West who wanted a taste of Eastern adventure. Tiger Tops in Nepal was his dream child, a luxury safari resort in the *terai* forest just north of Bihar. International clients from North America, Europe, and Japan were flown in to a private airstrip from Katmandu and met by teams of elephants which would carry them and their luggage back to the "camp" in the forest—a complex of rustic-looking but modernly furnished tree-house suites, a lounge, and a restaurant out in the middle of nowhere.

Tiger Tops is located within a wildlife preserve, the main attraction being, as the name would suggest, wild tigers. But there are many other kinds of game as well. When Coapman was in charge, tourists who came to Tiger Tops were taken on elephant back for "camera safaris," and were also provided with other opportunities for seeing animals in their natural habitat. What made Tiger Tops successful, however, was not just the abundance of wild animals, but the exotic disjuncture of elite, postcolonial taste—soft pillows, cool drinks, comfortable chairs, old scotch whiskey, and fine dining—with the untamed, wild, and potentially dangerous environment of uncivilized Asia. To a degree, Tiger Tops re-created the colonial adventure in microcosm by giving those with wealth and power a chance to try and see themselves by looking—from very close up—into an untamed jungle. In this context, Coapman provided the persona of a real-life adventurer. He was someone who had not just seen tigers in the wild. He had looked them in the face and hunted them down. From his clients' perspective Coapman added to the whole experience that necessary degree of intimate knowledge about something which would otherwise be utterly strange and incomprehensible. What Coapman did, among other things, was to tell stories about his adventures in order to maintain the aura of his persona. With great admiration, Dil Das would tell me of how Coapman, scotch in one hand, sitting beside the big open fireplace in the central lounge, would enchant his clients with tales of fantastic, dangerous adventure. One was never quite sure if Coapman was ever really telling the truth about anything, and yet there was always enough which was believable in his narrative to make one think that his fantastic experiences might just have happened. He was, in essence, a character who had effectively, and strategically, constructed his own identity, a man who had mythologized himself in order to make the fantasy of Tiger Tops seem that much more real.

Although mightily successful at pulling this sort of thing off, John Coapman was, I think, alienated by the extent to which he had mythologized and marketed himself as a persona for popular consumption. It was at least in part for this reason that he came back to where he grew up and tried to find himself by building a house in Pathreni. He was trying to escape a legacy of fuzzy truths, and was searching, quite frankly, for some sort of meaningful life that was simple and down to earth. However, Coapman was a dreamer, and even his attempt at simplicity could not escape the tyranny of his epic imagination.

Coapman tried to live up to his own somewhat legendary status and had developed a reputation for speaking his mind in four-letter words. In the conservative enclaves of Landour he was regarded as a shameless reprobate, but even in more liberal circles he was thought of as scandalous—all of which simply exaggerated the dimensions of his mystique. Coapman had many friends in both Mussoorie and Landour and enjoyed being the center of their attention. Many people enjoyed his company too, for there was no one to match his ability to tell a story or carry a conversation. When Coapman spoke—about how to skin a leopard, when to plant cabbage, or where to start a fish farm—everyone listened, both because they were drawn in by the power of his narrative and because he would not tolerate distractions, interruptions, or criticism. In this regard he had a personality well suited to both the hierarchies of corporate management and colonialism where the casual conceit of authority is both taken for granted and imperiously enforced. Coapman always spoke from an elevated position where he seemed to be in control not only of what people did, but how and when they listened.

Were it not for the fact that Coapman was, in fact, larger than life, his style of interaction might have been, depending on your perspective, either offensive or comical. As it was, however, he was both intimidating and, I think, rather pathetic, not because of his own shortcomings, but because he seemed to embody, albeit with tremendous style, the essence of colonialism. India was there to satisfy his desire, a place which he could use to define himself, and, to a degree, a place that was never quite real, in the sense that one could simply take for granted one's place in it. For him India always had to be explained and explored; it could not just be home.

And it is the significance of that word—home—which matters most, but is hardest to understand. For one of the things I have grown to find most disturbing about having been born in Landour is the way in which power, personality, and desire often merge to such an extent that authority becomes an almost casual way of life; a fact of life which is encoded, among other places, in the casual use—and that use's acceptance, even under conditions of intimacy and friendship—of the title *sahib*, a title whose meaning is less bound by culture than a history of alien hierarchy. Postcolonialism, perhaps more so than its nonprefixed imperial form, seems to be an ideology where the sharp distinctions of institutionalized power become normative cultural artifacts of a present whose only legitimacy is nostalgia. While Coapman seemed to celebrate the incipient nature of this transformative convergence, it always made me cringe—and still does, although now with impatient anger rather than embarrassed guilt—to watch and listen to the hundred daily dramas of hierarchy where status was and is defined by an imperative order and refined in a tone of voice which bespeaks, in its very grammar, an earlier time; a time when my grandmother would, for example, as a matter of course, have the barber boil his "dirty" scissors, comb, and clippers before letting him cut my father's hair.

I do not want to suggest that Coapman was some kind of swaggering buffoon who shouted orders as though everyone was a servant. There was something more subtle about him which took respect for granted even from those who were denied polite intimacy. Something about him made it seem perfectly natural that he did not buy or cook his own food, make his own tea, or wash his own clothes. In this respect, however, it would be wrong to single Coapman out, for I think he simply manifest, in a larger-than-life nonapologetic way, the latent, anachronistic conceit of postcolonial Landour. Whether we liked it or not, there was a little bit of Coapman in all of us who were born into the kind of power and privilege which money can buy but only history can define. And it was for this reason, I think, that Coapman's persona created problems by reminding us of our own veiled pretensions.

Long and rectangular, with one big room and a kitchen, the house he built and the home he tried to create on the ridge opposite Pathreni, is a cross between a chan, a makan, and a European hunting lodge. It was built by local village masons who made the walls extra thick and the windows extra big but who otherwise constructed the building along local Pahari lines. A huge fireplace occupies one end of the main room, and kerosene lamps and candelabra stand on special ledges built into the wall.

When Coapman finished the project in the early 1980s the unfinished walls were festooned with watercolor paintings, etchings, and countless big game trophies—an ibex shot in Kashmir, a *cheetal* stag from Rajasthan, an enormous *sambar* rack, and five or six ghoral and kakar heads mounted on polished cherry wood shields. Ghoral, kakar and spotted deerskins covered much of the floor. Old and refurbished bookcases with glass fronts, bought from Vinod the antique dealer in town, contained the classics of English literature, translations of the Hindu epics, and dozens of newly bound old hunting stories. Two extra-large custom-made *charpais* [cots] were positioned along the wall at the opposite end of the room from the fireplace and were covered with bolster pillows, thick, rustic-looking throw rugs, cotton comforters, and woolen blankets. Small tables were positioned next to and at the foot of the beds, each containing an artifact of some sort: a bronze image of Shiva dancing, a marble icon of Ganesh, a miniature painting from the Kangra school of Krishna playing his flute, and a polished, almost translucent granite Shiva *lingam* set in a garland of marigolds. On top of the bookshelves, mantelpiece, and window sills were etchings by early colonial artists, framed samples of Arabic calligraphy, Urdu poetry, and

Tibetan prayer wheels, each carefully chosen and carefully displayed. Opposite the fireplace, on either side of an ornately carved oak table and facing the skin of an eight-foot leopard, were two massive planter's chairs which seemed to evoke, along with everything else, the somewhat nervous essence of imperial comfort, and the studied compulsiveness of colonial leisure. It was the kind of place that Sir Richard Burton might have lived in if, overcome by self-doubt, he had needed to remind himself about his place in the scheme of things.

A narrow hallway led out past the kitchen into the garden. Although the house was "finished" in a literal sense, it had been built in such a way as to allow for an additional guest room, or series of rooms, to be built on the northeast end. The walls, which were made of thin, interlaced pieces of slate cemented together with mud, were left rough so that a new wall could be easily joined on to what already existed. The yard behind Coapman's house was long and narrow, overlooking a deep, steep and rugged ravine. Above it was a vegetable garden and a water tank, lined with plastic and tar, which was connected to the spring on the road above by a long piece of black rubber pipe. The yard itself resembled an English tea garden. There were six or seven variety of roses grown from cuttings taken from gardens in Landour, Mussoorie, Dehra Dun, and Meerut. Benches and tables had been made from large, flat pieces of slate, and the whole area, no more than twenty meters by five meters, was landscaped with bushes, trees, and shrubs left strategically in place while the rest of the forest was cleared away.

The house itself was a fantasy which many might dream of but which only Coapman had the temerity to build. Down to its last detail everything was a product of his imagination. The roof was made of long, thick, pine planks, and I do not think there was a person in Landour who believed that a wooden roof would last through one monsoon season. If it didn't rot, the sun would surely cause it to shrink, crack, and leak. But Coapman went ahead, regardless, because in his mind the aesthetic appeal of a wooden roof was far more important than any practical consideration. I think he took endless pleasure in pointing out, to Landour's motley array of doubting Thomases, that after two years of heavy rain there were no water stains on his knotted ceiling, and no dampness on the inside of his two-foot-thick walls.

The debate between Coapman and his friends on the Landour hillside about the relative merits of roofing material was couched in practical terms but had, in fact, much more to do with identity and self-expression than keeping out the rain. You see, in the North Indian hills—from Kashmir through to Burma—corrugated metal was the colonial roofing material of choice. Every house in Landour, bar none, has a "Cherokee red" corrugated tin roof, although the red paint on many, including that of Miss Campbell's old house, has long since given way to large, rusty stains. Village houses, on the other hand, usually have slate roofs, although these are becoming less and less common as corrugated metal—not to mention flattened out kerosene and rusty cooking oil tins—is taking the place of local materials. In any case, Coapman steadfastly refused either to abide by precedent, listen to reason, or follow the direction of change. He decided, instead, to build a roof which flew in the face of both tradition and nature, history and environment. He built a roof which matched his own self-perception as man who wanted the best of both worlds on his own terms, regardless of the consequences.

But one is rarely ever able to escape or ignore the consequences of one's actions, particularly when they are enigmatically reflexive. And so it seems to me quite appropriate, almost eighteen years since the roof went up and fifteen years or so since Coapman left, that the dairy farmers who now rent the cottage from Mr. Jain's widow and use it as a chan have wisely—and with practical rather than romantic concerns, if a certain degree of unintended postcolonial criticism—nailed on sheets of rust-proof aluminum to keep their buffaloes dry and to stop the wood from rotting away.

Coapman had said he would meet us at Dil Das's chan and that we would leave from there to go hunting. I looked along the path but could see no sign of anyone but Rukam filling the canister with water. I went back in and sat down on the edge of the cot. Dil Das had poured us each a full measure of kacchi, and with a knowing smile he quickly handed one of the metal glasses to me. It was still too hot to drink, and we hurried to try and cool it down before Rukam came back and caught us in the act. Dil Das didn't really mind sharing his brew with his brothers. But given the cost of collecting firewood and water, and buying *gur*—not to mention the fact that it takes upward of an hour to "drip" a single bottle full—kacchi is a rather precious fluid. Whenever his brothers dropped by, Dil Das would always try, with various degrees of resolve and good humor, to hide the full bottles from them and pretend, despite tell-tale signs to the contrary, that no one was drinking. Sending Rukam out for water had been a ploy to sneak a quick drink.

Like everyone else I have met in India, Dil Das drank his kacchi in one long gulp as though trying to avoid its taste. Even if you like it, kacchi is not something you sip politely. It is not in the least like a cocktail. You drink it down fast as possible, a tumbler full at a time, and then relish the effect. And while the effect is like that of any alcohol, kacchi is thought to evoke heartfelt emotions. Under its influence one is able to reveal the truth about one's feelings, a truth which might otherwise hide behind the many masks of sober propriety. Although I never grew to like it—in fact it makes me gag and gives me migraines—the memory of its smell and taste, which catches you halfway up the nose and back toward the ears, evokes a powerful feeling of gross identification with the harsh pleasures of village life. It is a common practice to spit afterward—to clear the palate, let us say, rather than show distaste.

Kacchi is an illicit commodity in the villages around Mussoorie from which some are able to derive a regular, if dangerous, income. However, Dil Das tended to brew it for his own private consumption, to drink with friends, and clearly gave the impression that selling it to strangers left a bad taste in his mouth. For him the whole point of drinking was to evoke a mood of emotional friendship which cash transactions tended to undermine. Dil Das took intense pleasure in carefully pouring out equal measures of his brew, and then inviting all who were given a share to drink deeply and to freely enjoy. And sitting in his damp, run-down chan-without-animals, there was clearly a sense in which he was sharing something of extreme personal value.

The irony, however, is that brewing and drinking kacchi can be held directly to blame, at least in part, for a number of serious social, economic, and medical problems such as domestic violence, malnutrition, and poverty. Calculated in terms of poor health, lost labor, and misspent gains, kacchi has played no small role in the socioeconomic demise of Garib Das's family. The money spent on gur alone—about fifteen rupees per canister, or five rupees per bottle—could buy enough food to feed a family of four for one day. It is for this reason, and the fact that drinking is primarily a masculine vice, that placing a ban on brewing kacchi has—with some well-placed post-Gandhian prodding—become a primary concern of grass-roots women's organizations in and around Mussoorie. And so, for Dil Das in particular, that which inspired true heartfelt emotions came at the direct expense of health, wealth, and happiness as calculated in the public register of social value, a contradiction which forced at least some kind of ironic rationalization about the relationship between self and society. And looking back on those good times we had together there is also the growing, uncomfortable realization that our friendship was perhaps not some kind of postmodern, transcultural experience which challenged social facts with the romantic innocence of heartfelt truth, but, like poverty itself, just another symptom of alcoholism, capitalism, and colonialism. Dil Das was fond of saying that friendship was, in essence, an ineffable "matter of the heart" which cut through historical differences and social distinctions, and yet it may also be true that it was those same differences, those same distinctions, which turned our friendship into a fetish of hope about the meaning of our lives.

Rukam and Coapman both arrived before we had a chance to drink another glass, and since the fire had died down we decided to put the still aside and get a move on. It was now fairly late in the morning, so we decided not to go far, but simply on down the narrow ridge below the saddle to try our luck spotting ghoral on the slopes below the village. We followed a narrow trail along the crest of the ridge which led down steeply to a place where bamboo used to grow in abundance and where the undergrowth is thick. Droplets of water clung to the bushes and stunted trees encroached onto the trail. Before we had gone more than a hundred meters our shoes and pant legs were wet through. Since the rain had stopped, many birds had come out to feed, and as we walked down through the forest a flock of magpies screeched and screamed before darting off into the shadows of a thicket lower down in the valley. Startled, a purple-black whistling thrush went darting down after them in a jagged flurry between the sagging oak branches and moss-green tree trunks, making, despite its rather poetic name, the sound of fingernails scratched across a blackboard.

We slowed down and walked more quietly as the trail moved off the crest of the ridge and angled down below an outcropping of boulders. It was on the other side of these rocks, in a shallow depression, where we planned to stop and scan the opposite slope. In the lead, Dil Das left the path and moved slowly up and around one of the lower boulders while the rest of us fanned out below, Coapman moving carefully along the wet rocks holding onto one of his many custom-made walking sticks— a polished piece of knobbed cherry wood with a forked piece of deer antler stuck in one end. We were just above Bandar Chowki, and true to its name there was a troop of about thirty black-faced gray langurs sitting in the oak canopy above the sheer cliffs which fell away down into the ravine some hundred meters away.

The slope opposite us was almost a cliff, and not so wooded as our ridge. However, there were thickets of scrub, large jagged rock faces, and wide expanses of grass on the edges of which we hoped to find ghoral browsing. Lower down in the deep ravine the undergrowth was thicker, and it was likely that kakar would make their way to the upper edges of this to feed on the new grass. The distance to the other side was between a hundred meters straight across and two hundred meters at the upper and lower extreme of our vision, all well within range of the rifle.

We crouched down, moving slowly, so as not to make a silhouette against the western sky and sat down so that the rocks were behind us. Now it was simply a matter of sitting, waiting, watching, and listening for the telltale sound of rocks being dislodged as ghoral moved about on the narrow ledges below the pine trees.

We had been sitting for about twenty minutes when a fine drizzle began to fall and a rolling bank of fog moved up the valley from Seraghat. There was nothing to do but sit as the bank moved silently closer.

Looking down I focused on the silver-gray back of a langur and watched as he dissolved out of sight into the blowing mist. During the night a spider had made its web between the bare branches of a dead bush, and now, as the light drizzle blew up the valley, small droplets of water condensed on the threads and made the web sag and sway gently in the breeze. My arms, too, were dusted with the same tiny droplets, shining pearl-like on the ends of each curled hair. Soon the sound of dripping water was all around us as the fine rain pooled and then ran off each leaf and blade of grass.

There was no harm in smoking now, since the smoke would not give our position away, and I passed cigarettes around while Coapman tried to light his pipe. Up above us, just below the pine forest along the path which leads to Donk, we could see three women from Chattarmani's household loaded down with body-length bundles of grass jogging back toward the saddle above the village. Earlier we had seen them working across some of the upper slopes, and as we sat down among the boulders it was possible to hear the muffled jingle of their bracelets, their laughter, and the sharp, rhythmic sound of sickles cutting wet grass.

We sat on for some time smoking and contemplating the thickness of the fog around us. And then it began to clear, not lift exactly or blow away, but gradually disappear, giving us first a shadowy view of the lower ravine, and then a brighter and clearer view of the mountains around us. A kestrel hung on a heavy, moist current of air that rose up through the ravine. Watching the kestrel my mind began to wander, eyes focusing in and out of the shadows cast by the rocks and grassy knolls on the slope across from us. I could always imagine what ghoral looked like much better than they actually appeared—a disembodied patch of white on a lifted throat, twitching ears, a shaking tail. It was always the parts which first came into view, but however many times I hunted I invariably made the mistake of looking for whole animals, just as at other times I listened for whole stories. I wanted to see them stand out, apart from the rocks and trees, as a life is set apart from language and speech, naked in the light.

Dil Das and Coapman must have seen the ghoral at about the same time. Enveloped in fog and wet with rain, it had come out into the clearing to dry itself off, and the shaking of its coat and ears had given it away. Dil Das leaned over and grabbed my knee while keeping his eye on the goat, trying to line up my sight with his.

"There. Do you see it?" he said, and he pointed down into the valley. I looked in the direction he indicated, hoping that the ghoral would jump into view, but I could see nothing but rocks and trees. "There, just below that pine and right above the patch of kala ghas. It's facing away from us and up the hill. There, there, it's moving now, up toward that bush. Do you see it? Can you see it now?"

"No," I said, after looking down the length of his arm and off the end of his finger. "Where?"

"Just there, down below the boulder with the white streak."

I still could see nothing, and so Dil Das began to talk my eyes into the right place, constructing as he spoke a verbal map of the mountain in front of us, a kind of mantra, I suppose, which would make the ghoral come alive and stand out whole against the shadows.

"You see that kestrel there," he said, picking a point of common reference.

"Yes, yes."

"Well, look down straight from where it is to those pine trees below the rock slide."

"You mean those three trees over there, above the patch of open ground?"

"No. No. No. Not that ridge down there, further up this way near to the big dead oak," Dil Das said.

"That oak tree way up there, you mean?" I said, getting somewhat confused.

"No. Lower down. Do you see that one?"

And so our dialogue went, slowly tracing an imaginary trail from bird to rock to tree. As it went, and the scale changed from panoramic to something less, our points of reference and phrases changed as well, from stilted prose to a poetry of sorts which closed in on the prey.

"That oak tree?"

"Yes."

"I see it now."

"Look across that patch of grass."

"To the right? Yes. OK. I see it, yes."

As the ghoral moved, I finally spotted it, gray brown against the green grass. It was moving slowly up the slope, looking occasionally down into the valley as it casually browsed, flicking its ears now and again as though to rid them of dampness. It looked much smaller than I had expected. They always did from above and far away. Slipping off the safety catch I lifted the rifle off my lap, where I had tried to keep the scope and breech as dry as possible, and slid down off the rock so that I could face down into the valley. Dil Das moved back to give me room. I wrapped the shoulder strap around my arm, and rested my left hand on a patch of moss on top of a boulder. Lifting the butt into position I sighted through the scope until the ghoral came squarely into view, filling the lens with its compact body. I took a few deep breaths to steady my aim and waited to see if the ghoral would move again, trying as I did to keep the crosshairs steady. It was looking down and away from us so that my perspective was on its narrow back. I was hoping it would turn one way or the other, thus giving me a side shot at a shoulder. However, it seemed oblivious and quite content standing where it was. Gradually I squeezed the trigger, holding my aim low on its back as the bullet, given the steep trajectory, would raise to a point straight above its heart. I felt the heavy rifle kick against my shoulder and smack against my cheek as I fired.

The ghoral had been standing about 175 meters away, and the 150 grain copper-coated lead bullet smashed it to the ground. It slumped backward, caught for a moment on the trunk of a small tree, and then rolled down into the thicket out of which it had come a few minutes earlier. I pulled the bolt action back, expelled the spent cartridge, and pushed another into the smoking chamber waiting to see if the ghoral was dead or just wounded.

A second or two later a rapid movement caught my eye halfway up toward the crest of the ridge above where the ghoral had been standing. Another one was making its way quickly up the steep slope, running as fast as possible away from us and away from where its companion had fallen. It zig-zagged back and forth from rock to rock, moving up the face of an almost perpendicular cliff with graceful precision, leaping so that it would land, all four hooves together, on a small ledge before jumping again toward another narrow purchase, and the eventual safety of the ridge above and the wooded valley beyond.

We must have all seen it at just about the same time, and Dil Das pointed upward as I lifted the rifle again and tried to aim at the moving ghoral. I watched it through the scope as it jumped from point to point dislodging rocks as it surged upward. It was working its way up a narrow, shallow ravine and showed no sign of slowing down. Then Coapman gave a loud, shrill whistle and the ghoral stopped short on a patch of grass above a steep cliff. It jerked its head around, ears erect and twitching, and looked back across the valley toward us, as though intent on pin-pointing the location of the sound. I let the crosshairs drift down to a point at which throat and chest come together and once again squeezed the trigger and felt the rifle buck as though jolted alive. The blast from the barrel echoed once against the slope in front of us, and then again, a little later, off the more distant eastern ridges, finally returning again to rumble off the western massive before finding its way down the valley and into the vast plains below where it seemed to carry through the air like distant, rolling thunder.

For a moment or two it seemed as though nothing had happened. The ghoral stood frozen above the cliff looking back toward us. Then it seemed to crumple as its muscles went limp. Its back legs buckled, its neck bent back, and its head rolled over to one side. And then it fell sideways onto the steep grassy slope and began to somersault, gaining speed and losing all sense of grace and compact balance, before bouncing once off the top of the cliff and then down, silently spinning over and over for what seemed like a long time. Out of control, its dead weight came crashing through the branches of an oak tree, hit the ground with a dull thud, and disappeared into the dark shadows of the ravine just above where its companion had landed.

It was a long and steep climb down into the valley where the two dead ghoral lay, almost side by side. But Dil Das and Rukam had both cut grass and bamboo on the slope almost every day since they were young boys working for their father, and knew the way well, moving carefully down from tree to rock to bush. When they got down to the ghoral, Coapman and I could see them searching for vines with which to tie the hooves together such that fore and back legs came together like shoulder straps on a boy scout's rucksack. They each squatted down, leaned back, and then squeezed their arms through the space between the bound legs and the sagging white stomachs of the dead animals. As they stood up, the ghoral heads rolled back, and their limp bodies sagged lower and lower down the backs of the slowly climbing men, and the dead weight shifted backward such that, from far away, each goat looked something like a monsoon leech, still stuck firmly in place on the skin of its host, but gorged on blood to bursting point, ready to be flicked away. As Dil Das and Rukam came closer we could even see the reddish brown stains on their shirts and pants as blood from the wounds dripped down.

After they reached us on the ridge and rested a while we all set off back up the path to the village. It had now cleared somewhat, and although clouds still blocked out the sun, and mist covered the topmost peaks, there was a certain brightness to the day and so we decided to take advantage of the break in the weather and go on down, past Chattarmani's house, to the ridge from where it is possible to look across to the big cliffs of Bari Dhang. There are almost always ghoral there on the rugged expanse of rocks and grass below the pine forest which stretches down almost all the way from the village of Moti Dhar and the old broken-down rest house on the Mahant's road. Rukam stayed behind, however, and Sundar, Dil Das's nephew, joined us.

Leaving the ghoral to be skinned and butchered later on, we set off up the trail toward Rutnu's chan, past the muddy water hole, and down the rocky trail which cuts above and behind Chattarmani's family home. From there we followed the path down further across some barren fields, and then down even further along the crest of a steep ridge which leads on down another five hundred meters or more to Koldighat in the valley at the base of the big cliffs where Dil Das used to keep his buffaloes.

About half a kilometer down from the barren fields the ridge levels off for a bit before plunging down steeply to the southeast, forcing the trail to zig-zag sharply from the edge of one precipitous cliff to another. We stopped here on the level ground, sitting down on a blanket of damp pine needles for a moment before heading off on a narrow path which leads due east over to one of the many slopes from which Chattarmani's wife and children cut grass.

The path angled down into a ravine and then turned sharply up, across the face of a grassy knoll, before turning around the edge of another ridge and over to a cluster of rocks from which it was possible to look, from a distance of two hundred meters or so, over the full panorama of the cliffs.

Between the ridge where we had stopped to rest in the grove of pine trees, the grassy knoll from which grass is often cut, and the rocky ridge on which we were going to sit, a water course angles down ever more steeply until it ends abruptly in a cliff which falls away almost down to the Koldighat stream another one hundred meters below. We were walking along the path above the water course when Coapman, who was just in front of me, slipped on a smooth, moss covered rock, landed on his back, and then bounced down over the side of the trail backward as his cherry wood walking stick clattered away. It happened so quickly, and without warning, that we could do nothing but watch as all three hundred plus pounds of Coapman rolled head over heels down toward the cliff.

It is one of those scenes that does not dull with the passage of time, and I can still see his khaki-clad bulk, bouncing like a large gray boulder, sweeping shrubs, bushes, and even small trees away as though they were only leaves of grass. We all knew what was at the bottom of the slope, and as he passed out of sight over a lip of rock we knew that it was all over; a fact which the sudden, total silence seemed to confirm. I turned around and saw the shock on Dil Das's face as he beat his chest and shouted out, "Oh my god, he is gone; he is dead."

Both of us threw down our guns and ran down the path to where it crossed the water course. From there we cut across the slope, back under the path we had run down, hoping to make our way above the cliff to a point at which Coapman had either stopped or gone over the edge. Dil Das was in the lead, and we had not gone very far before he shouted out, "There he is, over there at the base of that tree." We scrambled over as fast as we could and found Coapman firmly wedged, with one leg turned back at a seemingly impossible angle, between a rock and the trunk of tree. Half conscious, he was breathing heavily and groaning.

I remember once, when Dil Das and I were coming back from some village late at night, meeting a *dairywalla* on the path below Donk. Kerosene lantern in one hand, he and his brother had been leading a buffalo up from the plains to their chan when the animal, spooked by the shadows of the flickering flame, angled into the hillside, bounced outward, and then lost its footing. It had not fallen far, but had broken a leg and damaged a lung, and there was nothing the men could do, even with our help, except stand there, listen, and watch as their buffalo died. Later on, when panic and fear had changed into memory, and there was time to make analogies, it was Dil Das, telling his version of the story about Coapman's adventure, who saw in the event more of a bovine accident than a wild ghoral's fall; and, I suppose, more of a comical farce than a colonial tragedy.

Seeing Coapman all twisted and covered with blood and dirt, my first impulse was to go for help, so I grabbed Sundar, told him to hold on to the rifle, and turned to run, back up to Chattarmani's, or maybe all the way back to school; in the moment of initial panic I had not stopped to think. Before I got far, however, Coapman began to regain consciousness and told me to shut up—for I was thinking out loud about the logistics of carrying a crippled man of his size all the way back into town—and come back to give him a hand. I did, still wondering, but to myself, if he would fit into a tin tub strung up on a pole; which is the way sick people and pregnant women from nearby villages are taken to the hospital.

What had seemed at first glance to have been any number of possible serious injuries, however, turned out to be mainly superficial. As we sat there on the slope above the cliff and gradually untwisted Coapman from the roots of the tree and the branches of broken bushes, we realized that despite grotesquely contorted arms, legs, and neck, miraculously nothing was broken. However, as Dil Das, Sundar, and I tried to get him to stand—by lifting, with all our strength, from under his arms—it became clear that there was something seriously wrong with his lower back, and that any movement was extremely painful.

It was now about five in the afternoon, the sky was cloudy, and the climb back up to Chattarmani's was almost vertical along a narrow, zigzagging rocky trail. Although Coapman was able to stand, with our combined support, each step caused him excruciating pain. But we had to start moving; otherwise, in the cold of the night Coapman would stiffen up and find it impossible to move. If he lay down, it would be for a long, long time, and given the weather he needed to be taken to a warm and dry place where he could rest.

After much stumbling and slipping, shouting and cursing, we finally devised a relatively effective way to move up the mountain. Dil Das took the rope we had brought along to tie up ghoral and wrapped a few lengths loosely around his shoulders. Coapman was able to grab onto this and lean back far enough so that his back hurt a little less. From behind I placed my hands and arms along his back and pushed while Dil Das pulled. Sundar carried the guns, and step by step we moved along. Even so, progress was very slow, and by the time we got back to the pine grove only fifty meters up the trail it was already getting dark and raining intermittently. We sent Sundar on ahead to get help from Chattarmani's, but even when help arrived our progress remained slow. The road was too narrow and awkward for us to try and carry Coapman, and anyone who tried to lend a hand simply got in the way.

From the pine grove up to Chattarmani's house is only about three hundred meters or so, but with all the twists and turns it took us until about 10:30 at night to get there. The moon was nearly full, but it was hidden most of the time by the clouds, and so we stumbled our way up through darkness, relying on the soft, diffused light of the fog to at least follow in one another's footsteps as we leaned into the side of the hill, unable to see the edge.

In great pain, and tired out, Coapman was less able than ever to keep his abrasive personality in check, and he cursed us all every step of the way for not pointing out a slippery rock or a protruding branch, or for trying to make some kind of encouraging remark about how close we were getting to the crest of the ridge. Our initial plan was to stop at Chattarmani's place for the night, but when this was suggested Coapman protested vigorously, and so we were forced to pass up the Brahmin's "goddamn, sister-fucking" hospitality—as Coapman ungraciously put it—in order to get to his own place on the ridge opposite Pathreni.

With great difficulty we worked our way down from the spring, under the long-needle pines, and through the scrub oak to Coapman's front door. Once inside he sat down on the edge of his double bed while Dil Das and I got a basin of water and a cloth to wash away the blood and mud which rain and sweat had not already rinsed off. Coapman took out a large bottle of talcum powder to soothe his scratched, rashed, and leech-scarred skin; and then, with a mighty groan, and our help, he lay back slowly onto his bed. While Coapman was covering himself with powder, Dil Das had lighted a fire in the fireplace and put some candles on the ledges. As the fire blazed into life and the candles sputtered, light filled the room full of trophies, casting enormous, dancing, disembodied shadows of a rather small barking deer and a lifeless cheetal stag on the bookcases, rough rock walls and knotted wooden ceiling. I remember falling asleep, laying in the bed next to Coapman, listening to his groans and heavy breathing, looking up at the mounted head of a ghoral—any one of a hundred or more whose story had been told—whose unblinking marble eyes glinted a reflection of the fireplace and candles, making it look almost alive.

The next morning Coapman could not move out of bed, and so while Dil Das stayed with him, I ran as fast as possible back up to Oakville to see what could be done. Fortunately Dr. Olsen, a missionary physician on the more conservative side of faith, was at home on the Landour hillside and not off on one of his mobile clinic gospel tours down into the Aglar valley. He kindly agreed, with black bag in hand, to walk down to Pathreni and take a look at Coapman's back. His presence was reassuring but really unnecessary, for without x-rays or laboratory equipment there was little he could say about the condition of bones and kidneys and little advice he could give beyond the obvious: stay in bed and rest.

Somewhere along the way up from where Coapman had fallen, perhaps around Chattarmani's house, I remember being struck by the fact that we were in the process of acting out, albeit with heartfelt groans and moans, the script of what would become a story about real-life adventure. Coapman's fall would not just become an integral part of Dil Das's life history; there was something about the drama of that night which seemed to confuse event and narrative, memory and moment. Indeed, as we got closer and closer to Coapman's house, we began to talk, reflexively, and with the laughter of exhaustion, as though the present were already past. And I think there was something about this confusion which made me realize, as we stopped along the path near the spring and I pulled another cluster of fifteen black, slimy leeches off of Coapman's massive white calves, that although we had made a heroic effort and overcome great odds, that what I had really discovered was that Coapman's fall made all the difference in the world for how Dil Das would remember and tell his own life story. The fall must be taken seriously as a pivotal event in Dil Das's narrative, not because it changed his outlook on things, but because it seemed to reveal to him the nature of his role in a precarious colonial encounter, a kind of farce which undermined the pretense of friendship.

It was almost three weeks before Coapman recovered enough to walk, stiffly and with the aid of one of his many canes, the rest of the way back up to Landour. Dil Das and his wife stayed and nursed Coapman back to health, for long before then I had to leave and go back to school in the United States. Eventually Coapman recovered, and he stayed on for a while in the lodge he had built, but I think the fall made him realize that he could not stay there forever; when all was said and done, he was passively mortal. He could not aggressively live up to his own expectations of a kind of life which brought him down to earth while allowing him to freely cultivate an epic persona. Living between Landour and Pathreni was simply too dangerous for a person like him; there was too much at stake in terms of the meaning of self and other. After a few years in Jain sahib's jungle, I think Coapman grew tired of the fact that the free-

dom afforded by the strategic confusion of categories also demanded
the constant hard work of self-definition. He could not simply live in the
jungle without the constant fear of falling into someone else's concep-
tion of him—of loosing his mystique—and so he left India altogether
and escaped the horns of a colonial dilemma.

As for Dil Das, Coapman's departure marked, in essence, the end of a
close encounter which defined his life, the end of a relationship which
gave a literal context to his mutated biography. After Coapman's fall,
Dil Das himself fell—in what he came to regard as a kind of intimate,
parallel tragedy—and, finally, his wife died. From 1982 on, he became
more and more obsessed with the illusive meaningfulness of friendship,
but also, I think, aware of the fact that he did not control the terms of
intimacy.

It has been more than seventeen years since Coapman left and thirteen years since Dil Das died. While I was visiting my extended family at
Oakville in the early 1990s we all went out to the haunted house for a
picnic. My father brought a pair of lightweight hunting binoculars along,
and we stood at the edge of the yard and looked down in the jungle at
the lodge, which was clearly visible in the bright May sunshine. For a few
years after Coapman left, and before Dil Das died, it was taken over by
the Mussoorie Gramin Vikas Samiti as a base camp-cum-storehouse for
village development work. But after Mr. Jain's untimely accidental death,
and given the informal nature of the deal Coapman had negotiated with
regard to the forest land and its use, Mr. Jain's widow got nervous about
the building's ultimate fate and asked the team of field workers to move
out. With unintended irony, she now rents the lodge out to migrant
dairywallas from Jaunpur whose more permanent alien status ensures a
degree of security regarding the ownership and control of property.

And looking down through the field glasses from Miss Campbell's
house I could see five buffaloes comfortably tethered on a rose garden
terrace below a wooden roof over which rustproof aluminum had been
nailed.

Chapter 5
Hearts of Darkness

"At that time Coapman—John sahib—was in Delhi with the Coca-Cola Company. Harper was with him. It was November and Campbell was in the Punjab. Where was it now? At Amritsar, I think. At least that is where his elder brother was. What was his name? Ah! I have forgotten! Oh no . . . yes . . . Lauri. That is right, Lauri Campbell."

"Anyway, Coapman invited me to come to Delhi. So I went. Early one morning we went duck hunting to a place called Samphla. It was early in the morning and the fog was very thick. You could not see a thing or tell what was what. It was very, very cold. We were joking around and I said, 'sahib, don't shoot any cows by mistake!' "

"Now Harper had on a rubber suit and rubber waders. He had everything to go right out into the lake. There was a dog with us as well; a retriever to go and pick up the ducks we shot. But it was so cold I thought we would die! Now, we were joking around, and Coapman and Harper made a plan to play a trick on Campbell. You remember, now, that Campbell was my guru; he was my guru, you see. But we were just fooling around. So this is what we did. Harper took one corner of the lake, Coapman took another, and I took a third. But then we placed Campbell out in the middle of the lake saying that it was the best spot! But what was he going to shoot from there! It was like this; we were joking around."

"In the end John sahib shot twenty-nine or thirty ducks. Harper shot twenty-five or twenty-six. Something like that, anyway. I am only estimating. Since I am a mountain hunter and did not have the proper judgment or 'estimation' for hunting in the plains I shot only seventeen or eighteen. The dog with us was a retriever and it would go and fetch the ducks we shot. It could swim, you see."

"After a while, when Coapman, Harper, and I had finished hunting, we sat down, ate, and drank some hot tea. It was very cold. Later on Campbell came up in an irritated mood, took off Harper's rubber suit, and started gathering up the decoys which had been brought from America. He didn't say anything, just gathered everything up. Then, obviously mad as hell, he said, 'Let's go!' Now John sahib, who had provided us all with hot coffee and tea, took out a cold Coca-Cola and offered it to Campbell! A cold Coca-Cola, mind you! To this Campbell replied, 'Friends, you have frozen me to death by putting me out in the middle of the lake, and now, on top of that, you are offering me this cold drink! What are you trying to do, finish me off! I am your guru, but look at what you have put me through today. So let's go!' We just put the ducks in the car and headed for home."

"They had called me to Delhi in order to have fun. 'You have your money,' I said. 'I have come here and you have given me money to spend. Whatever you have done, you have done. But there is one thing; one thing above all else: Campbell sahib, you are my guru.' And a guru, after all, is a guru."

"And then Campbell said to me, 'Yes, I am your guru.' "

Well, to this John sahib replied, 'O.K. Campbell, you are Dil Das's guru, *magar guru to guru rahe gaiya, or chela ban geya shakkar.*'* But I said to John sahib, 'No, this cannot be. A guru is a guru, and that is that. One must respect and show deference for one's guru. That is how it is.' "

"We came back to Delhi then; to house number 101 in the Golf Course area. I bathed and changed my clothes and got myself ready to go. . . ."

"Listen, Joe my friend, that time is forgotten now. It is gone. But in those days I had my gun and plenty of ammunition. Everything was set and taken care of; it was organized. However, in those days, when I was young, I did not know which gun was which. Campbell sahib would say, 'This is the gun for tigers, this is the gun for pheasant, and this other one is a .22 rifle.' One gun had two barrels, and there was an air gun and two revolvers. . . ."

"There were three of us on this ridge; at Bandar Chowki right here below the village. It was long ago. Long, long ago. . . . There was a *kakar*. I had the carbine which fired thirty rounds. Thirty rounds, I tell you! And was the ammunition my goddamn father's? No! Never! . . . But the barking deer; the sister-fucking *kakar* was mine! . . . That time has gone now; those days when we would go down to Bandar Chowki on the ridge below the village."

*   *   *

"I had to go down to Dehra Dun to get my first shotgun. I bought it from an old Gurkha for one thousand rupees. When I got the gun, and

---

*"The guru has remained a guru, while the chela has come out ahead." There is a play on words here since *guru* sounds like *gur*, unrefined molasses, and *shakkar* means refined brown sugar, or the higher quality, improved form of *gur*.

had it licensed, I also got an 'all-India' permit made. But if you get a gun you also need to get shells and a belt to carry them on, a belt on which to show them off, a belt that goes across your chest, like this. I paid something for the permit, I don't remember how much now, and about twenty or thirty rupees for the taxi down and back. The whole thing came to about 1050 rupees."

"Back then Mr. Powell lived down below Allen School in a big house. He was a hunter and had devised a system for calling leopards. He sold the contraption to John sahib, and we got a permit made and took it with us hunting to the Nali forest block."

"The leopard call of Mr. Powell's was made from a rope and an old *ghara*, a clay jar that is. We would tie the rope tightly to some branches and then pull the ghara along so that it made a roaring sound when the sound of the rope sliding through a narrow hole cut in the bottom of the pot echoed off the insides before escaping through the mouth."

"We positioned ourselves on the ridge below Nali, and after calling for some time, a leopard answered from the ridge above Koldighat and started to make its way toward us. It moved slowly and then, when night fell, it stopped altogether. It got dark, so we left and came back up to the forest bungalow."

"Well, we made the mistake of not staying longer. We came home the next day, and that night the leopard we had called over from across the valley killed two of the forest guard's goats. It was searching for its mate and got angry when it realized that there was no other leopard around. Then it went on down the ridge to Sarona and killed two goats right in the middle of the village. It was a very angry leopard! It caused much trouble, so we did not tell the people there at Nali that we had made the leopard call."

"Powell sahib was a great hunter. He killed many leopards and tigers. But in the end he sold everything. Even his house he gave to the school. He used to come over here to the village quite often. He was the first one to show me a double-barrel gun for shooting tigers, the kind that shoots very thick, fat shells. I did not know about guns back then. It was only later that Coapman explained all types to me."

*   *   *

"Once John sahib and I went to Rothakpur. His friend Harper sahib, who also worked for the Coca-Cola Company, was there too. We were hunting *hiran* [blackbuck]. I had a double-barrelled rifle, and Coapman had an over-under combination rifle-shotgun."

"The hiran were out on a flat plain covered with fields. They would run very fast, and then leap high in the air as though they were flying.

What was going to happen? How could we even aim at these creatures? But then, it was incredible, John sahib shot one as it jumped; it was in the air. I swear it is true! And then, as another jumped, Harper did the same thing. Now it was my turn, and I was excited. There were fields all around us and the blackbuck were running. I aimed and fired and one fell down. We had shot three. After I had shot mine, John sahib said that he had doubted that I would hit it. But I told him to forget about it. 'It is just a matter of shooting properly, that is all,' I said. However, the blackbuck I had shot was really out of range; it was too far away and I had been lucky. So it was my mistake."

"Once we got back to the camp I told them all that I had to go home since my mother and wife would be worried. But John sahib wouldn't listen. He insisted that we beat some sugarcane fields before I left. I said, 'OK.' He was like that, you see, telling everyone what to do and when to do it. 'Do this, do that!' he would say. He told me to forget about my wife and mother. 'Women are like that,' he said, 'they worry.'"

"Anyway, there were a few hundred beaters who had been hired from the nearby villages to flush out whatever animals were hiding in the sugarcane fields. All of them were paid. We shot quail and many other things as well. We also brought back five tiger skins from Rothakpur."

"At that time Coapman's eldest son, Johnny, was quite young; Mark was even younger, and Katey, well, she was the eldest. We would all play cards together and just sit to pass the time. I didn't drink then; I didn't even know about it."

*   *   *

"Coapman was hunting with the Nawab sahib at a place called Kanya ki Gauri in a forest near Delhi. They had shot two tigers. Coapman sent a message up to my village telling me to come down and join them. They sent money for my fare. Everything was arranged."

"So I traveled down from here and found my way to the place where they were camped. When I arrived I found that they had all gone off somewhere, so I asked the cook where the sahib was. He, poor fellow, was distraught, and said that whenever he went to call the sahib, that the sahib would curse at him. He had no idea what to do! He warned me about the sahib's temper, but I told him to just tell me where he had gone and that I would go and find him, cursing or no cursing. You see, Coapman had told the villagers that they should not make any noise; that they should not disturb him. When they did, he would get very mad. But when Coapman heard my voice, he called out: 'Oh, so you *have* come!' Then he sent someone to call the Nawab sahib who was down by the river while I stayed up in the village with him and the children."

"After some time, I asked the villagers there about leopards. They told me that they were having trouble with a number of them. They told me the whole story of their troubles; how a leopard had killed many of their cattle. So I went off into the forest to the place they had indicated to see what I could find. After searching for awhile, I found the tracks of leopard and concluded that it must be the one which was causing them trouble, since its tracks were around where there were the tracks of many cows and buffaloes."

"I told Coapman what I had found and we made a plan to sit up for the leopard. We got a calf from one of the villagers and tied it up along the track where I had seen the pug marks. Then we built a *machan* in a tree not far away and the Nawab and I figured out a plan to shoot the leopard. I said to the Nawab sahib, 'I will hold the spot-light, and all you have to do is shoot straight.'"

"Well, during the night the leopard came and killed the calf. Then the Nawab sahib got off a quick shot. All was quiet. He must have missed. However, we couldn't be sure. We waited. Quite a bit of time passed, and the Nawab began to get impatient. I said, 'Let's just wait and see what happens.' So we waited, and waited. . . . Finally, after three hours, I heard some rustling in the *sal* leaves, and I thought to myself, 'OK, here it comes.' It came up to the dead calf slowly and started eating. This time the Nawab sahib shot straight, and the leopard died on the spot."

"Now, the Nawab sahib gave up to one hundred rupees apiece to those who skinned the tigers and leopards which were shot. I had no idea how skinning was done, but earlier I had stood by and watched while some of the men worked. I learned by watching. When it came time to skin the Nawab sahib's leopard, I skinned it myself, right down to taking the cartilage out of the ears! This is not something just anyone can do, but I did it. You have to be a hunter in order to know these things. I got nothing for it though, no money."

* * *

"One day a man had come to go hunting at Koldighat. He was an acquaintance of Coapman and had brought two friends with him. They had hired three coolies as well, so we were a large party. We decided to go down to Koldighat and then work our way up to Moti Dhar."

"Well, on the way up to Moti Dhar we shot two mountain goats. Then we had another chance when we saw a third from that place where you shot the kakar. Do you remember? It was from that very spot, where it is very dangerous. That is also where I fell, you know. Anyway, the man who had come, Coapman's acquaintance, took a long time aiming and fixing his glasses, but when he did finally fire the third ghoral fell down dead."

"With three animals in hand we decided to go back down to the chans at Koldighat and fix something to eat. Our wives were there and said they would fix some of the ghoral meat. So we butchered the animals and they began to prepare the livers."

"Now, there was a forest guard not far away who heard about what was going on and said that he would put a stop to our hunting. Just as food was being prepared he showed up and demanded to know what was going on. Well, John sahib said nothing; he didn't answer. Instead he told the guard to come with him up the ridge above the chans. I went with them. As we were sitting on the ridge a ghoral ran out and the forest guard started shouting: 'Shoot! shoot!' Quickly Coapman aimed and fired. The shot went straight and the ghoral fell down dead. Now we had shot four. Coapman told the forest guard: 'This hill hunting is a difficult thing. You have to be quick and you can't get nervous.' Then the forest guard himself went down and fetched the goat and Coapman gave him some meat. That was that! The poor fellow was at our mercy! He could not so much as move! His strength was completely gone! And we did not even have a license."

*   *   *

"Work went on, and I kept hunting. But then my wife died and my heart was broken. She had fallen sick, so I had come home from Ludhiana to make arrangements for her treatment. Dr. Chappman had operated on her twice, but she died; she died and my heart was heavy. My daughter Dharma, who just left with her husband to go back down to his village, was born by ceasarean section in the Landour hospital, you know. But my wife died."

"Now, back then Coapman was working in a hotel in Africa. That is what I heard, anyway. He heard about what had happened and thought that since my wife had died that I might run away from the village. So he sent letters to me and gave me money."

"It was not long after this when Coapman decided to go to Katmandu. So he wrote me a letter and said that I should leave Pathreni and come with him. I decided to go. Everyone wanted me to go because they all thought that I would otherwise run away from the village on account of my wife's death."

"I arrived in Katmandu and then we went to Tiger Tops near the Bihar border where I started working. I led tours, told people what to do, and showed people animals. Tiger Tops was still under construction then and we were also involved in building houses. One was a big round house in the middle of the compound. Ours were off to one side. There were also stables for the elephants. Oh! How can I explain? It was a city in the middle of the jungle!"

"Now, at Tiger Tops everyone drank except me. Even so, I was entitled to three pegs of whiskey per day. Everything else I had to sign for, and it would be deducted from my pay at the end of the month. So it was not long before I started drinking. But I only drank after I had finished all of my work properly, and before I returned to my house."

"On the safari tours in the game park I would be the one to hold the light and point out the animals. If a tiger came out of the jungle in front of us, I would be the one to shine the light and get it to move. The light was the only way to control the animals. So once a group of people had come from Japan. They were all terribly scared when a tiger appeared in front of us, but I shone the light directly on it and told them not to be afraid. But then, instead of moving off, the tiger roared. It wouldn't move for the longest time! It was very, very close!"

"It was like this that I learned to drink liquor in Nepal; when we had to face tigers and not shoot. I survived three close encounters with tigers and one with a bear. It would have been dangerous even if I had been able to shoot. All I had with me was a *khukari*—you know, one of those thick, curved Nepali knives—and I thought to myself, if I am attacked I will cut off their paws! I held on to the khukari firmly while the others, the people on the tour, stood behind me. I told them to stand quietly. The tigers growled a lot. There is a grass there in the forest near Tiger Tops called *dhudi*, or elephant grass. The tigers ran into this grass and hid, and we had to go in after them. I pissed in my pants I was so scared. Now, anyone can get scared, but when you are scared silly to the point of going crazy, then what! I just said to myself: 'Kill me if you wish, tiger. That is it. We will see.'"

* * *

"When I left the village I traveled to Tiger Tops on my own. Along the way, just across the Nepalese border at Birganj, I was sitting in a restaurant with some Nepalese. They were drinking, so I thought I would also have a drink. I asked them if there was any liquor to be had, and they told me to sit with them. They asked me what I would like. They asked if I wanted chicken. When I said yes, they brought it out and I ate it. Then they gave me a jug full of liquor. Now, it had been two or three years since I had anything to drink, and the trip had already been long, so I asked if I could take the liquor back with me to my room in the hotel. However, it was not really legal to drink, so they said I could not since I might get caught. In the end I had to drink it all there."

"When I had finished and was ready to go, I took out an Indian ten-rupee note in order to pay. However, we were in Nepal and they said that I could not use Indian money there. Fortunately, though, the people in the restaurant agreed to change some money for me so that I would have enough for the bus in the morning."

"Since I had enough time, I decided to go to Katmandu for a visit instead of going directly to Tiger Tops. I knew I would not have another chance. In the morning I caught the bus. Now, half way between Birganj and Katmandu there is a place where everyone stops to eat. The people there were all drinking openly. They were all Gurkhas and Nepalese; not a Hindustani among them. I sat down and ate and drank as well. Now, this fellow who was traveling with me—I guess I was not alone—didn't drink. He was afraid of what might happen to him if he got drunk."

"Now, the distance we had already traveled that day was as if you were to go from Dehra Dun to Tehri via Rishikesh, about one hundred kilometers. We got back in the bus and drove on. I saw sugarcane growing beside the road, and by six in the evening we got to Katmandu."

"While traveling I had made friends with a Gurkha and asked him to give us directions to a hotel. However, he told us to forget about the hotel and come stay with him at his home. I said fine, but the fellow traveling with me was scared and thought the Gurkha might try and take advantage of us in his house. I told him to forget his troubles; to relax. Then I said, 'Listen, this is neither your country nor mine, but we will go together as brothers.' I made him understand, you see, made him understand that there was nothing to fear."

"The Gurkha took us to his house, fed us, and showed us around the town. Later on, I asked him how to find Dr. Fleming's home, you know, the teacher from school. He gave me directions, and I took a taxi. I found my own people! We met. We got together. Bobby was there along with his father and I told them what I was doing; that I was on my way to Tiger Tops. Bobby showed me all around town and took me to see the temples as well. There is one thing, though, the *bhajans* and *kirtans* (devotional songs) they do there in Nepal do not compare to the ones we do here; their songs are not on par with ours, that is. They do have one custom which is better than ours, however; they are rajputs (the sons of kings), and meat eating is all out in the open."

"When I had to leave Katmandu I got a ride on a truck back to Birganj. The driver was a friend of Bobby's. In Birganj I went to the bank and asked if they knew how to get to the place where John sahib was. They said yes, and told me that the road to Mangoli left right from there. At Pashutap it turns. I caught a jeep from Birganj to Pashutap and arrived in the evening. I stopped at a hotel. The owner, who was an old man, told me how to get to Tiger Tops from there. But it was already late, so I decided to stay the night and go the next day."

"Now, everyone there was drinking liquor. The fellow who was with me wouldn't touch any. He was worried that something might happen to us if we drank. He kept complaining, so I locked him in our room with a bottle and said that I was going down to bathe in the river and have a look around. He was afraid someone might attack me, but I told him to forget about it, that I could take care of myself. I walked around. Food was provided by the hotel, so we ate and drank there."

"In the morning I got a ride up to Gangoli where the Tiger Tops airfield is. It is really just a big field with white rocks on it. Just as we arrived a plane full of people landed and at the same time Johnny came out of the jungle leading a line of elephants to pick up the guests. There were also people there to guard the plane. They were fixing their food. Then Johnny saw me and we exchanged greetings. He was surprised that I had found my way, but I told him that the address I had been given was correct and that I had no problem."

"The elephants carried us through the jungle and across the river to Dunga where there was a fleet of cars waiting to carry us to the hotel. What a jungle! When we got to the hotel I found them all playing cards: John sahib, memsahib, and the kids. They were all very happy to see me. I looked around and acquainted myself with the things in that place."

"I rested for two days and then started work on the third. 'What kind of work?' I asked. Well, my job was to show people animals; all sorts of animals: rhino, blackbuck, swamp deer, leopard, and tiger. We would tie up buffalo calves at Surang Ka Nalla and at Dakhari Nalla in order to attract the tigers. I had to get up at three in the morning to make arrangements, but I was always ready. Many of the guests who I showed around were scared, but I just always told them to calm down and relax."

"You see, this is my addiction; my infatuation! I am a hunter! I did good work there, very good work indeed. The work was good."

"Then the king of Nepal, who was a friend of John sahib's, died while his children were visiting the park. Now there was some kind of conflict going on. I told John sahib that running a hotel was hard work, and that those who knew the king, but were opposed to what John sahib was doing at Tiger Tops, were talking behind his back. I did not know their language, but I could understand what they were saying. In the end they gave John sahib a bad name and he had to leave. They were all old retired military types there: Gun Bahadur, Beet Bahadur, and so forth. Now some of them were good, and some were bad, but John sahib would not listen to me. In the end he was forced out. He would have listened to Campbell sahib, you see. But he was a man of his own heart and would not listen to others."

*   *   *

"Once Murphy sahib from Tiger Tops came here to Pathreni to go hunting. I told him not to worry about a permit as it would only cause unnecessary trouble."

"I remember that at Tiger Tops Murphy sahib would have a glass of whiskey in his hand as soon as the sun went down. We would collect huge *sal* logs for a bonfire and sit around and talk. My job was simply to make those who had come to the park happy. That was all—make them happy and show them a good time."

"Once a man who had come to take pictures got so frightened when a rhino and tiger started fighting that he could hardly move. I told him to just relax and take his pictures."

"We had elephants there to take the guests around. One was named Sundar Prasad. I would command the elephants and say, 'Sundar Prasad, go carefully; beware!' When driving Sundar Prasad, I would tell him to drag his back legs down the steep slopes so that his back would stay flat and the guests would not fall off."

"Then there was Champa Kali, the tame elephant who would scare off the wild ones. They sharpened her tusks and would give her four bottles of liquor to drink. I would tell her, 'Champa Kali, leave some for me!' She would leave me half a bottle to drink!"

"One day our elephants stole two bottles of liquor and got in a fight with some wild elephants. Our elephants were surrounded, but there was nothing we could do. We were not able to shoot, of course. That was the problem, you see. We had all had something to drink, the elephants and those of us who were looking after them. But it was the only way to go in and do the sort of things we had to do. A man's heart is weak."

" 'Bal Bahadur, you fool, what are you doing!' we shouted. 'Don't let those elephants go in there!!' But they had already gone into the forest. Sundar Prasad pinned one of the wild elephants up against a *sal* tree and ran it through with one of her tusks. When her mount brought her back he cursed at her: 'So you ran away did you, sister-fucker,' he said. 'You thought you could run away?' This was our game; our fun! Yes, it was our work, but it was our fun as well. Certainly we had our expenses, but we also had money to spend."

"I tell you John sahib has done many things, but nothing to compare with Tiger Tops. He taught the people who are there now. What they know he alone taught them. But let me tell you friend, it will never be like it was in our time."

"There was a place called Bhimlar Chowki which is flat and open like Dehra Dun. We could not take our cars there, but we had built a place that was set up with lights so that the guests could take pictures from the edge of the plain. I tell you, the animals there were amazing. Some had horns as big as my arms, the sister-fuckers!! What can I say! And there were lines and lines of wild boar, but we could not shoot them."

"One day I was driving along in the reserved forest with a fellow named Ram who was a driver for Tiger Tops. I told him to just casually run over a wild boar if he ever had a chance. We had not had any meat for a long time, and this way we could get some. Well, he did it! There were six or seven of us in the jeep and we got some liquor from the village nearby. And what sister-fucking meat! I tell you, those Gurkhas are expert at this sort of thing. They got a cooking pot, filled it with meat, and fixed the boar right there. The next morning we left. We didn't leave a single trace, not even any bones. This was my thievery there!"

"There were also rhino poachers in the park. They would come across the river which marked the boundary between India and Nepal, kill the rhinos, and then take the horns back with them into India. There is a type of grasslike bamboo called *babula* which we cut and use for our chans over here. We also make it into rope. Well, these fellows came across on the pretext of asking us to let them cut some from the park forest. They wanted to buy it from us, but we told them that we had none to spare. We had use for it ourselves. There were eight or ten of them all together; all thieves—big men—from the nearby villages. They were all wearing *dhotis* [loin cloths]. Sahib told us to give them tea. We did, and they drank it and left. They were all Nepali; Gurkhas. I don't know where they had hidden their guns. But right after drinking the tea, they left saying that they were going home. Then, at about four o'clock we heard a shot fired down near Sungar Nalla. They had killed a rhino. Now, they don't have any forest guards in that forest, only Gurkha military fellows. Anyway, the soldiers went after the poachers, caught them and turned the rhino horn over to the government; to the *Shripanch* [head man or local leader]."

"I tell you, it is a dangerous place there. People used to get killed by tigers in the forest."

*   *   *

"Hunting was not permitted in the forest reserve around Tiger Tops, so we got a permit to hunt at Nawalpur down in the terai forest. There is a river there and John sahib made a boat with his own hands from material brought from the United States. We used it for hunting ducks. My job was to start the engine. Whenever it came time, I would say: 'Give me half a measure of whiskey and I will have enough strength.' You see, I was afraid the boat might sink, but John sahib said that was out of the question; there was not a chance."

"Later on we went leopard hunting and made a machan up in a tree. Now, as you know John sahib is very heavy so he wanted to climb into the machan and make sure that it was strong enough. Mind you, this was not just any old machan we had put up, it was big enough for four people to sleep in comfortably and we had covered the bottom with branches so it could not be seen from the ground. Big men were coming to hunt from the United States, and they needed a solid, sturdy machan."

"Now, I told him not to go out too far on the branch, but he did not listen. The branch broke, and he fell. It was a tall sal tree and he fell straight down and hit the ground with a tremendous thud: bhaaaaat!! I ran over and found that his mouth was clamped shut, so I took a hand-kerchief out of his pocket and ran down to the river about a kilometer away to get some water. I ran back with the wet handkerchief and found that the others were fanning him. His teeth were still clamped shut so I squeezed some water into his mouth as best I could. At first he just made a gurgling sound, but then he revived."

"I tell you, I broke down and wept! There was no one else there who I knew; none of my own people. I told him, 'Listen, you have called me here where I don't know anyone and then you go and just about kill yourself. What is the meaning of this!' Anyway, I massaged his shoulders and gradually he revived. And then what did he do; what do you think? Even with great difficulty, and obvious pain, he climbed into the machan and shot a tiger. John sahib was sly. You see, he knew that if he did not shoot the tiger that I would! Nothing got past him. But I tell you, I was the one who made the tiger dance in the torch light!"

"He and I have been together since we were young, and we have grown old together. . . . He has spent a lot of money on me, and I have spent all of my life hunting in the jungle; but it is good, hard work, and not just any old way to live your life."

*   *   *

"There was an old tiger in the forest reserve just across the border into Bihar from Tiger Tops. Hunting was allowed there by permit. Now, the old conservator of forests was a friend of John sahib's, and so we had contrived to save the tiger for him to shoot."

"Well, you see, in their youth everyone is strong, just as you are. It is a matter of age. But the old conservator of forests was very feeble and unable to hold a gun steady, much less aim and shoot. And yet the poor fellow was very keen on shooting a tiger. So, John sahib and I sat around and thought about this for a long time; we thought about the old tiger which was being saved for the conservator. We had been asked to arrange the hunt, but were afraid that if the conservator did not shoot the tiger that the whole thing would be thought of as a waste of both time and money. As it happened we went ahead and made arrangements for the hunt, and the conservator sat up for the tiger but never got a chance to shoot. After a few attempts, he had to give up and go back to Delhi. So finally it was decided that we would shoot the tiger for the conservator. We had a plan, you see."

"We stayed on in the camp. Then one day, after coffee at about four P.M., we went into the jungle and crossed ravine after ravine looking for tracks. I was beginning to think that the whole thing was pointless, but then we found some pug marks in the sand. I measured them and we determined that it was an old tiger; that it must be the big one we were looking for. Going back to the village near our camp we tried to make arrangements to get a calf. We wanted to tie it up near where we had seen the tracks so that the tiger would return and kill it, but the Hindustanis who were with us were crooked and made some kind of protest. I don't know what the sister-fuckers' objections were, but in the end I told them each to take ten rupees and get lost. I was a guru regarding these things! If the tiger killed the calf we could sit up over it and get a chance to shoot. Finally, in the end, we managed to get a calf from the villagers and we tied it up on the path."

"The tiger killed that calf, and I immediately called Delhi to tell the old conservator that his tiger had been located. But by the time he arrived back at our camp the tiger had killed two more calves. Now the retired conservator was a very old sahib; an Englishman who in his prime must have been a good hunter. We sat around the fire in the evenings and drank. All of us drank. Now the old man said to me, 'Dil Das, I have the wisdom of age, but you are a young man and can work with your hands.' You see, he had been a good hunter once, but now that he was old he was worried that he would not be able to shoot straight. Anyway, I told him not to worry; that we had located the tiger and that everything would work out this time."

"We went and sat up over one of the dead calves. I held the torch and told the conservator to be careful. I told him to be ready for whatever happened. And then the tiger came! I flashed on the light and the old man fired at exactly the same instant. The tiger did not so much as move! The bullet went right through its throat! He could not have missed, you see. We had fun."

"You see, hunting is a very dangerous business! One must not be afraid. One must not get shaken. It is for this reason that I learned how to drink. . . ."

"Ah, my friend, John sahib has made lots of money, but he has friends all around the world. If he goes to Danda ki Beli he will find friends. There are friends of his at Dhanaulti, Jaunpur, Sarona, and Saklana, and friends in all the villages around here. He has been many places and done many things. That is why he is happy."

*   *   *

"While we were working at Tiger Tops, we went down into the Bihar forest where hunting was permitted. The conservator sahib was with us, and there were some filmmakers as well. We contacted the district forest officer in order to arrange for the hunt, and I explained to him who I was. I told him I was from Mussoorie, from the village Pathreni, out beyond Jain sahib's jungle and below the forest *chowki*."

"There were many of us with lots of guns and we wandered through the forest. It was here that the old tiger was being kept for the conservator sahib, the one that John sahib shot in the end."

"While the conservator was with us we organized a big beat, a huge beat over an area as big as all of Jain sahib's jungle put together plus Pari Tibba over there, and Chamasari as well—that whole area. Well, while we were beating this jungle a *serow* [small, short-horned goat] came out of the bushes and the conservator sahib shot it."

"Later, the conservator sahib said he wanted to shoot a leopard, so we had a machan made up in a tree where he could sit. However, we all had doubts about whether or not the conservator would be able to shoot straight. Then we had an idea. John sahib had shot a leopard the night before. We took this leopard, which by mid-morning had gotten stiff, and propped it up in some bushes not far away from the machan. Then we tied a long wire to its tail and trailed the wire off to some other bushes and hid it so that the old man would not be able to see what was going on."

"After the old man had climbed into the tree and had been sitting for some time, John sahib, who was with him, pointed out the leopard as though it had suddenly appeared! The old man aimed and fired. Just as he shot, at that very instant, I pulled the wire and the leopard fell over!"

"We did all of this just so it could be filmed, you see. If we had to wait for a real live leopard, and for the conservator to really shoot it, it would have been much more difficult. So the conservator was happy, and the film crew took their pictures and were very happy."

"From Bihar we came back to Delhi where John sahib went back to work. Now, I had to sneak past the guard at the Coca-Cola plant to try and find him since no outsiders were allowed into the compound. But the guard saw me and got suspicious. He said he would call the police. I told him that I was a friend of John sahib's and to go ahead and call the police if he dared. Who did he think he was! We got into an argument, but in the end he didn't believe that I was a friend of Coapman's, so I had to wait outside the gate. Later Campbell sahib came by in his red jeep. I told him that I had been waiting all day and had nothing to eat. We went and ate."

* * *

"Hunting, this was the only work John sahib did. . . ."

"Later on John sahib left his first wife and married a second time. She was very young. She must have been half his age. When I met her at the Savoy Hotel up in Mussoorie I told her that it was good that John sahib had not married anyone twice as old! John sahib translated for me. Johnny was also there, and they all laughed. Later he divorced this wife as well and then remarried again. He brought his third wife up to Mussoorie in June and wanted to go hunting. What was I to do! I managed to get a pass, however, and we went hunting bear out near Kimoi for a week."

"You see, it was in his heart that he should be quick to anger. That is why he was married so many different times. And now I have heard that he has remarried yet again!"

* * *

"Remember when John sahib fell? He just slipped on that rock like a buffalo and was gone. . . . He caught that tree, and that saved him. But even then, half dead, he was telling us to go on hunting! And the ghoral you had shot earlier in the day, we didn't even eat it. It went rotten right here where we are sitting."

"After you shot that one, and I went down and found it, why did we go on hunting? It was a big one. We should have been satisfied. . . ."

"It is good we didn't stop at Chattarmani the pandit's on the way back up, otherwise we would never have gotten him up and out the next morning. Even so he was so stiff that he could not get out of bed. My wife and I massaged him, you know. Ask him sometime and he will tell you. . . . And do you remember how your father went and brought that doctor, Dr. Olsen, all the way down here. He looked at John sahib and said, 'I can't see any bones for all the fat!' We died laughing! But, I tell you, it was really lucky that nothing was broken."

"He feared nothing. There was no fear in his heart. . . . I must say, though, I am convinced! He is a sharp man. . . . You see, he wasn't even a Pahari and yet he came out as the father of all Paharis! I tell you, he could curse and swear, rant and rave, but he escaped death by the smallest fraction. . . ."

"He had this house built, and that stone table over there. He called his whole family here. It will be here even after he dies. . . . You see, it is good. It is good. People will come and they will see that we were friends, and that we did this and that. Your brother Steve's son will come down here also. And your cousin Tommy's son as well.

"Wherever John sahib is now, I hope he is happy. . . . He has made money though. That is why his wife got angry with him you know. I talked with him and tried to make him understand, but. . . ."

"You see what happened was this. One day in Delhi it was Christmas time—but it was always the same, regardless of the holiday—and John sahib's wife said, 'Let's celebrate.' But all he wanted to do was go hunting. I talked to him and said, 'Why do we have to go hunting today? There is always tomorrow.' It was his *jid* [cocksure attitude] though—his personality—and he would not listen."

"And she worried about him too. I tried to tell him. I explained everything to him. I said, 'Don't go into the villages and drink. Who knows what will happen to you.' But he was like that, poor fellow. He did what he wanted to do."

"And remember! Remember how he yelled at us that day after his fall when we did not make his tea quickly enough? And just the night before he had been eaten alive by leeches! I tell you, what can you do, what can you say?"

*   *   *

"I will die here in Pathreni you understand. . . . I have land here in the jungle and I am happy. No one can stop me from hunting here. . . . But there is one thing. I speak from my heart as we are sitting here now. This jungle is not productive. It is our problem; a problem we must face. Go to Dehra Dun and you will see that there are fruit trees and many other things, but here there is nothing."

"I told this to John sahib when he and I were hunting with Bhutto. You know, [Zulfikar Ali] Bhutto, the prime minister of Pakistan. We had taken him hunting once and he told John sahib that if I wanted land in Pakistan it was mine for the asking. But John sahib said no. He told Bhutto that I would not go, that I could not go. John sahib has taught me what I know, and in Pakistan I would have no idea what to do."

Chapter 6
Land Masters
Purebred History

Dil Das and I had gone over to the garden behind Coapman's empty house to cut some roses that he wanted to send back up with me to give to my parents at Oakville. It had been many years since the bushes had been pruned, and the flowers seemed to have gone wild, growing big and floppy, having lost all refined qualities except for the richness of their scent. It was here as we cut hybrid roses that Dil Das told me the story of his encounter with the prime minister of Pakistan. He was serious, of course. And for all I know maybe he did go hunting with Zulfikar Ali Bhutto, and did "learn everything he knows" from John sahib. In any case, there was something fantastically real, in a tragic sort of way, about the way he spoke, first about his basic happiness and material well being, then his economic problems, and finally about an offer of land in the shadow of an epic event that seemed to partition a great many things while appearing to resolve a problem of poverty.

*   *   *

There is an old photograph of me as a child, one of many, mixed in with thousands of other slides. As I write it is being sorted, systematically into family history, by my parents who have retired from India.

The photograph was taken in Etah, a small, dusty district town to the east of Agra, where my father worked—long after the era of blind-faith conversion, in a time of transition from preaching and prayer to community development—as a village pastor, but where the work he and my mother did, among the poor and outcaste, was social reform. I am wearing a green checkered shirt and shorts, a uniform of a kind. My hair is blond and curly. I am standing among friends holding a pop-gun and pointing it upward at a green papaya. The photograph was taken beside our family car, in front of our home, a large, sprawling, dust-brown mis-

sion bungalow built with high ceilings, wide verandas, and thick walls
to keep out the heat. The photograph shows in the yard in front of our
house; the hard-packed flood-plain *doab*-dirt yard which faced the poul-
try farm, the pig yards, and the mission compound.

As I remember it, I spent a lifetime in Etah, a lifetime outdoors with
Charaunji the driver's children: with Edu, whose real name was Edward,
with Saroj, Kishan, Rajan, and Nagma. We played endless games and
went on wild adventures chasing rabbits through the garden, fishing in
the tanks, baking stolen potatoes in the oven-hot brick-kiln sand. We
were running, always running, fast and ever faster, with fear and trembling, across the mud-rutted coral where the huge stud boar lay, pink
eyes never blinking. Endlessly we ran across the barren canal-leeched
saltpeter-flaked *maidan* plain near the railway tracks, racing we ran to
see who would be first to reach and climb the mulberry tree.

But above all else I remember running to hunt doves with slingshots.
I remember making slingshots, looking at the branches of trees and
bushes to find the best wood for slingshots, searching, endlessly, for
scraps of old inner-tubing to put on slingshots, imagining the powerful elasticity of rubber tractor-tubing stretched back tight on slingshots,
one-by-one collecting cankerous *kankars*, deeply pitted, perfectly shaped
brick-kiln pebbles, that is, to shoot from slingshots. With meticulous care
Samuel, the cook's helper, would wrap the thin strips of carefully cut
inner-tubing around and around and around the forks of our slingshots
so they would not break, so that not even a fractional gap remained between rubber and wood.

While my brother Steve and I hunted with Edward and the others,
Charaunji and my father worked. And the work they did—at least in
part, and at least as I remember it, with images of warm incubators and
fat suckling sows—was breeding chickens and pigs. With respect to pigs
in particular the idea was to improve, through the simple genetics of reproduction, the quality of stock held by those who owned pigs, for meat
and night-soil consumption, in rural North Indian villages: untouchable,
outcaste sweepers.

Since no one else but the lowest of the low works with pigs—a veri-
table symbol of impurity, if not also something more substantial (since
human feces are here at the looping end of a very short food chain)—
the idea was to turn the terms of defilement into the means of hybrid
production, a profitable means of production which no one else but
sweepers could touch, much less buy, own, and sell. And so the fat, pink,
short-snouted American sows on the mission compound were crossed
systematically with the smaller, dark, bristle-backed "country" breed to
produce sounders of little pigs; pigs which, while still eating shit, would
grow up bigger and be worth more on the one hand, and yet retain a

high degree of inbred resistance to heat, dust, and disease on the other. The idea was, in other words, to cross-breed capitalism, caste, and the local division of labor in order to promote a kind of class struggle based on the fractured eugenic politics of an ironic moral economy, a moral economy of justice—rather than development per se—which managed, somehow, to slip past cynicism and still be blithely critical of oppression, strategically utilitarian, and yet fundamentally humanitarian all at once. It was a post-Marxian missionary endeavor in the best possible sense of the term.

But what I remember most clearly in all of this, in the converted world of poor, landless, pork-eating Christians, is the technology of reproduction, since at the base of everything was not just the fact of poverty, but the virtual necessity of turning, as much as possible, less than nothing of material worth into something of value. I remember Etah as an experimental workshop of sorts which seemed to grow, expanding upward and outward from pigpen genetics to other things, to handmade looms for weaving useless grass into useful dinner placemats, for example, and, finally—making a virtue of necessity in a world of chronic underemployment—to training the Christian sons of village sweepers in the practical, vocational skills of driving and repairing cars.

The Grand Trunk Road runs up and down the Gangetic plain right through Etah, and the cars that run on it, along with the buses and trucks that transport people and produce through the Hindi heartland, seem to be in a constant state of disrepair. Ours certainly was; a boxy old gray-blue Landmaster, made by Hindustan Motors in Kanpur around mid-century and modeled on the British Austin, it marked a point of industrial transition from colonial to national production. While denoting progress (ironically, of course, in a socialist era of land reform), it was, however, always breaking down, usually on the road to Kasganj or Mainpuri, on the way to and from other mission stations, on picnics and hunting trips, and, at least once, in the middle of Corbett Park. It was a slow, low-slung, bumpy car, a useless piece of engineering designed, at best, for the better-metaled infrastructure of another time and place. By 1963 or so our Landmaster was a machine of marginal utility in constant need of being fixed, and that, in one way or another, is what my father and Charaunji always did.

In this sense, the old Landmaster was the perfect car for a place like Etah; a place which—at its best—took pointed issue with the machinations of both tradition and modernity, with evangelical Protestantism, postcolonial progress, and the prejudice of pure breeding. But deeper down the experimental work of rebuilding was also much more than this, for it was a recognition that there was something of great value in constantly fixing things which seemed beyond repair, of taking up, by choice and by design, the old, worn down parts of broken, useless things and making them work; not perfectly, to be sure—for that was not the point at all—but making them work almost in spite of things so as to control, in as much as possible at least, and with compassion, the nature of dispassionate change.

But I have not been entirely honest here, for the allegories of faith—of the will to reform—lose a great deal in translation. And motor-driven technology, as an immaculate concept, is ultimately keyed to a different history than that of a history of landlessness and semi-skilled vocational training. Saroj drove a milk truck for some time on the Grand Trunk Road between Agra and Etah, as did his father after my family and I left and made our escape into the hills; Kishan and Rajan, I am told, are mechanics now; and Edward, along with tens of thousands of other young men for whom education has not paid off and being Christian is neither here nor there, has moved to Delhi and now works, I believe, as a driver for a development agency. Edward is a fleet driver of Toyota Land Cruisers, Isuzu Troopers, and Ford Broncos, perfectly luxurious First World tanks (with tubeless, puncture-proof tires, no less, and maybe the emblem of a dove on the doors) deployed in the war against Third World poverty—which is, I suppose, back again, the long way around, to reconversion; to pure-bred, blind-faith evangelism.

In light of this, and in light of Dil Das's dialogue with Bhutto and Coapman, I am more than simply critical about the work of development, and not simply because there is bad faith in neo-colonialism, and something insidious about the obscene salaries involved, the channeled flow of First World capital, and the spawning industry of highly technical knowledge. I have become critically skeptical of all development on account of a deep ethical deception which can make, if one is not extremely careful, a righteous fetish of oneself—one's class, status, and party, that is—in light of other people's problems.

I claim no moral high ground here, no privileged position as such, other than a postcolonial pedigree of sorts which strains against partition but prohibits resolution. I am just trying to reflect on where I stand, pen in one hand, sling in the other, in relation to land, power, knowledge, and the hunting stories told by the pork-eating son of a Christian convert whose name—Dil Das—translates, almost literally, into an enslaved confession of faith.

Part III
Shram Kand

THE BOOK OF LABOR

Chapter 7
Dairying

An Untold Story

I distinctly remember once while in junior high school earnestly telling my father as we walked along the Tehri road, which ran above our
house near the school, that I wanted to take pictures of the dudwallas
we met along the way so that I could show them to people in the United
States. I also distinctly remember that both the milkmen and those to
whom their pictures would be shown could be totally anonymous; their
identities did not matter. I had this idea in my head that it was somehow important for people "back home" to understand how people far
away lived their lives; for them to learn to appreciate an aspect of the
world upon which I thought I had a privileged perspective. I was interested in communicating difference and thereby making sense. But what
I thought then was that I needed to make sense of the milkmen. Despite
my daily encounters with them, they still seemed strange enough to in-
cite translation. Which is to say two things: that I could not just let the
milkmen be, and that it did not occur to me—at least in the same way—
that I should take pictures of people in the United States and spend
time explaining them to the milkmen.

In retrospect it seems quite clear that what I was really after was not
the milkmen's "strange identity" at all, but rather a clearer sense of my
own enigmatic self.

I can clearly see myself standing on the road watching a group of
milkmen walking toward me, from around a bend, underneath thickly
foliated oak trees, with their sheet-metal milk containers strapped to
their backs in woven, rope fishnet bags; each milk container capped with
a wooden plug pressed into place over top of a wad of leaves fanned out
like a hand of playing cards, or a twist of grass, set in place to keep the
milk from spilling out when sloshed from side to side by each successive
stride. I can also see myself, years later as a professor, standing in a class-
room talking about milk containers, net bags, and the daily routine of

walking into town while pointing to an image on a screen that reflects my own perspective while depicting what I take to be a distinctive scene. My projection of the milkmen's strangeness, and my appropriation of their still images, lets me define my own position by claiming and proclaiming knowledge about someone to someone else. It is the curious status of translator which appeals to me as the only secure point of reference I have when trying to locate myself in relation to a world at once familiar and strange. And while this perspective certainly helps to flesh out and texture the production of public knowledge, it is a position which leaves both Self and Other seeming rather two-dimensional and fragmented.

For his part, Dil Das spoke very little about that of which I had first sought to make adolescent sense. He did not reflect on his life as a milkman. In fact, many years after I wanted naively to photograph the milkmen, I tried to capture them in a more sophisticated academic manner. In trying to interview Dil Das about dairy farming, however, I discovered that he was a terrible informant when it came to collecting data on anything concrete. He would give the simplest, shortest answer to a direct question, in a flat, disinterested, and painfully formal tone, and would not elaborate at all. He seemed to regard the business of dairying as both horribly mundane and somehow alienating.

And yet, despite his rather ambivalent attitude toward his life work, he was commonly known throughout Mussoorie as *thekedar* sahib, or "Mr. Contractor," given the fact that he had been, for many years, a successful, large-volume dudwalla. In spite of Dil Das's reluctance to locate himself within the bounds of a political economy which at least nominally defined him, I have been able to pick up enough information over the years to reconstruct a plausible account of his life as a dairy farmer. What I have done, therefore, is to force Dil Das's life story to come to terms, at least on some level, with the basic context of its telling: the peasant world of Garhwal. I have added this largely unspoken story as the "silent" subtext to Dil Das's own narrative, because it helps explain an important dimension of his character and the economy within which he lived. It is powerfully ironic, however, that in representing what many readers will feel—with a sigh of relief, no doubt—is the "real-life" ethnography of a Pahari villager, I have been forced to reconstruct an autobiographical fiction. In order to translate a private life into public knowledge I have had to make up half the story. I have also used that which makes most academic sense, and that which most clearly locates me in both text and context, to deconstruct a biographical myth by writing ethnohistory. So that which sounds most real to life, to the truth, as it were, is really much closer to fiction than is the more fantastic biography Dil Das chose to narrate.

It was Dil Das's grandfather, Garib Das, a man whose name seemed to seal the fate of his lineage, who first settled in what is now Pathreni. Garib Das was from a place called Rohilla up in the high Himalayas to the east of Uttarkashi. He was one of four brothers, all of whom would trek back and forth between their village home and a camp in the lower Himalayas, spending six months in each place. The primary purpose for coming to the area around Mussoorie was the market it provided for bamboo baskets and for woven bamboo matting. After six months the family would use their earnings to buy up a supply of salt, oil, and other essential items and head back to their family home.

On account of not having any sons, sometime around the end of the nineteenth century, Garib Das adopted one of his brother's children, a boy named Gur Das. A number of years later, perhaps through a second marriage, Garib Das had four more sons and a daughter. By this time, however—between 1922 and 1925—Gur Das had already married and had two children of his own, the eldest of whom was Dil Das. At some point, it is not clear exactly when, but probably when Garib Das became too old to travel, Gur Das decided to settle near Mussoorie. He built a family home below a young walnut tree on the saddle of a ridge within easy walking distance of town and near a good supply of bamboo. When Dil Das and his four uncles were young, Garib Das and Gur Das would go down into the jungle below the village and cut thin, scrub bamboo from the shaded valleys. They stripped these into flexible weaving cane from which they produced winnowing baskets, vermin-proof storage bins, bread containers, and a host of other essential components of the village domestic economy.

While weaving was primarily a village and intervillage industry, bamboo matting and containers became valued urban and suburban commodities for a relatively short period of time after Mussoorie came into its own as a colonial resort town around the turn of the century. According to Dil Das, Oakville, my family home, built by Colonel Young in the first half of the nineteenth century, was at one point furnished with bamboo floor coverings made by his father and grandfather. It is now furnished with waste baskets, laundry hampers, flower baskets, and lamp shades made by the youngest of Dil Das's uncles.

In the early part of the twentieth century, Gur Das and his father had a standing contract with Woodstock School for floor coverings and refuse baskets—carried on the backs of sweepers to collect litter—which they would deliver to various houses and offices in Landour. However, with the introduction of jute and cotton carpets on the one hand, and tin trunks, gunny sacks, and plastic bags on the other, the bottom fell out of the local weaving industry. After he had already started taking on tailoring work as a sideline, Gur Das started selling water buffalo milk in the 1940s in order to supplement his income from bamboo. His much younger brothers also sold milk and worked in construction, among many other things. They remained, however, primarily bamboo weavers. Although in age almost a contemporary of his uncles, Dil Das was a whole generation apart, and therefore never learned how to weave. Instead, expanding his father's herd of water buffaloes, he developed the dairy business into the family's primary source of income.

If you were to think of an animal suited to the Himalayas, it would certainly not be a water buffalo, which weighs two thousand pounds or more. Gravity is only the most obvious thing with which it is at odds. Narrow, slippery paths with jutting rocks and sharp, hairpin bends precariously accommodate its wide, swaying bulk. But there is also something about the aesthetic of its contours—sagging belly, broad back, and wide, splayed hooves—which seem at odds with the vertical world it is made to live in. Cows, particularly small "mountain cows," are much more sure-footed and can graze on the steep slopes of the lower ranges where agility is virtually coded in the tell-tale sound of the bells around their necks as they negotiate the criss-cross trails which bear their name. However, they produce only a fraction of the milk that a stall-fed buffalo can, and although milkmen often have a stock of free-ranging cows, their "purer" milk is usually kept for ritual use and home consumption. From across a valley, tethered outside on a bright sunny winter day, a cluster of five or six water buffaloes look, unlike their sacred cousins, both incongruous and somehow profane, like thick black ticks stuck in the fold of some great animal's skin. But appearances aside, they are the life blood of many who live in the lower Himalayas and sustain themselves on the uncertain business of dairying. It has certainly been so for Dil Das, whose daily routine for years has been structured by the rhythmic demands of bovine needs, a demand so all-consuming that a common greeting in the hills inquires nominally after the harmony of one's household, whereas the real question—the critical condition of harmony—as Dil Das's uncle Tulsi once told me, has little to do with the human condition, and everything to do with whether or not one's buffaloes are safe and comfortable: milked, watered, and fed.

By the late 1950s, Dil Das had a contract to sell milk to Wynberg Allen, another Christian boarding school, and soon had upward of ten buffaloes. Like most others who got involved in the milk trade, Dil Das and his family continued to farm the land around their settlement. Gur Das had built terraced fields in order to provide at least a portion of the wheat, lentils, ginger, garlic, potatoes, and vegetables his family needed. However, the land around Pathreni is not very productive and the family has never tried to maximize its agricultural output. Over the past twenty years more and more of the fields have been left fallow. The demands of dairying are such that single-commodity capitalism plays a much stronger hand than broad-based subsistence farming.

Dudwallas like Dil Das walk into town daily in order to deliver milk. Their business is governed by this and other routine activities. In order to sell milk on whatever scale one must be able to supply a set volume, at a set time, every day. One must, therefore, establish a fairly rigid schedule of activities which ensure the most efficient production and delivery of milk. The milkmen who walk along Tehri road leave their villages just after dawn in order to get their milk into town sometime between nine and ten in the morning.

Milk consumers differ greatly in scale. Large hotels at the west end of town like the Savoy and Hackman's, and boarding schools like St. Georges, Guru Nanak Fifth Centenary, and Oak Grove, contract upward of seventy liters a day. Middle-range hotels, restaurants, and confectioners may buy twenty-five or thirty liters. Individual households often get as little as one or two liters a day. Unlike large-volume dealers like Dil Das, who only contracted with Wynberg Allen and Woodstock, most milkmen who sell milk to the middle-range customers prefer to have at least three or four clients, to protect themselves if one or even two contracts fall through. These milkmen, who are more numerous than the single-contract dealers, tend to move through town slowly, stopping off at various points to dispense their milk. After lunch, which is sometimes provided by a hotel owner or confectioner, they spend the afternoon buying supplies, meeting with other milkmen, and negotiating deals before setting off to get back home in time to milk their buffaloes at dusk.

Milk is delivered only by men. As in Dil Das's case, the volume being delivered is often too much for one man to carry. Ratnu, Rukam, and Sheri would often help their elder brother make his deliveries. When Dil Das was absent, there was always someone to fill in. For a short period of time Dil Das followed the lead of some of his neighbors and bought a pack horse for transport. However, this proved to be more trouble than it was worth since the horse did not pull its own weight, and demanded more work from its caretakers than it did as a beast of burden. Dil Das soon went back to packing the milk into town on his and his brothers' backs.

Despite the appearance of a clockwork routine, dairying seems to be inherently capricious. Production and delivery is, of necessity, dependent on a whole series of variables over which a producer can exercise only a modicum of control. Consequently, efficient production is an ideal which is daily compromised by any number of unexpected factors.

Moreover, the annual cycle of production, based on a radical if predictable fluctuation in market demand, further complicates the process of running a profitable business.

When Dil Das was in business during the 1960s, and even now to a large extent, demand was extremely high in March, April, May, and June at the peak of the tourist season, and extremely low in November, December, January, and February when the population of Mussoorie was reduced by as much as one-third. Most of those who comprise this seasonal third of the population were the large-contract consumer such as hotels, schools, and restaurants, which close down for the winter months. With this in mind, a milk producer such as Dil Das had to be constantly making long- and short-term choices in order to keep the volume of milk flowing at the lowest possible cost to him in terms of both time and money. However, he had to be able to accommodate somewhat contradictory demands—a supply of milk that was constant, day-in and day-out, for about half the year, but which then had to be reduced, or stopped altogether, during the winter when demand evaporated.

While it is now possible to maintain year-round production, this is a fairly recent development. Throughout the past fifty years, the price of milk effectively dropped during the winter to a point where it was no longer profitable to sell, even if buyers could be found. What this means is that efficiency—calculated on a yearly basis—had to be compromised to the ability to produce large volumes in the summer but virtually nothing during the winter, while maintaining the overall health of one's milk buffaloes. If you were a large-scale producer this was difficult to do. Since the flow of milk cannot be stopped altogether without compromising the health of one's stock, some milkmen were, until very recently, forced to sell at a low price, to western-style cheese producers, in order to try to break even.

Dil Das was most successful as a milkman between about 1955 and 1975 largely because he had control over a big enough family to run a successful dairy operation. He had four brothers and four uncles of whom six were married, making a total of fourteen working adults. On account of bamboo weaving, not all fourteen were directly or exclusively involved in the dairy business, but Dil Das did have control over a large enough labor pool to ensure that there was always someone to do the necessary work. In order to be able to contract a sale of forty liters or more, Dil Das had to have the necessary labor power to take care of eight to ten buffaloes.

Unlike nomadic Gujars, who herd scores of water buffaloes up wide paths to high, flat pastures at three thousand to thirty-five hundred meters, dudwallas in the lower Himalayas, where there are no flat pastures and where many homes are located at the end of steep and narrow paths, must keep their animals tethered. Not only must food and water be brought to them, and their dung carted away to be put into fields as fertilizer, but they must be kept cool and comfortable; which means, as their name would indicate, some attempt must be made to keep their skin from drying out. Occasionally during the hot summer months, buffaloes are carefully herded along narrow paths to streams or springs where they are bathed in cool water—a requirement for the buffalo's general health, since unlike buffaloes in the plains there is very little opportunity for a mountain buffalo to wallow neck-deep in a pond or swim in a canal. Usually it is impossible for buffaloes to negotiate the small, steep paths which lead to nearby springs, however. And so, if rain water cannot be collected to keep the buffaloes watered down, they are, for better or worse, simply tethered indoors out of the wind and sun. In the late 1950s, Dil Das's family dug a shallow muddy pond on the ridge above Pathreni where some of their buffaloes could be safely herded to wallow, up to their knees at least, in what remained in April and May of the February rains. In any event, buffaloes spend virtually all of their time tied up. Depending on the weather, air temperature, and position of the sun, they either move in to their stall or out to a flat spot in the open air, keeping warm and dry in the winter from November through February, as cool as possible in the hot summer from late March through late June, and, ironically, as warm and dry as possible in the perpetually cool, damp monsoon season from late June through mid-September when care must be taken against various fungal and viral infections.

Given the climatic extremes of their mountain environment, Dil Das and others like him move their buffaloes between winter and summer chans, which are always located as close to fodder and water resources as possible. During the 1960s and early 1970s Dil Das used Pathreni, which is located at an altitude of about seventeen hundred meters, as his summer base, and would then, in the winter, move most of the milk buffaloes down six hundred meters to Koldighat in a valley to the east near a small stream about two kilometers away. Koldighat is considerably warmer than Pathreni, which often gets a dusting of snow in January and February. At the peak of operation during the mid- to late 1960s, Dil Das kept buffaloes at both locations year-round in order to use resources more efficiently. However, the problem with Koldighat during the summer is not only the heat, but also the more arduous walk into town to deliver milk. Even so, Dil Das felt that there was not enough fodder near Pathreni to provide for all of his stock.

Partly because of population growth, and partly due to the practical requirements of keeping large numbers of buffaloes watered and fed, more and more milkmen are, like Dil Das, turning their once seasonal chans into permanent settlements, calculating that their buffaloes can weather the climatic extremes. In fact, on the larger ridge structure on which Pathreni is located, which runs from a peak altitude of about 1,800 meters down to the confluence of two streams at about 775 meters, all of the settlements—with the notable exception of Chattarmani's *pakka* house—appear to be permanently settled chans.

In the early 1980s Hans Ram used to live at the lowest point just above where the cactus start growing on Devi Dhang, and now his widow and six children make their home in what remains of a dilapidated hamlet which is far from both water and fodder. Around the edge of the ridge, and lower down toward the stream which runs by Koldighat, is Tota Ram's chan. Further up are two contiguous chans where Shiv Dutta's extended family lives. Shiv Dutta and his adult son Narian deliver milk to town by walking down into the Seraghat valley and then back up a trail through Dhobighat, past the lower Woodstock campus, and up to the Tehri road about a mile outside of town. Shiv Dutta is also a large-volume dealer, but with only one son to help him out he regularly uses a pack pony. Both Shiv Dutta and Tota Ram settled permanently into their chans from Loharighar, a small Brahmin village one ridge, and about an hour's walk, to the east. At the crest of the ridge above Shiv Dutta's place is a chan where Banu Singh and his wife Soni Devi have settled. Banu still owns land and has a broken-down home in the village of Chamasari just across the valley to the south, but he now delivers a few liters of milk to the old Bhataghat tea shop straight up the ridge and to the west of Pathreni, and to Jabbarkhet, right below Oakville, my home. He and Soni have no children of their own. Before a pipeline was built and a standing tap was located outside their chan they managed, with the help of one of Man Singh's daughters, to care for their three buffaloes and eight cows. Now that water need not be carried up the mountain by hand, and because Banu has scaled back the size of his stock, he and his wife are able to manage on their own. Man Singh, who lives above Banu just below the big long-needle pine forest which stretches down the ridge from Pathreni, was until the early 1980s practically destitute. A cataract operation and a pair of glasses gave him a new perspective on things, and with the introduction of running water to his doorstep he has now managed to repair his home, plant vegetables, and persuade his sons to work hard. One works in the Landour post office while another has taken a job assisting the Mussoorie Gramin Vikas Samiti fieldworkers as a local liaison.

The Pathreni ridge is, essentially, comprised of families who settled there in order to take advantage of the Mussoorie market. As in the case of Dil Das, it was their fathers or fathers' fathers who made the decisive move, and many of them simply relocated into chans that were seasonal hamlets connected to permanent homes in the nearby villages of Loharighar to the east, Nagdwan to the southeast, Chamasari due south, and Moti Dhar to the northeast. All of these villages are within a few hours' walk from the Pathreni-Donk ridge, but living in a chan, which is closer to town and closer to fodder and water, makes more sense for a dairy farmer than living in a densely populated village where the competition for scarce resources would be that much greater.

During the 1960s when Dil Das had ten female buffaloes, no more than four of them were giving milk at any one time. This was typical and expected. Dil Das had to have enough buffaloes to produce the volume of milk he had contracted for—between forty and sixty liters—but he also needed "extra" stock to accommodate the natural lactating schedule of milch buffaloes. At any given time, four of the ten buffaloes had to be producing milk, and ideally Dil Das was able to rotate through the stock of ten by regulating the rate and schedule of each buffalo's pregnancy and calving.

One of the most complex problems in managing a dairy enterprise, however, is making sure that a lactating buffalo regularly produces a set volume of milk. By Western standards—where dairying is, effectively, computerized and industrialized—yields are very low, usually between four and seven liters a day, with five liters being a typically high yield for a healthy young buffalo who is four or five years old. Even a healthy buffalo's daily output varies during the course of her lactation, and so a five-liter yield represents the two-month peak of a seven- or eight-month production period, which may begin and end with as little as two or three liters being produced on an irregular basis.

A host of other factors also influence output. Aside from various illnesses, which are common but treatable, the single most important variable in maintaining a high yield is the volume and quality of feed and water; and it is here where the labor of women and children in a large, extended patrilocal family comes into play.

If two activities had to be singled out to characterize the daily chores of Dil Das's family during the 1950s, 1960s, and 1970s, they would be cutting fodder and carrying water. While a range of green vegetation can be used as fodder, by far the most common are grass and oak leaves, both of which grow in relative abundance. Grass is more commonly cut during the monsoon when it is green and grows rapidly, while oak leaves are used year round. Although relatively nutritious, both grass and oak leaves are bulky and have a very high fiber content. Consequently, buffaloes have to consume large quantities in order to get enough nutritional intake—about forty kilograms of grass or leaves per day; or about four hundred kilograms for ten buffaloes. Cutting and carrying this much fodder is no mean feat, and requires the combined labor of at least five or six adults working four or five hours per day.

During the 1960s and early 1970s Dil Das's younger brothers, Sheri and Rukam, along with the three elder brothers' wives, were engaged in cutting grass and leaves daily. They would go out in the morning after the buffaloes had been milked and fed and often walk up or down the nearby ridges for a few kilometers until they found a grove of oak or a slope of grass that had not been cut for a few weeks. They had established a fairly standard rotation cycle between the various groves and slopes nearby, but given the volume of fodder their buffaloes required, they often had to walk two or three kilometers—and up and down hundreds of meters—to find enough. Then, because they could not carry much more than sixty kilograms at a time, and because fodder needs to be fresh, they would go out in the evening for another two or three hours to collect a second load, returning home just in time for the buffaloes to be milked, fed, and bedded down for the night. As a young boy, Dil Das had to cut leaves and grass for his father's buffaloes, and it was, undoubtedly, the many hours he spent walking in the forest which helped develop his interest and skill as a hunter.

Unlike many other settlements in the area, Pathreni is relatively lucky as concerns the availability of water. Although a pipeline was built in the early 1980s, bringing water directly into the village, there is also a spring located about a kilometer away on the road leading into town. In the 1960s and early 1970s Dil Das had built—and continually repaired—a makeshift pipeline of bits and pieces of old plastic hose and galvanized steel pipe, which brought a good flow of water half a kilometer closer to the lower chans in the village. For a time the pipeline brought water to a cement tank built near the family's old house at the bottom edge of Pathreni, but this stretch of pipe gave out and was maintained for only a few years. For most of the time when Dil Das had to care for ten buffaloes, the four or five family members who were not cutting fodder were transporting water to the tethered animals.

Water is absolutely essential for maintaining a regular yield of milk, and during the hot season a buffalo needs to drink about forty liters per day, or four hundred liters for a stock of ten animals. At twenty liters a trip—the size of the largest *thekis* and *gharas* which are used to carry water—it is easy to appreciate the amount of time and energy required to walk even one kilometer, round trip, on a relatively wide, flat path. Before the construction of the pipeline, many of Dil Das's neighbors were not so fortunate. At Donk, down the ridge, Banu's wife Soni, for instance, used to walk two kilometers round trip, up and down two hundred fifty meters, to collect water for three buffaloes.

Although buffaloes can survive on oak leaves, grass, and water, a sustained high yield of milk also requires a certain amount of special, high nutrition feed. This feed, known generically as *pinda*, must be bought in town from merchants who specialize in rural commodities. It consists of lentil husks, salt, a mix of various "cheap" grains and oil seeds, and hard molasses known as *gur*, the same substance used to make *kac-chi*, although of an inferior, impure grade. Pinda is mixed according to various recipes and is priced on the relative content of its most expensive ingredient. On average pinda cost in the early 1980s between three and four rupees a kilogram. Although usually only buffaloes which are giving milk get pinda, it is difficult to say how much a milkman will feed to his stock. It all depends on cash flow, the volume of green fodder available, the "natural" capacity of one's stock, and the ratio of one's stock capacity to the volume of milk contracted. As a rule, most milkmen feed their buffaloes at least a few fistfuls of feed mixed with water per day, but some increase the volume of pinda to one or two kilograms in order to increase the yield by a corresponding number of liters.

The problem with this strategy is that pinda is both expensive and heavy to carry. Moreover, once a buffalo grows accustomed to high nutrition *pinda*, one must sustain this diet or run the risk of a sharply decreased yield, which can fall below the average. In other words, one cannot simply increase or decrease the volume of pinda in order to blithely regulate the flow of milk. Nor is it particularly cost effective—except in certain circumstances—to spend cash in order to increase yields, particularly if added labor can achieve the same end by other means. Under the circumstances, Dil Das's strategy was in step with the vast majority of milkmen in the area who only give their buffaloes a few fistfuls of pinda mixed with water as an evening tonic drink.

In an otherwise labor-intensive business—and pinda notwithstanding—the buffaloes themselves are the only significant cash investment which a dudwalla must make; an investment which is as large as it is risky. In general the price of a young milch buffalo has kept pace with inflation—around 800 to 1,000 rupees in 1960, 5,000 or 6,000 in 1975, and in 1998, close to 11,000 rupees or more. For a milkman like Dil Das who could expect a gross monthly income of about 1,200 rupees in 1975—much of which went into feeding the extended family—a buffalo represented a substantial outlay of cash. Like the vast majority of other milkmen, Dil Das could not afford to purchase a buffalo outright, and had to negotiate loans made against projected income in order to increase the size of his stock. As a large-contract dealer, Dil Das was often able to negotiate terms with his clients at Wynberg Allen and Woodstock School, but like many others he was also forced to borrow from local merchant-moneylenders who charged extremely high interest. Although government-authorized bank loans are becoming much more common, this is a relatively recent phenomenon. In the 1960s and early 1970s it was difficult for someone like Dil Das—who had very little collateral—to secure a low-interest loan from a bank. In any case, debt is virtually endemic among milkmen. Very few are able to build up enough capital reserves to replenish their stock of buffaloes every few years.

Although there is a lively buffalo trade between hill villages around Mussoorie, the best stock is available from nomadic Gujars who herd hundreds of buffaloes up into the high pastures for the summer. Moving down the *terai* in the spring, from as far away as Kashmir, these nomads sell buffaloes along the way in order to earn money and maintain the size of their herd. When Dil Das was in need of a fresh young buffalo he would often go down to Dehra Dun to negotiate a sale. With the buffalo in tow he would trek back up to Pathreni along the wide Mahant's Road. Named for the religious leader cum landlord who used to own much of the land around Pathreni before independence, this road is also used by the Gujars on their way up to Nag Tibba and further on to Deodital and Kathling. In the late spring long single-file lines of buffaloes can be seen stretching for a kilometer or two along this old pack trail, which connects the Pathreni area with Rajpur and Dehra Dun in the terai at the foot of the Himalayas and the Gangetic Plain on beyond the Siwalik hills.

A milkman may need to buy a buffalo for any number of reasons. Although he is able to maintain his stock when the older buffaloes give birth to female calves, it is often necessary to buy a buffalo which is giving or will soon start to give milk rather than wait for the young calves to mature. Moreover, a milkman must ensure that his buffaloes are not all the same age, for he cannot afford to replace them all at once when they stop giving milk. Given the volume of milk he has contracted for he may find it cost and labor effective to sell—at a premium price—a young buffalo that has just started giving milk, and buy one that will start giving milk in a year or two. He may also decide to sell, at some risk, a mature buffalo whose yield is known, and buy a younger buffalo in the hope of getting more milk for longer. The most difficult deal to arrange is the sale of a female buffalo who is past her milk-giving prime. In any case, Dil Das and his neighbors engaged in a great deal of buffalo trading with their counterparts in nearby villages, each looking to find someone whose buffalo for sale matched their ever-changing needs. Spring is the main season for such trading, in part because new calves are born then, and in part because everyone is gearing up for the high-volume summer sales of milk.

Unfortunately, it is not at all uncommon for a number of these sales to end in disaster as skittish buffaloes sometimes plunge to their deaths into deep ravines when guided along narrow village paths by the hand of a strange new owner. Needless to say, this and other kinds of accidents and illnesses can prove ruinous since a single buffalo represents a very large and carefully calculated investment of both time and money. I was walking with Dil Das once when we came upon a vacant chan outside of which were the carcasses of three buffaloes. They had apparently all died of the same illness, and the owner had simply packed up and gone back to his village. There was nothing else to do.

The least variable factor in the whole business of dairying tends to be the price of milk, which is roughly the same throughout town—about 6.50 rupees per liter now, 4.50 rupees per liter in 1985, and roughly 2.50 rupees per liter in 1968. Although the price is fixed generally on the basis of market supply and demand, the radical variability in demand and the annual surplus of milk has tended to keep the price relatively low. Milkmen, who tend to be highly individualistic and are not organized in any sense, cannot raise the price of their product without losing their contract to someone who is willing to sell for less. Contracts are won more or less on the quality of milk sold and the reputation of the trader rather than on the basis of competitive pricing.

Milk quality is a very knotty issue upon which the success and failure of many milkmen has been determined. It is virtually a commonplace among urban consumers to categorically accuse rural producers of diluting the milk they sell with water. I can clearly remember our family cook, who kept track of the daily milk delivery as it was poured out liter by liter into a stainless steel cooking pot set on the kitchen floor, complaining under his breath—and at other times more loudly—that the white liquid being dispensed was, in fact, water diluted with milk. Although there are technical means by which the butter fat content of milk can be measured, these are notoriously unreliable and only tend to exaggerate the acrimony between those who deliver and those who drink. There is a story told about an old missionary who, unwilling to take action without hard facts in hand, took his lactometer out to the village and measured the milk directly as it came out of the buffalo, only to find that it registered well below the official "scientific" norm. And this, of course, is what the milkmen themselves say to those who complain that the milk is not thick enough—it is, after all, the same as what all the other buffaloes produce. If it is watery, that is because of the grass and leaves they eat, and the poor conditions under which they live. Our milkman once told our cook—with an air of half-seriousness he had developed about the whole business—that the milk was "thin" because there was too much water on the wet monsoon grass that his buffaloes were consuming.

Variability in the real quality of buffalo milk notwithstanding, all milkmen do dilute the milk they sell with some water. In fact, they can get away with this because of the inherent variability—buffalo to buffalo and breed to breed—in the butter fat content of milk, different feeding patterns, health, and so forth. The volume of water added to milk is highly variable, and, needless to say, not something which is spoken of openly. On average, though, most milkmen can cut their milk with about 25 percent water without getting caught. In fact, milk with this much water added is referred to as "pure," whereas a 60-40 ratio of milk to water—the greatest dilution I ever recorded—is considered clearly adulterated.

From the perspective of a dairyman like Dil Das, it is easy to appreciate the incentive for adding water to milk. First, one is able to increase the overall volume of sale with virtually no cash or labor investment. In other words, Dil Das and others are able to increase the real price of milk by one-fourth and thereby make a clear profit by creaming off, as it were, 25 percent on every liter sold. The temptation, of course, is to add more and more water, but this is very risky given that contracts are won and lost on the basis of the quality of milk sold and the trust a milkman is able to instill in his customers.

Aside from the obvious financial incentive, dilution is also an important—and perhaps even crucial—factor in the economy of milk production. Despite their hard work, Dil Das and his neighbors are often in a position where their buffaloes are not producing the expected amount, even if this amount is calculated at 15 percent or so less than the contracted volume. Buffaloes get sick, have accidents, and die, and those who cut fodder and collect water also fall ill and cannot work. For whatever reason, when there is not enough milk to fill the daily quota it is fairly easy—and absolutely essential, given the market demand—to make up the difference with a little more water. The practice of dilution, therefore, adds a degree of fluidity to an otherwise rigid and uncompromising economy.

The practice of dilution also helps milkmen accommodate the dramatic annual fluctuation in demand. By producing as much as 20 or 25 percent less than the contracted amount of milk, for example, Dil Das was able to partially insulate himself from the 75 percent or more drop in winter demand when his boarding school clients closed down their kitchens during the holidays. Since fodder is of the poorest quality during the cold season and many buffaloes are in the early stages of pregnancy, he was able to reduce production to one quarter or half of the peak season volume.

Although financially and practically expedient, the endemic practice of dilution in the lower Himalayas helps isolate the way in which petty capitalism has poised many families on the brink of disaster. One way of looking at the phenomenon of dilution is from the perspective of production rather than sale. From this perspective it becomes clear that only an extraordinarily large extended family, such as Dil Das's during the 1960s, could provide the necessary labor to care for a large stock of buffaloes. Although there are a few small-scale producers who keep two or three buffaloes and sell small volumes of milk to one or two customers, everyone agrees that in order to turn a profit one must contract at least thirty or forty liters of milk, and that in order to produce this much milk one has to own a minimum of nine buffaloes. To care for these buffaloes adequately requires the labor of five or six adults and at least three or four children. Since the unit of production is almost always the family—I encountered only a few cases of hired labor—there is a tremendous amount of pressure for kinship to accommodate itself to the vagaries of a labor-intensive cash economy.

The problem, of course, is that families are inherently unstable given the fact that daughters grow up and marry into other families, and that sons grow up, get married, have children of their own, and eventually break away from their parents' and grandparents' home to establish their own households. To have three generations under one roof—or fed from one stove—is an ideal which ironically anticipates the inevitability of a generational cycle of growth and disintegration. The economy of dairying is based on the realization and long-term stability of an extended family ideal which is, in fact, highly unstable and unpredictable. This instability often undermines the productive base of the dairy industry.

Dil Das was married in the late 1950s, and his wife soon gave birth to a daughter named Dharma. His younger brother Ratnu was married soon after, and his wife also gave birth to a daughter. Sheri, the next oldest brother, was married in the early 1960s and had one daughter, born about 1962, and two sons, born in 1966 and 1967. Rukam was not married until the early 1970s, and his wife gave birth to a son about 1976 and then died in labor while giving birth to a daughter a few years later. One of Dil Das's four uncles fell off a cliff while cutting fodder and died in the early 1970s. The other three, Tulsi, Abloo, and Jankhi— all between fifty and fifty-five years old in 1970—were married to much younger women, and their children, of whom two are boys, have only recently reached working age.

Dil Das's first wife died in the early 1960s of cervical cancer, and it was at this time that he left and went to Tiger Tops in Nepal with John Coapman. He married again in the late 1960s, but his second wife died childless. He remarried in the early 1970s and his wife soon gave birth to a daughter. This wife also contracted cancer and died in the early 1980s when her daughter Gura was about eleven or twelve years old. Ratnu's first wife bore a number of daughters and he soon married a second wife who finally bore him a son after giving birth to two more girls.

Around 1970 Dil Das's extended family began to break apart. The major rift was between Dil Das and Ratnu. Personalities aside—since the sense I am trying to make here is economic—it had to do with the fact that Dil Das was in control of the business and made decisions, whereas Ratnu and his two wives provided a significant proportion of the labor. Eventually Ratnu moved his family to a chan on the ridge above the main settlement and started his own smaller dairy. For their parts, Sheri, Rukam, and Tara continued to help Dil Das, but as their own families began to grow up they followed Ratnu's example and set up their own households—Sheri in the main family home, and Rukam in one of the chans near his uncles. Tara, the youngest brother, soon left the village altogether to work as a technician for medical missionaries, and later as a pharmacist in the plains. None of them started their own dairy business. When not helping out their two elder brothers, both Sheri and Rukam took odd jobs doing road construction until Rukam moved up to Tibri to serve as the caretaker of Chowdhri sahib's orchard. For their parts, Tulsi, Abloo, and Jankhi stopped helping with the dairy business but continued to weave bamboo, turning their "traditional" skill to the production of "modern" wastepaper baskets, lamp shades, flower baskets, and various toys sold door to door on the Landour hillside.

By 1980 the only family members with a steady income were Tara, the youngest, who had left the village and maintained only sporadic contact; Rukam who earned a small salary from the absentee landlord whose orchard he protected; and Ratnu, who had expanded his dairy business to include six buffaloes. Aside from Ratnu, whose two wives and numerous young daughters worked unflaggingly to feed and water their stock, the rest of Pathreni seemed to slowly slump into economic depression from about 1977 on. Sheri's two sons have grown up and taken jobs outside the village—one as a shepherd's apprentice in the Himachal Himalayas, and, more recently as an assistant to his cousin's husband who is a building contractor; and the other, first as a baker in Delhi, and now as a truck driver's assistant in Barlowganj—sending back occasional remittances to support their surviving parents. However, Sheri, like his uncles and brother Rukam, was always short of cash, deeply in debt to local merchants, and always on the lookout for a "short-term loan" from old friends. Although similarly in debt and short of cash, Dil Das was able to support himself and his daughter on a small stipend paid to him by Ratnu in exchange for negotiating a large school milk contract.

One of the ways in which Sheri, Rukam, and their uncles were able to make ends meet was by renting out the extra space in their chans to dairywallas from further back in the Himalayas. The apparently generic title dairywalla refers, curiously, only to nonresident milkmen who settle in the area around Pathreni during the peak tourist season, and is quite a different title than that of dudwalla. These men, who come with their families from villages on the second range back in the mountains, are unable to deliver milk all the way from their remote homes. They set up with their stock of buffaloes in chans nearer to town and sell their milk from there. The number of dairywallas in the Pathreni area has increased dramatically in the past fifteen years, and it is not at all surprising that they are able to rent from local milkmen like Dil Das and his family who are not producing large volumes of milk. Even so, everyone in Pathreni realizes, with a degree of bitter irony, that the dairywallas are not only a new source of competition, but also a further drain on the limited local resources of fodder and firewood. However, renting to a dairywalla like Hukam Singh and his family is now one of the only sources of steady income for the widows of Ratnu, Abloo, Sheri, and Tulsi, and they cannot worry themselves unduly with how what they do affects Chattarmani, Banu Singh, Bhussi Pandit, and other milkmen nearby.

Despite the money earned from renting, selling a few bamboo baskets, and brewing illicit liquor, the surviving sons and brothers of Gur Das were, by the early 1980s—with the notable exception of Ratnu—living in a state of poverty; this was not abject poverty where there is daily hunger, but the kind of hand-to-mouth poverty where there is just enough to eat but not much more, and where everything from clothes to cooking pots is old and in need of replacement or repair.

Two basic factors contributed to the larger family's demise, the first an accident of fate brought on by an ideology of kinship, and the second a structural problem in the petty economy of capitalism. Unlike their father, who had five sons, neither Dil Das nor Ratnu had sons. Although, as Ratnu's success demonstrates, it is clearly possible to run a dairy with the labor of women—who do virtually all the hard work in any case—there is a sense in which the whole business is geared toward a patriarchal ideal of fraternal unity, an ideological vision of sons and brothers working together to inherit the fruit of their father's labor. In Dil Das's case the fact that he had no son simply meant, after a while, that there was no long-term goal toward which to work. This realization probably came at about the time when he and Ratnu went their separate ways, but was certainly well ingrained after 1977.

By the early 1980s, when I began to do research in the area, it was quite clear that Dil Das had lost heart. This is not to say that he was demoralized on an emotional level by the fact that he did not have a son; he had simply come to the conclusion that without a son there was no longer any particular reason to try and build something—a house, for example, or a business—to pass on to the next generation. For his part, Ratnu was quite explicit about the fact that he would never be satisfied until one of his wives gave birth to a son to inherit the business. When a son was finally born in 1987, he named him "53" in order to commemorate the age at which success was finally realized. Although Rukam had one young son, and Sheri two, neither of them had enough children or wives to risk buying buffaloes. Moreover, it would have been somewhat impertinent of them, as younger brothers, to try and compete against their older siblings rather than, if only nominally and not in fact, working with them.

A serious structural problem which also led to the family's demise is intrinsic to the economy of commercial dairying. Unlike land and other forms of wealth, buffaloes are only worth money while they are producing. A buffalo past its milk-giving prime is worth only a small fraction of its original value, and a dead buffalo is worth practically nothing. Hence, it is absolutely imperative that a milkman not let his stock get old or die before selling out or buying new, young buffaloes. A single buffalo represents a significant portion of a family's net worth, and to let it grow old and die while maintaining ownership is like throwing away money.

When an extended family like Dil Das's decides to split up, with each brother taking an equal share, the fragile balance of the dairy economy is severely undermined. If the buffaloes are divided up equally—a complex problem given age, health, milk-giving history, and so on—no one is left with an adequate stock. If, as in Dil Das's case, the two elder brothers buy out their younger brother's shares, they are often left with more buffaloes than they can care for, but not necessarily enough milk-giving buffaloes to maintain the volume of their contract. Under these circumstances a milkman can simply sell out and get rid of his stock before it loses value—but then what? Although he might recoup his initial investment, he is left with no source of income. If he sells a buffalo to buy food or clothes he will soon spend his way into poverty. And yet, there is no way to simply hold on to one's investment since a buffalo must be fed and watered. Even then it is daily losing value even as it eats up labor. Moreover, it is very difficult to sell out and put the money away for reinvestment later, since families like Dil Das's have no savings other than those represented by buffaloes, and no alternative source of income. Although many dairy farmers own land, the large contractors like Dil Das tend to dramatically reduce their farming activities in order to allocate a maximum amount of labor to dairying. Moreover, because he was a bamboo weaver, Gur Das never farmed on a large scale, and the land inherited by each of his five sons was very, very small. Dil Das and his other brothers simply could not return to subsistence farming. More significantly, they had grown dependent on a whole range of market commodities which the sale of milk enabled them to buy.

For Dil Das and many others the problem with dairying is that it is an all-consuming business which creates its own cycle of dependency. Once you are in, particularly in a big way, it is hard to get out with your investment intact. If you do get out, there is not much else to do since commercial agriculture—growing potatoes, vegetables, and ginger, primarily—requires land, water, and fertilizer. The land quality in the Pathreni area is notoriously bad, a fact which does not greatly affect those who sell milk—or those who weave bamboo—but further constrains those who cannot.

Unlike many older communities in the lower Himalayas which are surrounded by acres and acres of picturesque terraced fields, most of the village population just east of Mussoorie settled there about one hundred or one hundred fifty years ago to sell milk to the British and the personnel of empire they brought with them. They paid little attention to the niceties, or demands, of a purely agricultural mode of production since they calculated that cash would enable them to profit. Men like Gur Das were drawn in by a transformation in the relative value of milk. Whereas it had been a product for consumption, it took on a seductive cash value on the boundary of colonial expansion. Over time, exchange between the center and its periphery transformed surplus milk into a commodity whose production and sale has come to define—in a rather rigid and uncompromising way—time, environment, labor, and the structure of kinship, among other things.

There are, of course, a number of families who have successfully negotiated the pitfalls of dairying. Chattarmani, Dil Das's Brahmin neighbor who lives just below Ratnu on the opposite side of the saddle from Pathreni, is perhaps the best case in point. Chattarmani's father settled in the area at about the same time as Gur Das, but started selling milk earlier. Like his neighbor, the senior Chattarmani had a large family, most of whom were sons. Moreover, the second-generation marriages were virtually all "successful," and the third generation is now comprised of a large percentage of sons, all of whom, as the metaphor for unity goes, "eat from the same hearth." Chattarmani's extended family now produces upward of sixty or seventy liters of "pure" milk per day with the combined labor of thirteen or fourteen adults. They have three or four chans located at prime locations—a cool summer site from which milk is easily delivered, and a low valley site which is warm in the winter and close to both water and fodder. The family has stayed together—in the sense of working as a unit and contracting one volume of milk—in part because the family is so big, and their stock so numerous, that it is logistically difficult for them to all live in one place and "literally" all eat from the same hearth. In other words, they have successfully hurdled that critical point of family expansion at which Dil Das and his brothers went their separate ways. Even so, the house of Chattarmani is characterized by unusually amicable relations under the management of the eldest brother.

It is difficult to know what part Chattarmani's high caste has played in his success. All Brahmins do not do nearly as well. But, on the other hand, almost all low-caste villagers in the Pathreni area are, like Dil Das, comparatively poor. As a rule there is a clear correlation between low caste and poverty, even though many higher caste families are in similar straits. All things considered, therefore, Chattarmani's success is probably a positive function of exactly those negative factors which led to Dil Das's demise—the latent stigma of a demoralizing ideology, an inability to produce sons, and, finally, the extended family's breakup. The irony is that Dil Das and Chattarmani are good friends notwithstanding the fact that both fate and the political economy of dairying have dealt them very different hands.

Despite the success of some families, commercial dairying has created a market of extremely narrow dimensions with few realistic alternatives for men like Dil Das. Far from being innovative entrepreneurs, those who market milk have grown dependent on a mode of production defined and maintained by elite consumers. Calculated in terms of labor and natural resources, milk is probably worth much more than its market value, and yet there is no way to "consume" these resources other than by turning them into milk. What has enabled some, like Chattarmani, to profit in the short run will, I am sure, be their undoing when stricter controls are put on the use of forest resources, when the balance of trade shifts out of the hills and into the hands of dairy cooperatives in the plains, or simply when the precarious local history of supply and demand makes it impossible to sell milk for more than it costs to produce it.

It was not until after I had finished researching the economy of dairying that I began to reflect on what might be called the politics of consumption. I began to ask myself not just what milk was worth in straightforward, practical terms, but what it meant to those who drank it, and to those who sold it to be consumed. I began to reflect on the cultural implications of exchange, and on milk's moral value as calculated in terms which must be distilled out of the culture of postcolonial petty capitalism.

Milk is, of course, a vital fluid in Hindu gastropolitics and ritual. It is also a powerful symbol of nutritional value. The fact that we are all nourished on "mother's milk" also contributes to the reputation of all milk as being somehow hypernutritional—it is natural, wholesome, and pure. Along these lines, the milk carried to school on Dil Das's back was, in fact, assimilated into various "nutritional practices" which derived their significance from the symbolic and caloric value of this pure fluid.

In boarding schools, that diet is often regimented in order to accomplish the specific ideological goals which inform nutritional health. Milk, among other things, provides a crucial link in the transformation of physical well-being into intellectual development. As an academic institution, one of the things Woodstock was particularly concerned with was the health of its students. Various specific nutritional practices were also part of a discourse on physical, religious, and moral growth and development, an ideological compulsion to "build the body and train the mind," as one of the school songs put it. To achieve this kind of growth and development, the boys and girls in boarding were given a glass of warm milk every evening at nine just after an hour and a half of "study hall" and just before lights out.

There is nothing wrong with this per se, in the eyes of Dil Das, Chattarmani, or the Woodstock nutritionist, but it strikes me as a kind of cultural distortion, based on a whole series of almost farcically iniquitous interdependencies, that economic dependency in the lower Himalayas, and a degree of steady environmental degradation, is directly connected to the raising up and educating of upper middle-class doctors and lawyers in New Delhi, New York, Bombay, and Boston.

As a young boy growing up in the relative privacy and privilege of the principal's house, I never got to—or had to, as many with delicate palates felt—drink post-study hall milk. However, I was able to eat, with great gusto, various concoctions made from cream. The congealed milk-fat which formed on the top of boiled milk which was skimmed off every morning by our family cook before being whipped (with an old egg-beater whose staccato grinding rhythm I can still hear in my half dreams of waking) into a rich, thick, frothy paste that, over the years, and over apple pie, chocolate cake, brownies, pudding, and, every morning bar none, over hot porridge, and on *chapatis* with jam, found its way, as cholesterol, into the blood of my grandfather and older uncles who died of arterial sclerosis, and, I am sure, into the chambers and muscle walls of my own much younger heart. I was an athlete—a basketball player, a soccer player, a cross-country runner, and a track "star"—and the logic of the day, which often scoffed at the preaching of cautionary science, was that cream was good. In addition to tasting like heaven, it gave to those of us who ate it a kind of condensed high-energy boost.

Cream was not served to those who lived in boarding; it would have been impractical. Nor—for very different reasons, however—was it always available to those families on the Landour hillside who boiled their own supply of milk. When milk is diluted with water the relatively small amount of cream which raises to the top is one of the first things to go, and so, in effect, our high-energy athleticism struck a competitive balance—through the acrimony of accusations and counteraccusations between sahibs, memsahibs, cooks, and milkmen—with the child labor of carrying water, grass, and leaves. In the end, however, one can be consoled, depending on your point of view and the relative percentages of water to milk, either by the fact that most of the time we were really drinking low-fat "whitish water," or else that Dil Das and his low-cholesterol compatriots had, sardonically speaking of course, the last laugh in a curious postcolonial politics of health.

If you were to walk through Mussoorie it would be simple to find any number of examples of similar nutritional practices revolving around the local consumption of milk in various forms. *Halwais*, or confectioners, who produce scores of varieties of sweets, yogurt, and cheese, provide the best case in point. Many of the sweets are produced from milk solids which are derived when the fluid is boiled down to a pasty residue called *ravari* or *meva*. Eating sweets, drinking milk, or consuming yogurt is regarded by many as not only healthy, but also a sign of prosperity and success. In the leisure culture of Mussoorie, upwardly mobile tourists are perhaps more concerned with a display of wealth than they are with individual health. In any case, catering to the tastes of those whose status is linked to the richness of their publicly consumed diet allows many Mussoorie confectioners to thrive. Moreover, tourism creates an environment where basic needs are sacrificed to taste, where only cream and butter will satisfy the desire of those who strive to rise to the top.

Diwali, the late autumn Hindu festival of lights, is an occasion when themes of wealth, auspiciousness, and taste are ritually woven together. In early November we would walk into town from school and survey the shops along the mall filled with hundreds of different kinds of brightly colored fireworks—deep green, twine-wrapped "A" bombs, red and gold sky rockets, black and silver roman candles, earthen fountains covered with golden paper, meter-long strings of deep red "lady-fingers," and mountains of yellow, pink, blue, and purple cherry bombs. Each stall was festooned with bright lights to enhance the display, which often extended well out into the street. Usually on the night of Diwali my parents would take us into town to watch as the sky was filled with bursting lights and the streets seemed to shudder under the impact of huge explosions. Often one of the stalls would catch fire when a renegade rocket went astray, and before long we would all be marched off into the relative safety of a back road.

In addition to watching the fireworks and setting off a few of our own, one of the reasons for going into town was to see the fabulous displays of sweets. One of the gestures of auspiciousness and good will on Diwali is to give gifts of sweets to friends, colleagues, and clients. To accommodate the demand, confectioners produce mountains of sweets, which are put on display before being sold and wrapped up in kilogram and half-kilogram boxes. There is a degree of competition between the sweet shop owners to see who can put on the most spectacular display.

In the late 1970s the proprietor of Omi Sweet Shop, in Landour's Shivaji Market, removed all the tables and chairs from the seating area in his shop, set up a floor-to-ceiling tiered construction, and filled it with four or five kinds of *laddoo*, five or six varieties of creamy white *burfi* made with pistachio and almonds, *rasgoola, rasmalai, son halva, malai chop, gulab jamun*, and any number of other confections arranged in gigantic, meter-high, gold- and silver-covered symmetrical mounds. Behind the tiered construction he carefully placed full-length mirrors to give the impression that one was not looking into a sweet shop but an unending cavern of sparkling, precious jewels.

It is this image of Omi's opulent sweet shop, along with a memory of nutritional lectures on the correlation of milk, strong bones, and bright, shining teeth, which keeps coming to mind as I contemplate the economies of dairying and the politics of consuming milk. Milk has powerful significance, and rich nutritional value, because of being, all at once, a valuable commodity, a key symbol, and a highly condensed substance. But somewhere in the mix of meaning, money, and metabolism, relative value gets lost in translation. In coming to represent health and wealth among those who consume it, milk, for those who produce and sell it, has become a fluid channel through which resources are being drained away. Looking at Omi's mountain of milk-based sweets, or, in the Wood-stock kitchen's trays of colored plastic cups full of warm milk, one must inevitably conclude that there is something fundamentally wrong with the distribution not just of wealth, but also of health and a meaningful sense of self. The commodification of dairying has meant, ironically, that very little milk is consumed by the children of those who produce it, while their labor directly contributes to the girthy status of middle-class tourists and the physical fitness of missionary youth. Disparities of wealth are, of course, depressingly common, but given the multiplex significance of milk as a vital fluid in the gastropolitics of postcolonial India it seems that what might simply be characterized as an economic injustice is also, and more significantly, embodied as a hierarchy of health, within the core and periphery of Mussoorie's milk shed. It is a fact encoded in low birth weights, child mortality, and the brown-haired, big-bellied undernourished children, and brought home, with brutal simplicity, in the abject apologies made to me by Dil Das's wife when tea, in his chan-without-animals, had to be served black.

Although wounded by colonialism and capitalism, as Dil Das was often fond of saying, hunting had killed him. It was an obsession that enslaved him to the desire for adventure. This preoccupation could never be anything more than a form of leisure, a way to spend time rather than engage in productive work, even when rationalized by a logic of shooting animals to protect cattle and crops. It was in this nonproductive, recreational, passionate sense that hunting fulfilled desire while undermining a peasant economy geared to a routine of weeding, planting, harvesting, and, above all else, milking: a classic opposition which, in the larger scheme of another mythic history, marks the beginning of civilization, and, to borrow a phrase from Marshall Sahlins, the end of affluence.[1] Dil Das's passion for hunting turned him into an ineffective dairy farmer—a bad peasant.

Within this framework it is hard for me to lay the blame for Dil Das's failure as a dairy farmer anywhere but at my own missionary door, for it was others just like me who first planted the seeds of desire in a person who could not afford the luxury. Dil Das had his own gun, first an old muzzle loader and then a twelve-gauge shot gun, and he hunted on his own, but most of his hunting was done with others who had more powerful guns, more ammunition, and more free time. It was others like me who often persuaded Dil Das, with a promise of meat in exchange for a little time, to leave his fields and his buffaloes and join them in the jungle.

Because the meat of wild animals figures into the domestic economy of a peasant household as something whose value cannot be measured in terms of either labor or exchange criteria, one is apt to consider it a luxury item in an otherwise utilitarian arena—either a free gift, on account of the transaction being ultimate and final for at least one party involved (the hunted), or an item of surplus by virtue of the fact that while it has nutritional value, it is worthless as a commodity. It appears to be pure, free food in a context where almost everything else is carefully measured in terms of time, energy, and money. Whenever an animal was shot near the village there would be a feast, and huge volumes of meat would be consumed with great relish and gusto by all concerned, which usually included Dil Das's extended family and the party of hunters from Landour. In their excess, however, these orgies of consumption, taste, and desire did not so much supplement as undermine a diet of more meager composition. Despite the powerful myth of its being a free luxury, meat was in fact being paid for by trading labor for leisure in an equation that undercut the precarious balance of subsistence. Along these lines, I was once told by Tulasi, Dil Das's uncle, that milk is never drunk in conjunction with meat, because, among other things, the former is, figuratively speaking, a product of the latter. It is an act of symbolic violence against the natural order of things in a peasant economy where dairying defines the value of both time and energy as well as the propriety of taste. In any case, there is a certain amount of blood on my hands for having translated dietary protocol into the higher stakes economy of gastro-politics where meat and milk effectively cancel one another out, leaving precious little to eat or drink.

The question is not what we should or could have done to alleviate poverty, but how we were intimately and inexorably implicated in the very structure of that poverty as wealthy, postcolonial drinkers of milk. In other words, who we are subverts our best intentions. By taking for granted the asymmetrical relationship between elite consumer and subaltern producer, those of us who were Dil Das's friends were party to a structure of exploitation. Which is not at all to say that we valorized, in any sense, the structure of inequality. Quite the contrary, in fact, since liberal missionary practices are founded on a presumption of basic justice and human equality. However, equality is a slippery concept, particularly when the language of friendship, politics, and economics get confused. And so, in celebrating the people of Pathreni's essential humanity we were, and still are, blissfully unaware of our complicity in defining that humanity; in defining, by way of our own position as alienated, neoliberal moderns, the rustic meekness of those less fortunate than us. Which is simply to say, that for all we did or might have done for Dil Das and his family, the economic basis of the difference between us—class, if you will—was fixed and out of our control, defined by our respective histories. Colonialism had brought us together—from beyond Uttarkashi and around Mansfield, Ohio—and put us on the eastern fringe of a hill station where, amid invidious inequities, friendship and faith took the struggle out of class relations and defined, with strong ironic overtones, community development work.

For the past fifteen years or so my parents, under the auspices of the Mussoorie Gramin Vikas Samiti (MGVS), have been involved in small-scale development work in and around the village of Pathreni. Their work is founded on the assumption that development must be small scale, locally inspired, and community based. It is, for the most part, community work on a first-name, face-to-face basis. Their goal, ultimately, has been to inspire a program of self-development wherein men and women in villages like Pathreni will organize and take collective action to improve their lot. MGVS projects have been successful: a pipeline was built by the people of Pathreni and Donk, thus dramatically reducing the time and energy required to carry water from distant springs. An orchard and vegetable garden was established. Government grants and loans were secured for the construction of three new houses in Pathreni. Women have organized in order to coordinate family health care work and to advocate against the illicit brewing of liquor in their communities. A school has been built and staffed at Masrana on the main motor road not far from Pathreni. And the list continues. But the ultimate success of MGVS, as with any kind of development work, would be to render itself obsolete by having set in motion a process of "development"—for lack of a better term—that can sustain itself and thereby, at least on some level, combat the structure of "underdevelopment."

Because of his position between two worlds, and also the lack of a son,

I think that Dil Das had a rather ambivalent attitude toward material self-development. Rather than build things and "invest in the future," Dil Das chose to talk about encounters that enabled him to escape from a life of dependency, high-interest debt, and hard, unremitting work. But Dil Das's escape into the complicity of unusual friendship meant that he expected much more than, or something entirely different from, economic and political change. He demanded the moral equality of friendship — of being there, and knowing, as he put it, that our children would grow up and hunt together. He was demanding nothing less than the transformation of foreign missionary into local citizen. And this, I think, is a radical, monistic redefinition of community development. He was demanding that we let him help us put down roots of our own rather than try and root out the stigma of his poverty.

*   *   *

I had gone on a trek with my family and some school friends up to Deodital, a small lake located in a steep valley below the massive snow-covered peaks of Bandarpunch. Dil Das had come along, too. It was early summer and fresh green grass grew in abundance on the broad meadows where the snow had recently melted above the lake. Gujars had recently arrived from the plains and had rebuilt their homes on the edge of the meadow where their buffaloes could freely graze. In need of milk and curious to see how the Gujars went about their herding, a number of us climbed up the ridge behind the lake to one of the encampments. We were graciously invited into one of the houses and began to talk with an older man and his adult son. I do not remember how many buffaloes they had, but they appeared legion. All of them were enormous, and tremendously fit from having walked over two hundred fifty kilometers in the course of a month. Their coal-black hides seemed to give off a deep rich luster, and somehow the fact that they were not perpetually tethered gave them a far less docile demeanor than their low-altitude cousins.

The Gujars seemed to have more milk than they knew what to do with. Most of it they turned into *ghi* for sale, but they also consumed vast quantities in the form of butter, cream, buttermilk, yogurt, and cheese. Instead of the usual tea, we were each offered a three-quarter liter *lota* of fresh milk to drink, and it was milk so thick with cream that most of us were hard-pressed to finish what we were given. We sat and talked for a while about the price of buffaloes, the relative cost of going on pilgrimage to Mecca, and the abundance of grass on the meadows. We then invited the senior Gujar's son down to our camp. On his way past the lake the previous day he had seen that we had brought an inflatable raft with us and was curious about how it worked. After some hesitation he agreed to take a ride out into the middle and sat nervously bemused while we rowed around in the deep, dark water of a holy lake, if not quite Manas. He was probably in his early twenties, and with sharp, chiseled features, tremendously broad shoulders, a thick chest, and narrow waist he looked as though he stepped out of a Mogul miniature. He was, in essence, a picture of health.

This young man was the only person I had ever seen who carried himself, unselfconsciously, with a sense of majestic power—until I got to Banaras, many years later. We were all struck by his appearance, but not at all confused by his rural-born regal physique; after all, it came as no surprise that here was a man who embodied the "natural" nutritional practices to which we, in other contexts, had aspired, but which market forces had conspired to spoil. Like the rest of us, Dil Das was awestruck by the volume of milk which the Gujars had at their disposal, and also at the general health and fitness which they all seemed to take for granted. In a way, the young Gujar embodied a kind of fantastically ideal persona—a latter-day Krishna, if you will—in which Dil Das and I were both able to see, or at least would have liked to see, ourselves: a persona in which the politics of consumption and the economy of production did not work at cross purposes; a persona capable of uprooting development. With the young Gujar in mind it would have been possible to write about the heroics of dairying rather than hunting. In other words, the young Gujar, whose father proudly proclaimed that he drank milk straight from the buffalo's teat, succeeded in giving form to a narrative which colonialism and petty capitalism had elsewhere conspired to silence. I like to think that the young Gujar's biography might have been the only story about dairying that Dil Das and I—producer and consumer—could both have written from a common perspective, a perspective from which my singular "romanticism" and vacillating post-Marxian rhetoric, and Dil Das's oblique references and large silence, might have given way to some kind of con-fused truth.

Chapter 8
Slippage

Out of Work, Through Hunting

"In the hills it is this way: if one does not work, does not graze the cattle, then nothing gets done. When there is only one person alone it is very difficult. I worked. I grazed the cattle and did other work, and slowly I grew up. When I was older, I would walk to Woodstock School where we delivered milk. This was during the time of Mr. Parker. I would carry the load for my father. I worked and worked. On the way home through Jabbarkhet I would stop and pick up supplies. Then I would go and say to those at home: 'Here, here is the dal; the lentils.' You see, I was young and strong and did all the work. After returning from the school I would go out and cut grass for the animals and bring it back home. Only if you feed the buffaloes properly will they give good milk. All of this work I did with my own hands. It was profitable. I worked and worked and then did much, much more work."

*   *   *

"From the time I started this dairying business I have never left the school. I have never sold milk anywhere else. Just last year they called me in and asked me to take the contract. I told them I couldn't though. I said I didn't have the resources to do that kind of work anymore."

"You see, about fifteen or twenty years ago I had seventeen or eighteen buffaloes and forty cows. The last of the cows died about three or four years back. Then my wife died, and that was the end of it. I used to transport eighty liters of milk on horseback to Wynberg Allen School, and forty liters to Woodstock. All of us brothers were together then, and we farmed as well. . . ."

"If you have enough people working you can get everything that needs to be done, done within a day. You can cut grass. Everything; ten or twelve people can do everything. It can all get done. True, it is hard work, but it can get done. . . ."

"They asked me to come back and take the contract at Wynberg Allen. I was a good, old-time milkman, and they wanted my kind; not like this Prakash fellow who buys milk from the dairy in Dehra Dun. . . . Yes, and then the dairywallas came from back in the hills."

"Now I am in the business of growing these fruit trees here in the village. Wasn't that forest officer who came by impressed when he saw the plantation!? It doesn't matter if some trees die, others will live. . . ."

"But it only works when we all get together as brothers, you see. We used to have fields down in the valley at Koldighat where we would grow ginger. There was water down there, and the crops were better. . . . An orchard would do well down there, oranges and tangerines, but you would need to have someone to protect them. Water could be piped in from below Moti Dhar. All you need is men to do the work."

*   *   *

"If I have fields to plow and no children then what will I do? I should get married and have children. True, I should not have seven wives just to increase the size of my family! But if I do not have children and the work load keeps increasing should I hire a worker? No. I should get married. In this way I get a wife and later children who will work. Thus I save money. And through my wife, and later when the children get married, I also get relatives. If a person has money, he should get married. That is how he will become important. He will earn more money, harvest crops, and buy cattle and land. All of this is in the family! His children do the work. This is a hill custom, you know."

"Now look at Jain sahib, the younger of the two brothers. He has no children, but his wife goes to the hospital to see if there is anything which can be done so that they can have children."

*   *   *

"One day I had planned to go to Nag Tibba to hunt. My father was in a rather strict mood, however, and said that I would have to plant the wheat before I could leave. At that time we had two young bulls that had been raised together so I harnessed them up and plowed and planted four of our fields."

"I told my wife not to call me until noon when food would be ready. However, I decided not to eat and to just work right through the meal. I plowed and planted, plowed and planted. At three o'clock I only had three fields left to go, but I took a break to eat something and feed the bulls. Now, by the time I got to the last field I was very tired. The plow was falling out of my hands, but my father didn't offer to help. He was really in a strict sort of mood. Anyway, I finally finished and we all sat down together and ate. I was tired out though, so everyone massaged my legs and shoulders. We were all together then."

*   *   *

"Right here in Pathreni I have seen snow up to my chest. Snow right up to here. The road in to Jabbarkhet was completely closed down."

"On the day of the big storm, my father had gone to visit my sister who was married to the night watchman over at Library bazaar. This was right after my daughter Dharma had been born. He was on his way back when the weather got bad. Then, even though he didn't smoke, he bought a box of matches and put them in his pocket. By then it was snowing hard, but he got as far as the school, where he met Austin sahib who at that time was staying at Fir Clump. Austin sahib said, 'Listen Gur Das, stay here for the night.' But my father said he needed to get home."

"I guess he drank some tea and then started out. He got to the gap above Jabbarkhet and started down but the snow was too deep. Finally he made his way around and down to the Seraghat valley. Then, with great difficulty, he made his way along the lower path. Slowly, slowly, slowly, slowly he went and finally got over to those chans at the bottom of the ridge. No one was there. There was so much snow he practically died! He quickly got inside one of the chans and then took the matches out of his pocket. Had they not been there. . . . Well, you can imagine. Anyway, he took a handful of thatch and started a fire and managed to keep himself warm."

"Meanwhile we were sitting at home waiting for him to get back. We were worried and wondered why he had not come. All through the night we worried. Then, just as it was getting light we saw someone coming along the path; you know the place, where that LG [large-game shotgun shell] went off accidentally. It was just ahead of there on the path where the rocks stick out. We watched as the person came along the path slowly making his way through the snow. He came very slowly and it was about three o'clock in the afternoon by the time my father arrived here. The snow was that deep."

"Well two days later the weather had not improved much. Two shopkeepers from over at Arooghati came by along the lower road through our village. They were from over Dhurmala side, over at Rudhmora. They had run out of salt or something and needed to get into Mussoorie for supplies. We asked them why they were coming through the village and they explained that the upper road was closed. They asked how the road was on to Jabbarkhet and we told them what had happened to my father. However, we told them that had been two days ago and things might have improved. None of us left the house though, and my father advised them not to go. But there were three of them, all young and energetic, and they decided to try."

"Well, they got as far as the road leading up to the gap and could go no further. They tried to find a place to camp but could not find any chans. With great difficulty they made it back to Pathreni by nightfall. At that time our house was down below the road and they came down and said, 'Brother Gur Das, today we have died!' We invited them in."

"Now, whenever it snows one must have hot water ready to heat up one's hands and feet. It hurts because of the cold but it helps. They soaked their hands and feet and then we brought out a bottle of liquor. My father had also shot a kakar three days before when there wasn't any snow. We had gone down to graze the cows and had shot one. Since most everyone had gone down to Koldighat to look after the buffaloes we had not eaten much but had hung up the meat to save. Well, sir, that night we cooked up the meat and sat through the night eating and drinking. They stayed with us the following day as well. Then on the third day they went back home without ever having made it into Mussoorie."

"It was during that same snowstorm that Chattarmani's big brother—the one who was sitting over there at Kaphlani the other day when we went by—had gone into Mussoorie to deliver milk. At that time he had his buffaloes in the valley below Nali. Well, they got into Mussoorie and it started to snow so they took their thekis and went down by way of Dehra Dun and then up the valley to their chans by way of Kalapathar."

"That same year it snowed and snowed. We had plenty of rice but our flour was gone. We were tired of eating rice and wanted a change. We wanted bread. I decided that we would try something different. Two of my buffaloes were giving milk so I took a pot of milk and got it ready. Then I took another big cast iron pot and put it on the fire. Into this I put some unground *cholai* and roasted it up good. We made balls out of this and then soaked them in the milk. These we ate for two or three days. They were all right, but eating the same thing over and over again is not good."

"The snow that year was all the way down below Donk as far as Seraghat, all the way down to the stream where the mills are where we used to grind our wheat. The question was, who was going to take the wheat down and grind it? Well, I told my mother to clean the wheat, add a little cholai, and I would take it down to see what could be done. Everyone told me not to go. It is too dangerous they said, but I told them that it was only the jungle and that anyway someone had to go. I had a pair of crepe-soled shoes, but by the time I got to Sungarghati they broke and were useless. At this point I could not go back up, so I jumped and hopped all the way down to the mills! At that time there were three of them in operation so I split the wheat into three portions and got all of them working to speed things along."

"Coming back up was a problem. My feet were numb. By the time I got to Hans Ram's chan I was sweating. I could not feel the cold anymore, but I kept on going. Further up I met Banu's uncle. He told me to sit down and have some tea but I said, 'No, no, I must keep going. If it is all ready, I will drink it here standing up, but I cannot sit down. If I do I will not be able to get back up.' He said it was all ready, so I drank a glass standing right there. They all said that I would die, but I told them no such thing could happen. I had to get the flour back home by that evening."

"By the time I got home it was dark, but they had hot water waiting for me. Friend, I tell you, I didn't move from bed for three or four days after that. Nobody could have survived in those conditions, but somehow I managed."

"That year I even cut leaves for fodder in the snow. We would take a little liquor to drink, you see. The old people would say, 'Drink some, it will give you strength.' It was our medicine. We would get a little drunk and run out to do our work."

*   *   *

"In the monsoon one cannot go into the jungle. . . ."

"We would go to the mill at night after all the work was done to grind our flour. We would drink there as well. And then, as soon as it was light, we would go and cut grass or get wood. I would bring back my load of grass before the others had even got started. I was quick and very sharp back then. I still am!"

"Whatever work I need to do, I do it quickly. My back hurts now, since I fell that is . . . which slows me down, but the pills your father gave me are good. I took three a day and felt fine. . . . But I tell you, those bags of charcoal we were making for the MGVS project were heavy. I could only carry five while Ram Lal carried thirty. We will start that work again in October when the rains end and things dry out."

*   *   *

"Some people say that we live in filth, in the jungle, in the village. They say it is not good—and that is OK. But they don't really know *how* we live; that they do not know."

"Now, no one who is an outsider can come into our village. Sure, if someone comes through and asks for directions we will tell them where to go! But they cannot just wander around. Even a policeman will ask before coming in."

"For a while I had my buffaloes down at Salarni in the valley toward Dhobighat. In those days I carried my milk up the road by way of Dhobighat to the boys' hostel."

"One day a policeman had stopped some of the Chamasari milkmen at Dhobighat. He was an outsider and was trying to earn a little extra money for himself. He told them they would have to 'pay' him for inspecting their milk containers, and you know what that means."

"Now I was the third milkman to arrive on the scene, and it was just about this time that Bhusaiya, the Dhobi *pradhan* [headman], started shouting at the policemen. I told Bhusaiya to take it easy. I told him and the policemen that we would be glad to open up our containers, but if we were only carrying pure milk which had not been adulterated then we would have to be compensated for being inconvenienced. What if we had nothing to hide?"

"Well, Bhusaiya said that this was a fair agreement. But by this time all of the Dhobis had arrived on the scene and got involved. We are all one, you see; they know who we are and we know them. So I got tough with the policemen and said that if they did not find anything wrong with our milk that we would not let them go. We would not let them cross back over the road they had come on. You see, now the matter had to be resolved. There was no backing down. So, my friend, it was a showdown at Dhobighat!"

"Finally, however, the police *had* to back down out of shame. They were shut up! None of us had to give even one single rupee! We were young and strong, though, and the Chamasari fellows wanted to beat the police up right there on the spot to teach them a lesson. We let them go, though, and I went on with the others. What kind of thugs and cheats did the police think we were! It was our place. We had surrounded them and that was that."

*　*　*

"Once I had left my thekis of milk at the school and had gone back to Bhataghat. I had told the men in the kitchen to wait for me. I told them I would be back. You see, I was going to have a drink and then come back and pick up my things."

"When I got to Bhataghat I told the shopkeeper I had a bottle of liquor and wanted some *pakori* [batter-fried salty snacks] to eat along with my drink. He served up a plate, and I sat back and relaxed. But then, while I was drinking, I saw two policemen and a dog coming along the road from town where that corner is beyond the *pradhan*'s shop; where they have widened the road now. Back then the new road was not yet built and the corner was much sharper. The policemen were coming along where the hill has fallen down and I did not notice them until they were quite close."

"Now what was I to do? I couldn't throw the bottle away, so quickly I said to the shopkeeper, 'Give me some more glasses.' I poured everyone there a drink, which they quickly drank down, and then I emptied the bottle. The police came up and said: 'What are you doing; what is going on here?' You see, they did not realize that I had had something to drink, but they had been tipped off that I had brought some liquor with me. I remained calm and said, 'Nothing, I came up from my village and stopped here to have some pakori. Down in my village I had something to drink, but here I have just bought some pakori. Here, have some.' Then I told them that my village was Masrana."

"Now the policemen must have realized that I was not telling the truth. They were after me. They didn't do anything right there, however, because I guess they figured they could catch me out along the road at the place where the path leads off down to Kimoi. Well, just beyond the chowki at Bhataghat there is a path which leads down to our village. It is a well-worn trail now, but back then it was hardly anything more than a track, and all overgrown with stinging nettle."

"We had sat in the shop for some time and I was quite drunk. I wasn't about to go until I knew I could get away. Finally, however, something had to be done so I said to my uncle Sukka, who was there, 'OK, let's go.' But he was afraid of what might happen, so he stayed back at the shop. Nevertheless, I set off with a group of men. The police thought we were going out along the road, so they came after us, but kept their distance. Well, I made a quick move and jumped down the trail into the stinging nettle and the policemen started shouting: 'What are you doing; where are you going?' I shouted back, 'Nowhere!' and jumped a little further down the track. How were they going to catch me now? They thought they could drag me back up to the road, but when one of the policemen came down, I caught hold of him and dragged him into the nettles! How, you say! He could hardly move! That's how. And the other one was left standing up on the road. He was afraid of the steep hillside and all the nettles. I am a *pahari* man and so I just jumped down the hill. The one policeman followed me down to the big deodar tree but was badly stung by the nettles and I lost him there in the jungle."

"I came on home through Jain sahib's jungle and had a hot bath. Up at the toll, they told me the next day, they had asked the policemen why they had tried to catch me. They said that I was just going home and not doing anything wrong. The shopkeeper said that I had just bought pakori. I tell you, the poor policemen were frustrated and hurt!"

*   *   *

"This is a story about a flood. . . ."

"I had nine buffaloes then, and there were three of us young men down in the chans at Koldighat, Rukam, Sukru from Nagdwan Gaon, who is related to us, and myself. The children were all up here at Pathreni, but we were down there with the buffaloes because water and grass were plentiful. True, it is much further into town, but we would usually come on down from Pathreni after it was dark in any case, so it didn't really matter. We did not lose any time."

"I had just returned from a trip down to the Song River near Raipur. It was during the monsoons and had been raining very hard. I got back to my chan at Koldighat after dark and went right in and went to sleep. In the morning when I woke up it was still raining hard. I looked out and the water in the stream was the color of smoke! I looked around and was shocked. I said to myself: 'What has happened? Where are all the trees?' They had all been washed away in the torrent! I looked and saw that the raging water in the stream was cutting in toward the chan and I realized that we were in trouble. Rukam and Sukru woke up and they were frightened. They wanted to make a run for it across the stream to the road on the other side but I told them to hold on. Rukam shouted out: 'Now we are going to die!!' But I said: 'Wait; hold on; don't worry.' The water was cutting into the bank but there was nothing we could do. The buffaloes were tethered inside. I told Rukam and Sukru to go back inside and try to sleep but they could not."

"Finally, however, the water subsided and the danger passed. We were saved by that big boulder behind our chan. It diverted the water from the stream and saved us. But there was an area behind our chans where all the pine trees had been swept away and only bare rocks were left behind."

"Now Chattermani, the pandit's father, was standing up on the ridge when we made our way up the trail. He figured that the three of us must have died in the flood. But when he saw us coming up the ridge he shouted out and told everyone that we were safe. When we got up to his house he told us to sit and make ourselves comfortable. He knew that our buffaloes had been washed away, and kept saying that it was a terrible thing. He kept saying that we were all lucky to be alive. 'Don't worry about a thing,' he said, 'at least you are safe. Let the nine buffaloes go.' Then he told me: 'The nine buffaloes will be made up for, they will be replaced, don't worry. I am just happy to see that you are alive.'"

"We came on up to Pathreni from there and arrived at about ten or eleven in the morning. There was one cow and a buffalo in the village, you see, so I had to take less milk than I usually did into town. Then I left for Mussoorie to make the delivery to Wynberg Allen."

"The next day Coapman's son Johnny, and his friends Manmohan and Rajindar, came down to Pathreni. They went down to take a look at what had happened and came back saying that there was not so much as the name of a tree left in the valley. There were only stones and rocks. You remember that place where I told you Campbell sahib had fired three shots at the ghoral, well that hillside fell during the flood. It was washed away, and now there is a straight fall, a cliff all the way down to the stream below."

"Well, Johnny wanted to see this for himself. I told him it would not be possible since all the grass around the top of the slip was wet and pressed down by the rain, but he had a mind of his own and went anyway. I told him that it was dangerous and that he would slip and kill himself, but he wouldn't listen. He went and looked over the edge and saw what happened in the valley below. It was amazing!"

*   *   *

"Back when I still delivered milk to Woodstock, John sahib sent word that he would be coming up from Delhi. When he arrived at Kulukhet, the toll gate on the road up to Mussoorie, he called the school. I had just arrived from the village with my delivery of milk so I took the call. He asked how I was, and then got straight to the point. Arrangements needed to be made, he said, for a hunting trip. I protested and told him it was the middle of June, and that it would be impossible to make any arrangements for off-season hunting. But, well, you know how he is—and also, I guess, it was a different era then—so he told me that he would pay ten rupees for every shot fired! Austin babu* and Justin were there in the accounts office at the school when he told me this, and they agreed with me that it was no time to go hunting. But John sahib was persistent and he told me to meet him at the Hackman's Hotel on the Mall as soon as I could. He said he would be there shortly, and then added, 'If you don't meet me there I will have your hide, do you understand!!' I swear this is what he said! You see, he was cursing again!"

"I told him that I had milk to deliver, grass to cut, and work to do, and that I would not be able to meet him. I could not go to Hackman's.

---

* *Babu* can mean "clerk" or "accountant." It was used by Dil Das as an honorific title.

I needed to go back to the village. I told him I would meet him the following day after my work was done. But then in the end I went anyway."

"You see what had happened was this. Mr. Schoonmaker, whose children went to Woodstock, had come up from Delhi a week or so earlier and gone hunting out near Dhanaulti, on the ridges down below the Tehri road. In the Dhanaulti bazaar there is a shopkeeper whose name is Dalebu, or something like that, who comes from a village called Dandu Beli. Not Beli, mind you, which is the name of another village, but Dandu Beli."

"Now Schoonmaker had shot a *barasingha* [a 'twelve-horned' deer], but some of the villagers from Dandu Beli who he had hired as coolies to carry his supplies ran off with the kill. Schoonmaker was mad and demanded that the barasingha be given back. Word of this got back to Dhanaulti, and then back to the school. So when I spoke with Coapman on the phone, he told me to go on ahead and sort the matter out with Dalebu. He would come later."

"So I decided that I would ride a horse, as this would be faster than walking. I was young and the horse was a good one, so I ran it hard and got to Dhanaulti in good time. I was able to find Schoonmaker and ask him what had happened. He was still mad, and told me that many of the men at Dhanaulti were bad characters, and that they had stolen his deer. Well, I was in a funny mood, and told Schoonmaker that I was a 'bad character' too! I said this with the same strength and carefree attitude that John sahib would have. He would say things like that, you see! Anyway, I worked things out with Dalebu and we got the deer back."

"Later on Schoonmaker and the others who were with him told me that there was a woman who lived on Mullangar hill back in Landour to whom they wanted to send some of the meat. They wanted me to take her one of the barasingha legs. Well, it was already late, so I spent the night there at Dhanaulti, and in the morning had some tea before leaving. Then I asked the sahib to write a letter to explain things to the woman. I saddled up my horse, mounted it quickly, and pressed my knees into its sides. I raced that horse as fast as it would go the whole twenty kilometers, and got back to Mussoorie by about ten or eleven in the morning. I ran that sister-fucking horse like you wouldn't believe!"

"When I got to Mullangar I went straight to her house. I had to deliver the goods. I didn't stop anywhere. I went directly."

"Now, on my way back from Dhanaulti I thought to myself, if I go home with the horse and spend the night, then I will have to pay extra. There would be no point in that; it would be a waste of money. I knew the man from whom I had gotten the horse, and sent word telling him to meet me at a particular place. So, after delivering the meat, on my way back from the school to Tibri, above my village, I met the man at the place we had arranged. I told him that I didn't have any money to pay for the horse, but that he should go to the school and get reimbursed there. I told him to check with *babu ji*—Austin babu, that is—with whom I had left a letter explaining my intentions. Later he went and picked up his money, and I was able to go straight on over to the hotel and meet Coapman the next day."

"Now, the manager of Hackman's was a fellow named Bhora, who is also from the hills near Pauri. I went straight to his house and asked if John sahib had arrived. I said, simply 'Where is he?' not bothering to specify, except with a little extra emphasis, who I meant. Bhora replied: 'This sahib of yours has a very sharp tongue. He is dangerous!' Then he gave me the room key and showed me where to go."

"Both Coapman and Harper had come, and they had brought their wives along as well. They both worked for Coca-Cola, and I knew Harper since I had stayed with him in Delhi. Harper sahib smoked Charminar cigarettes. They had a waiter with them in the room and ordered things from him."

"Coapman asked how things were going. I told him that I had eaten breakfast with Schoonmaker at Dhanaulti, lunch with the woman at Mullangar where I had taken the legs, and had then come straight to the hotel. He gave me twenty rupees to get some food. When I got back we started to make plans for the hunt and to catch the thieves who stole Schoonmaker's barasingha."

"The next day we left, and the women rode horseback. There were also horses for the children, Suzy and Mark. Johnny walked with us. We had a full entourage of coolies as well. We left in the morning and arrived at Dhanaulti in the evening. As soon as we arrived, Coapman said: 'Call the hunters.' By this time Dalebu the shopkeeper had come. It was his son's teashop we stopped outside of on our way to the wedding you know. He is the one with the long nose. Anyway, everyone was assembled and Coapman asked: 'Who is the guilty party here? Who has stolen the barasingha?' We found out who it was, but they were not of Dalebu's village. They were from some other place."

"Later we went down the road which leads to the plains. We sent Harper sahib, who had brought his wife along, down one ridge, and we went down another. Coapman and I figured it was a good spot for them; that they would find animals there. Now, as they were walking his wife got thirsty, so Harper fired a shot to attract our attention. I heard the shot and said to Coapman: 'Good, they must have found something.' We picked up our things and quickly ran to where they were. But then when we arrived, Harper told us that his wife was thirsty and wanted a drink of water. Can you imagine!"

"Well, sir, John sahib got angry at this and said: 'Look, you have called us all the way down here just for this! You have made us stop hunting for this kind of nonsense. Why did you bring her along anyway? What do you think we are doing here?' Well, poor Harper sahib was left speechless! After all, his wife had wanted to come along while Coapman's wife had stayed at the camp. She should not have come where she didn't belong. Coapman was very angry and said: 'This is mountain hunting. You only get one chance and that has now been ruined!' "

"After all of this, John sahib told me to go hunting with Harper since he was mad. We sat on a ridge and Harper smoked his Charminars. Then I saw a kakar in the bushes below and pointed it out to him. It was a big buck with horns. Paat!—he shot it and it fell. Now, as soon as that one fell down dead another one appeared out of the bushes and paat!—he shot that one, too. When John sahib heard this his anger began to cool."

"We hunted like this for some time, and John sahib shot a ghoral. Finally we came back to the camp and John sahib proposed that we go and shoot some partridges. We walked this way from Dhanaulti, to the east back toward Pathreni. You know the place, it is right where our car broke down coming back from the wedding. There is a place there called Utiyanu where there are many fields and chans and a good path. What we did was to place a gun on each of the two ridges which border the fields. This way we flushed the partridges back and forth. I hid in the middle. The birds didn't know where to go! They just flew back and forth, back and forth! We laughed so hard that day we could have died! Things went so well that we returned home late that night and fell right asleep."

*   *   *

"A man from Delhi had come up to hunt with us. I forget what his name was, but he wore glasses. John sahib and I were down at Koldighat where I was keeping my buffaloes. The man with glasses came down and met us there and we took him out hunting along the big cliffs above the chans. We walked up onto the pine-covered ridge and hunted up there for some time. Finally one ghoral came out in a clearing across the way, and we told the man with glasses to shoot, but he was not fast enough and the goat ran away. It was all right though, and we thought nothing of it and went on."

"Now, below Koldighat, further down in the valley below Shiv Dutta's place and Tota Ram's, there is a road that leads off toward some chans. We decided that we would go along there and sit to look for ghoral on the opposite slope. We had been sitting for some time when three ran out across the hillside. The goats were moving fast so we told the man with glasses to shoot quickly. 'Shoot! Shoot!' we said. But—can you believe it—this time he carefully took off his spectacles, took out a hand-kerchief, and then started to clean the lenses! Can you believe it! I tell you! . . . Well, John sahib was disgusted. He got very angry and told the man to go clean his glasses somewhere else. We left him there to hunt by himself and went on to Loharighar and then to the village of Chamasari."

"It was at Chamasari that we ran into the forest guard. He was stand-ing above us on the ridge and was shouting down telling us to stop hunt-ing. We stopped there, and so he started to come down toward us, still shouting. But by the time he got down to where we were sitting, he was all apologetic, very courteous and meek! Now you tell me, Joe, why had he suddenly lost his backbone. He was standing up there on the ridge shouting at us as though he would confiscate our guns!"

"Well, while this was going on a ghoral ran out on the slope across from us, and John sahib shot it. He then turned to the forest guard and told him to go and pick it up. Imagine! Now you tell me, had not the forest guard been turned into a coolie! And then, to add insult to in-jury, we began to make plans, right there in front of the guard, to pick up some liquor from the mule drivers who ply the road from Beli! What could the forest guard do? All of the people there in Chamasari were friends of John sahib. They all would ask him into their homes. He had no enemies. I tell you, he is the guru of shikar; the master of hunting."

*   *   *

"One day a sahib came hunting and we went over to the chowki near Moti Dhar. When we got there I said, 'Sahib, would you like to fire a shot?' That is all I said. I didn't say what I had seen or where it was. 'Be sure to shoot accurately,' I said. Then I showed him the ghoral I had seen. He aimed, fired into the bush, and hit the ghoral which fell down. We decided to leave it there and go hunting further on."

"Later when we came back and I went down to look for it, however, it was nowhere to be found. I told the sahib I would go on down into the ravine below Kala Pathar to search. I thought I knew where it was. But I could not find it even though I was sure the shot had hit. The sahib was sitting up above on the path, and I told him that even though I couldn't find the ghoral it was all right; I had found some blood. There was a big clump of bamboo which had been all torn up. I said to myself, 'It must be right here. It won't take long to find now.' But then some boys from nearby came over and said that I would not be able to find it. 'Why not?' I said. 'Don't you think I can search for it?' So I went a little fur-ther down and there it was, right there. I told the boys to pick it up and carry it up to the sahib. You see, these villagers can be real bad charac-ters sometimes. The boys were just trying to get me to go away so that they could take the ghoral back with them. When I got back up to the path I said to the sahib, 'You see, did we find it or not?' "

"Then we went on down to Koldighat and had something to eat. Now, the sahib had a twelve-gauge pump action shotgun that carried five shells. He said that he was going back to school so I told him to leave the gun with me and that I would bring it to him in the morning. He did, and then left. Meanwhile, I went up above the chans to look around. I saw a hawk circling and thought that a leopard must have killed some animal. There was nothing else that had died in the valley that I knew of. As I walked along I realized that there was something walking on the trail in front of me, but it was out of sight. I didn't know what it was. Maybe a porcupine. So I kept walking and walking and whatever it was kept walking as well. Then it walked along beside me, still out of sight, but I could hear it. We walked and walked and walked. The hawk was still circling above the ravine, but then it flew off. I could not figure out what was going on. But then I put it out of my mind and made my way back to the chan and went inside."

"Rukam Das was with me at that time. I had my buffaloes at Koldighat, some of which were giving milk. I also had a number of male buffalo calves tied up on the flat plain near the forest not far from the chan. Well, I got back to my chan in the evening, and soon after heard some noise coming from the forest. I paid no attention and sat down to eat. Sheri's wife was down with us then and she had fixed some meat. She asked if I was ready to eat, and after thinking for a little while I said I would. But the noise outside kept on. While I was eating the noise got louder still and I realized that a leopard must have come upon the buffalo calves on the plain. I took a look outside but it was dark, so I went back in and grabbed the torch sahib had given me. However, the batteries were very weak; it was only bright enough to walk by. I shone it outside anyway, but could see nothing. Nor was the leopard afraid of the feeble light. I waited there quietly for some time but could not see or hear anything."

"I went back inside and sat down to eat again. I said to Sheri's wife, 'Do you have anything to drink? I am tired.' This is what you do in your own house. This is what you do, right? This is what you ask your family. She said, 'Yes, I have some; I have it.' So I told her to bring me some. I was tired and wanted to go to sleep. Meanwhile, I changed two of the batteries. Then I heard more noise outside and told Rukam to give me the torch. I had just picked up a bone from my plate, and as my hands were full I left the gun inside leaning against the wall. I walked out onto the dung heap and turned on the torch. The light was now bright, and it shone directly onto the leopard! It was right there in front of me! I said to myself, 'Oh my, the gun and the cartridges are inside and here I am standing outside with just a torch!' The leopard was just standing there looking at me. I was sucking on the bone!"

"So I took the torch and circled it around and around until the leopard backed into a bush. I went inside quickly and told Rukam to come with me. I told him there was a porcupine outside and that we would shoot it together. This was quite some time ago when Rukam was much younger; probably somewhere between Beeji and Gura's ages, about 9 or 10. Like Kamala here, but bigger and stronger. I did not want him to be afraid."

"So we went outside and I shone the torch into the bush again. The leopard was still there but did not appear to be afraid. I said to myself, 'If I fire now I will die, and so will my brother.' The leopard was too close, and looking at us. So I told Rukam that we would go up above the chan to get in a better position. When we got into place I told Rukam, 'Friend, shine the light exactly where I tell you; shine it right down the barrel of the gun.' I told him exactly when, and as soon as he turned on the light I fired; I fired straight into the bush—dhaaar!"

"Well, you don't get sister-fucking LGs like that anymore! The leopard let out a loud roar and I grabbed the torch from Rukam for fear he might turn it off. I thought I might have to fire another shot quickly. I told him not to move or run. What was he to know, he was just a young boy. He stayed right there standing beside me and said, 'My big brother is with me, what do I have to be afraid of.' So I took the torch and shone it down to where the leopard had been. I could hear some strange sounds coming from below and behind the bush. I thought that if I turned off the light the leopard might come back up. But nothing happened, and I concluded that my first shot had hit it squarely. We left and went back down to the chan."

"In the morning I milked the buffaloes and told my brother to deliver the milk to the school. I went off hunting to Moti Dhar where sahib had his camp. They had a license, a permit, I mean. Kapadia sahib from the school was there, too, but he was still asleep. I told them all what had happened and I told the grass cutters not to go into the valley where the wounded leopard was. I was at the chowki talking to them and then left and made my way down the ridge. Along the way I saw a chicken, shot it, and put it in my bag. I then made my way over to Bari Dhang and sat down to look for ghoral. Soon I saw one, fired, and it too fell down. All of this happened in the morning and I walked on slowly until I came back to my chan. My wife was there along with the children. Everyone was there."

"I sat for a while, and presently Shiv Datta came by, the old rascal. He had brought the forest guard along in an attempt to catch me. Now, the sahib had come down by this time as well and had gone into the chan to take a rest. He was in the part where we store the grass. I told the forest guard not to bother him since he was asleep. I said, 'If you have anything to say, say it to me. Talk to me. What is it you want? If you want meat, I have some. I have shot a ghoral. Take some.' But he did not listen to me. He said that I had no permit, no license. He wanted to see the papers. Now, sahib was sleeping but I went in and got the permit anyway. I showed it to them and said, 'We have five more ghoral to shoot. We have only shot one so far.' I tell you, the forest guard was silenced! He looked at the permit and said, 'I see, well then let me at least have the head and the feet to take home and eat.' I told him to forget about it! He got nothing! The rest of us all ate, drank, and made merry. We were all happy, in great spirits."

"Now, the leopard I had shot the night before had died behind the bush as I suspected, and we went to retrieve it. But how was I to skin it with Shiv Datta and the forest guard nearby? They finally left, however, since they could do nothing. We had a permit. So we were all sitting down near my chan at Koldighat, and my wife made tea which we drank. Then I realized it was getting late, so I went to where the leopard was, skinned it, and then brought the skin back all wrapped up. When I got back down we heard another leopard calling. It was searching for the one I had shot. I had shot the male and the female was looking for him. She was big and came right down to the back of the chan during the night. Sheri's wife and Rukam Das were alone in one chan and were very scared. They stayed awake all night making little fireworks out of matches to try and scare the big leopard away."

"In the morning I came back down to Koldighat, to where they were, after spending the night up at Moti Dhar. I had to milk the buffaloes. Rukam was so scared he didn't want to go to school to deliver the milk for me but I told him to go anyway as it was light out and he would be safe."

"After finishing my work I went back up to Moti Dhar. Sahib was very tired, so we sat there for some time. Finally I told him I would go hunting and that he should go home. I decided to go to a place which was not very far away. One or two men from Moti Dhar came with me. Along the way a ghoral jumped out in front of me. I fired and it fell down. Then I saw another one standing nearby. Quickly I reloaded, aimed, and fired. This one fell down too! We turned around and brought both back to the camp. It was all very good; a great hunt . . . except that the villagers there in Moti Dhar stole the sahib's knife."

* * *

"Whatever god there is—whatever *malik*—he is in the heart. One need not go looking around for him. There is no use in that. If you believe in your heart, that is good. Tell me, though, what is the point of going around searching for god? Yes, people go to church—after all, they must go; it is expected—and that is good. So go. After all, don't we who are from the village go to the Sirakanda temple. These are things which are done, things which are expected. But really it is a matter of believing. Isn't that right?"

"But along with god, there is also a *shaitan*, a demon. I have seen him twice. Let me tell you about the first time."

"One night I was coming back from Library bazaar. My brother-in-law was the night watchman for the maharajah who lived over there, the maharajah whose estate is near the Savoy. He was married to my elder sister. You know, he got shot accidentally.

"My brother-in-law was cutting bamboo and was shot by accident. Some hunters mistook him for an animal, and so my sister became a widow. One must hunt carefully. Look before you shoot."

"There was a court case against those who had shot him, but it was pointless. It was simply an accident. That is all. I told his people that if there was going to be a court case, it would have to be initiated by the government, not by them. In the end the case was dismissed. . . . But what was it I was talking about . . . ? Oh yes, the demon."

"I had gone to my brother-in-law's place one day because he was having a party. I got into a fight with my sister about something. I stayed to eat, and then went to sleep for a short time. When I woke up I told everyone I was going home. I stepped outside, took a piss, and then started off past the toll gate and headed for home. It was late and the whole town was asleep. Well, I walked and walked and finally got as far as that place right below the school gate. What is it called . . . ? You know the place where the road goes down to the church. . . . What do you call that place? I have forgotten. Is it Pinerock . . . ? No? No. Oh yes, Palisades! Yes, that is right. Taftan is up above the road and there is a big oak tree down below; many oak trees. Right where the road divides there is a very thick one, and above it is that place they have built for studying. . . . What is it called . . . ? The library? Yes, that is it, the library. . . . No? No. No, no!! Not now, I mean back in my father's time. Yes, now I remember; that is right: Parker Hall."

"Well, anyway, I was traveling at night on the road above the church and below the school. I looked down below on the road leading to the church and saw the light of a lantern. On the road there is a corner, a few stairs and a gate; it was right there. Now, by the time I got over to where they have recently made the car park, I thought to myself: 'What is going on?' You see, now the light of the lantern was shining all around. I could see a tall man dressed all in white carrying it in his hand, but the light was shining all around."

"Well now, I was frightened. So, you know that middle road that cuts through to the kitchen area of the school? I went that way instead of heading on along the main road where the path leads down to the church. I was frightened. I found the night watchman who was on duty at the school and sat with him for some time. I also knew other people there. So I decided to spend the night back where the servants used to stay; where there are storage areas now. I went the rest of the way home in the morning."

*   *   *

"One day I had business in Dehra Dun and was coming back late. This was when my eldest daughter Dharma's mother was alive. It must have been about nine P.M. by the time I got back to Pathreni. My father told me to go to sleep and not go on down to Koldighat as it was late. I wanted to go on down, but decided to stay and get some rest. Since I had work to do, however, I got up early. It must have been around three A.M., but it looked like the middle of the night. I had no watch on, you see."

"I started out for Koldighat and got down below those big fields below Chattarmani the pandit's house when I saw a man making his way up toward where I was. He had on a white hat and coat and to me he looked like Chattarmani's son. Our chans were together over on the Nali side of Koldighat. Since I had to collect fodder for the buffaloes anyway, I decided to just stay where I was and cut the grass while waiting for him to come up."

"Well, I didn't know that this character was a demon. I figured he was Chattarmani's son out cutting grass early in the morning. He was making his way stright up the ridge above the level patch of ground below which John sahib fell. I stood still for a while, waiting. I had my gun in one hand. As he came up closer I ran down to meet him and shouted out, 'Hey, Daya Ram, what are you doing up here so late at night?' He didn't answer even though he was as close as you and I are now. I ran over to him and was just about to grab hold of his shoulder when I stopped. 'Maybe this was a thief on his way up from Nagal down in the valley,' I thought to myself. Then, suddenly, the figure disappeared! I decided to sit down and wait. If he turned up again I would shoot him, but he had disappeared."

"I continued on my way down to Koldighat. Just as I was nearing the chans I saw Daya Ram coming out to take a piss. I coughed so as to let him know I was there. This is what we do in the villages. He was staying in the chan slightly above the others. I remained quiet. There is a saying here in the hills that one should not speak to another person while on a path. It is bad luck, or something. But then he saw me and called out. He asked me what I was doing up and about so early. Then he invited me into his chan for tea. His wife was there, as were his children, so I told him I would sit outside since it was quite warm and I didn't want to wake the children. I sat outside. While we were drinking our tea I said, 'Daya Ram, I thought I just saw you up on the ridge.' He said it was not possible; that he had just woken up and had not been up there yet. He said it must have been a thief."

"Later in the morning we both carried our milk up the same path together. When we got to his house on the ridge we met his father and told him the story. He said, 'Son, listen, this walking about in the night is not good. Sometimes it is bad, that is. No, not always. If you insist on walking around at night, however, sooner or later you will run into the demon.'"

Chapter 9
The Terms of Friendship

Daya Ram, a relatively well-to-do Brahmin friend and neighbor, invited Dil Das into his home for a cup of tea. Dil Das chose not to go in, but accepted the gesture of friendship on the neutral ground between two chans, his own and that of the pandits. He also chose to remember the event and recount it as a noteworthy episode in a ghost story, just as he remembered his high-caste neighbor's words of reassurance after the flood: "He told us to sit and make ourselves comfortable. He knew that our buffaloes had been washed away, and kept saying that it was a terrible thing. He kept saying that we were all lucky to be alive. 'Don't worry about a thing,' he said, 'at least you are safe. Let the nine buffaloes go.' Then he told me: 'The nine buffaloes will be made up for, they will be replaced, don't worry. I am just happy to see that you are alive.'"

After so much about the history of encounter through hunting and work, it will seem odd, no doubt, that I should choose to end my account of Dil Das's life by bringing things back, abruptly in the last part of this book, to caste and the contested moral biology of "untouchable" interactions—the biographical structure of a seemingly different kind of difference. Yet, I think that in some ways caste-based distinctions defined, for Dil Das at least, the basic, underlying problem of identity, perhaps not consciously, but on that fundamental level of the question "who am I?" Dil Das could not simply ignore, or shout down, as it were, the answer that culture had given to this question. And yet, because he simply could not accept that answer, he spent his life, and particularly the time he spent talking about his life, trying to construct an answer that was more in keeping with his self-image and more in step with the history of his experiences.

Like many others who have borne the burden of ingrained prejudice throughout their lives, whether by virtue of an oppressive ideology or a specific history of exploitation, Dil Das seemed to be at once resigned to the fact and yet deeply resentful of the stigma of untouchability. What strikes me as most significant, however, at least in terms of biography, is the way caste rules and regulations have almost completely defined the mechanisms—both narrative and experiential—by which means he tried to "re-write" the ethics of social interaction in order to re-define himself. In other words, I think it is possible to see in Dil Das's life, even outside the explicit domain of hierarchy, a tragic confluence of categories and conceptions about friendship, and how an escape from caste into conviviality is made precarious by the logic of encounter.

This becomes apparent, however, only in light of the fact that Dil Das did, occasionally, speak out directly and forcefully about injustice. As we shall see in the last part of this book, he clearly articulated his position on the whole issue of hierarchy. But, in a curious sort of way, a reading of these critical narratives reveals, I think, a much larger and more invidious structure of power which worked through the emotional agency of anxious intimacy—that which was made possible, or even necessary, by the confluence of caste, capitalism, and colonialism: a breakdown of interdependence, the construction of dependency, and a search for alternative frameworks of meaning.

Male bonding of various sorts is, of course, not at all unique. Moreover, in North India there are many institutions of fraternity, both formal and informal. But for Dil Das the meaningfulness of personal relationships was all-important. In his view, friendship was the definitive trope of biography, an essentially moral point—defined in highly personal terms in an otherwise impersonal world—around which particular events revolved, and to which the ethics of social interaction—truth, honesty, respect, and generosity—were keyed. In keeping with this, Dil Das seemed to be almost obsessed with the meaningfulness of sharing food and drink with others in a context where status was defined in terms of the "mixed-up" mutual respect of an eat, drink, and be merry lifestyle, rather than in terms of the sober, clear-cut hierarchy of caste-based distinction. In fact, his narrative seems to speak out against the structure of hierarchy by mixing things up, by having people enact daily dramas of dietary fraternity at almost every turn: on the road to Katmandu, for example; at Tiger Tops around the fire; with policemen on the way back from Kathling; with strangers in a tea shop while escaping from the police; with Chattarmani the Brahmin and various high-caste friends in Kimoi; with strangers in a snowstorm; with friends duck hunting in the Punjab; with doctors in Ludhiana; with Daya Ram while talking of demons; and, as we shall see, with patients in a Delhi hospital where his wife underwent treatment for cancer.

Most of the time these dramas seem to have nothing to do with purity and pollution as such, and I would not speak of them—as either event or story—as forms of protest. Dil Das did not deconstruct "this *jat/pat* business," as he often put it, by articulating a rhetoric of protest. I do not think that he was even aware of the fact that while telling stories in which food and drink figured prominently as the medium of contact that he was anxiously trying to construct a world of friendship in order to circumvent the terms of "biological" difference. Nevertheless, whenever he told stories, it was obvious that he regarded eating and drinking together as supremely meaningful and significant—if also fraught with a degree of fear and trembling—and I think that for him the sharing of a meal with others of varying status signified, if nothing else, the moral contingency of the stigma into which he had been born.

And this is probably a good thing, for it gave him a critical perspective on power as well as a positive sense of self. Yet ultimately, I think, it created a kind of ambiguously structured psychological space wherein friendship was made to bear the full burden of what is usually distributed equally on the "webs of culture." Intimate colonial encounter provided a highly problematic, open-ended response to the basic question about identity, which had been defined as so critically important by caste but for which caste provided no answer at all. And so, for Dil Das, autobiography bespoke both the euphoria of heroic independence from "falsehood" as well as the terror of having engaged in a translation of truth into something too personal, too close to the heart.

While I was conducting research for my M.A. thesis in 1981 Dil Das was away in Delhi for much of the time looking after his sick wife, so I talked at length with Tulasi Das, Dil Das's elder uncle, about life in the village of Pathreni. I also interviewed others from the community. While transcribing the tapes of these interviews and discussions, sorting out information, and generally trying to make sense of that which was said by writing it down in various ways, I remember being struck by the fact that friendship was such an important social fact to so many people whose lives "ought" to have been structured by kinship, ritual, and ecology, or at least by something which could be securely nailed down as ethnography rather than some sort of ghost story.

Despite my search for the criteria of impersonal exigency, I recorded, in 1981 or so, what I came to interpret, later, as an emotional commentary on economic change and ideological conflict; in this commentary character was defined as a kind of residual goodness that not even the poverty of colonial economic history or inbred cultural prejudice could assail. This is a condition of tragic irony wherein the terms of self-consciousness evoked what I can only describe as a confusion of pity, respect, and displaced hope. It is a condition that I thought was perfectly articulated, over and over, in a common phrase used by Tulasi Das, a poet of sorts in his own right, to describe his friends, and the oxymoronics of virtue and reality in cross-caste, inter-class friendships in particular. It was often used by others in what seemed to me as a kind of fateful curtailment, or karmic qualification, of human kindness and the spirit of goodness in personal achievement. While shaking his head wistfully as though to mark off the limits of comprehension—the limits of heroic escape—Tulasi would intone this deeply tragic refrain: *acha admi hai, bichara.* "He is a good man, poor fellow."

In rereading my analysis, in listening again to the taped interviews with Tulasi Das and others, in talking further with friends of whom I had asked pointed questions fifteen or sixteen years ago, and, finally, in trying to translate Dil Das's life out of intimacy and into some sort of public knowledge, I have come to realize that all the talk about friendship was directed at me—a pandit of sorts, in my own right—and, by extension, at those who had once been close to Dil Das but either were born to grow up and leave, or were simply born twice. The discourse on friendship is not, therefore, what I originally thought it was. It is not so much a contained critical commentary on caste or class as it is a personal appeal to make the terms of our encounter more meaningful than culture or history will allow.

I do not for a moment think that it was a Christian ethic, born of the transmuted ideals of Renaissance Europe—carried first west by pilgrims and then back east again along the trajectory of a different colonialism by the missionary heirs of Puritanism—that inspired Dil Das to resent his oppression. That would be the ultimate conceit of postmodern logic. And yet, colonialism, and Christianity—and also capitalism, if one may speak, in a parallel way, of a less than holy trinity—are directly to blame, I think, for having defined the moral alternative to hierarchy in terms of a universal utopian truth about freedom and equality, a utopian truth that is all but meaningless in the face of practical experience. And here, somewhere between the transnational interface of ideology and utopia is where Dil Das was caught trying to define himself in terms of a tenuous, tertiary category whose significance depended not on a revelation of meaning or its final realization, but on the perpetual translation of self into other in order to articulate an illusive truth. This was a kind of interlocutive quest whose observance required my participation and that of those others in Landour, Koldighat, and Donk who were Dil Das's friends.

By keeping our distance, however—through writing, by living and eating apart, and by simply conforming to the comfortable conventions of our somewhat down-at-the-heel postcolonial elitism—we made that translation both necessary and impossible, both meaningful and meaningless. By going away, however, we have forced the issue of difference. We have made the work of translation sound like the ramblings of a lost man talking to himself. We have let the mutuality of encounter fall back into the cultural solipsism of untouchable, binary categories and must accept the fact, therefore, that we cannot escape the demon of paternalism—for how else can one explain the use of *sahib* as a term of endearment, "guilty" charity as a perquisite of conviviality, and the fact that, although we often ate in Dil Das's home and often ate together on neutral ground, he never ate with us at our table in the huge dining room of the bungalow built on the periphery of town by Colonel Young of the Dehra Dun Rifles in 1848. It would not have made sense, on anyone's terms. And so, being a good man, poor fellow, I cannot escape the stigma of colonialism by hunting for friendship, a friendship that, finally, can never come to terms with the tragically intimate power it reveals.

Part IV
Uttarkhand

HIMALAYA

Chapter 10
The Heart of the Matter

"Are we not men? I mean, I ask you. This 'jat, pat' business, this business of caste, is all an artificial construction."

"In reality there are only two jats: male and female. It is really a question of what is *made* different: this, that, and the other thing. Otherwise everything is all just a human construction, nothing more than that."

"You see, if I make shoes, I become a *mochi* [cobbler], and that is OK. But what people don't understand is that making shoes is a skilled trade. If you make somebody into a *chamar* [leather worker], into an untouchable, it is pointless. What matters is how a person does his work, and not the kind of work he does."

"You see, now sardars—Sikhs from the Punjab—are making shoes in factories. Before they did it themselves, with their own hands, but now they have employees. There is one fellow in particular. What is his name? Ah, that's right, Hajara Singh. He would lend money to anyone in Mussoorie, to sweepers and everyone alike. Whenever they would receive their wages they would go to him and pay the interest they owed. And also that fellow at the clock tower, that sardar. It was the same with him. Well, his brother-in-law has a taxi now. He got rich by giving the mochis money and learning their trade. He stole their work, you see. The mochis are finished now. They have nothing. This is jat. It is nothing."

*   *   *

"And these pandits, who do they think they are? They need an umbrella, a coat, and a pair of boots when they die. Remember how they were all dancing there in the village while we were sitting to one side?"

"It is the same as I have said before; it is a matter of the heart. If there is a conflict between hearts then there will be trouble. Problems. It is a matter of the heart. For friends you will butcher a goat and keep your heart pure. After all, what is the point of fighting? Distrust and doubt come into the heart and do this; they cause one to dislike others. But all of this is false. It is false consciousness."

"Take Hanuman for example. When they asked him where god was he ripped open his chest and said, 'Here, in my heart.' Truth cannot hide; it cannot be hidden, I mean. An honest man cannot be put down. You are whatever you do with your hands."

*   *   *

"This jat, pat is stronger over near Tehri and Sakhliarna than it is here. Once while I was traveling there my shadow fell on a big man, a Brahmin. He rebuked me and said, 'Hey, what are you doing?' But I ask you, what is in a shadow? I tell you, this jat, pat business was that strong over there back then. Can you imagine, it was only my shadow! Now it is better, though. But even so, it is not good. It is going away, but it is not yet completely gone. There are not many who talk like the Tehri Brahmin did anymore. Many people will sit and eat and drink with us. The old customs are no longer kept in the heart."

"Now, just because I am from Pathreni, the big men there in my in-laws' village would say, 'I hear your daughter is getting married.' I knew what they were after, but what could I say but yes. Then they would say, 'OK, I will spend one night with her. Her wedding night!' Had they become her fucking mother? I tell you, I would shoot them inside the house. Inside! On the spot! . . . But they had strength, so what was to be done? They had control. They had power."

"But those men who did these things have lost control now. Their houses are broken down and in ruins below Kadukhal, beyond Dhanaulti, and also over where my daughter lives in Sinipur. I'll show you sometime. We couldn't go near there with our shoes on. It was like that, and we were scared. But we had relatives there and wanted to visit them. We had to go. But if we were caught by the big men they would put us to work in the wheat fields, or to work at whatever was growing at that particular time of year. They did this for no reason at all. We also could not pass through Magra. It was forbidden. It is finished there now, however."

*   *   *

"Once a pandit came along the road and sat down below the pine trees above the house here to take a rest. John sahib offered him some tea and some food. But he refused. He just said, 'It's OK, it is all right,' but he did not accept our offer. He did not want to eat what we had touched, I guess. So John sahib said, 'Look here pandit, god has given us all the same food to eat. What is there that shouldn't be eaten? Why not eat what we offer you? After all, you are alive; so eat.'"

"Now the Arya Samajis write that people should not eat meat or drink liquor. But if you are in trouble, you must eat and drink whatever there is. If you choose not to eat certain things on principle, then just hurry up and die!"

"Well, the pandit had to shut up. He could not say anything! He understood, you see. After all, if a person dies they are dead. There can be no argument."

"But these pandits, they want to have a stick, a hat, and a dhoti in order to go where they go. That is their life; their work—but five meters of cloth in payment for services! That is just too much!"

"You see, one day a pandit came to our house and for his services wanted some yellow cloth—how much? Five meters of the stuff! Can you believe it, five whole meters! Well, I kept quiet and was writing his request down. But I had heard enough. So finally I said, 'Listen, pandit, if I can't find five meters, is it OK if I bring you a scrap of the yellow stuff?' But I was not finished with him yet. No sir! I said, 'Listen, there are plenty of tailors in Mussoorie, how about if I just get you a pair of pajamas made?' I tell you, I really don't understand this custom of giving cloth as payment. What did he want with five meters anyway? But that is the way the world works. It is just the way it is."

"But tell me why I should not eat certain foods? I have ten good years left and will enjoy them. Some people listen to what the pandits say: don't eat this, don't eat that. They say that eating certain things will have an effect on your life. And it is true. If you believe them, that is. If you believe them it will happen."

"They come here to the village and try to read our palms to tell the future. I tell them to go away. Whatever is written is written and doesn't need to be read."

"Once I was down at Ashley Hall in Dehra Dun. I was on my way to visit my daughter Dharma, and there were some others along with me. I was laying down sleeping when this pandit with ash stripes painted on his forehead came up and pestered me. I told him to bugger off and leave me alone. I was tired. I just told him to go away."

"I was up at Gorikund once with Hilliard and Bollinger; you know them, the two staff members from school. There was a pandit sitting there by the bathing tank and he asked me what my jat was. He wanted to know my caste. Well, I told him straight away that I was a male, and that if he wanted to look closely he could see for himself! He was intelligent. He should have been able to see for himself that I was a man. Didn't he know the difference between male and female? He also wanted some sort of donation from me, but I told him to get lost. Why should I have given him *dan*? Why should he get a gift from me?"

*   *   *

"One day a pandit came to my house because Gura was sick with a sore throat. He looked at her and told me to give her away to someone who could look after her properly. Well, sir, I got mad and said, 'Listen here, pandit, I gave her life, so stop talking nonsense.' Now I ask you, if I had given her away where would I be now? That pandit would really have made a mess of things had I listened to him. He said that I would save money by giving her away, but I told him that it was through spending money that I lived, not saving it! We got into a big argument and finally I told him to leave. So it goes."

"These pandits are real cheats; just out to make money. Didn't you see up at the Sirakanda Devi temple they were selling coconuts for five rupees each! The cheats were all inside making their offerings. I tell you, if you are clean inside then everything is all right, if not then everything is hopeless and there is no value — no point that is — in making offerings to god. Pandits say, 'Don't eat this, don't drink that,' but I say they don't have to eat and drink what they don't want. God has given man these things to enjoy, so eat and drink. True, one should not drink and then start cursing at people. Those kind of fools come to my brother's house."

"Nobody comes to my house just to drink. They come and call me brother, friend."

*   *   *

"Some of these pandits say they don't drink. But in their own houses they, well . . . well, you know these big men! When they come out of their houses, they call themselves pure! Yes, it is all right. I know. I have drunk liquor. This I will tell you. I have not hit anyone, nor have I been hit by anyone. I have not fought with anyone. I have drunk and I have eaten; I have sat in the courts and watched the fights go on."

*   *   *

"There was a pandit from over at Jhalki; you know, the place where they have those orchards. He told my father that he needed a *kandi* (woven basket) made for picking up cow dung. My father agreed to make the kandi but he was a little late in finishing the work and did not deliver the kandi on the day he had said he would."

"My uncles and he were down cutting grass by that big tree where I shot the kakar. From up above the pandit came down to the village and started shouting and cursing at my father for being so late. It was a matter of that time, you see, a different era altogether. You see, the pandit was in fact just a government servant, only an employee, but here in our village he was acting like a big, important person."

"Anyway, my father told the pandit that the kandi was ready, and that he would be right up to get it for him. He left the load of grass he had been carrying down on the path by the tree. My mother retrieved it later. My father was the head of the household, you see."

"Well, the pandit came down nearer to our house and again started shouting and cursing. My father told him to wait, he was just on his way up. Then, when he got up to where the pandit was, he suddenly took off his shoe and hit the pandit with it twice saying, 'Listen, friend, everyone has mothers and sisters, so why are you cursing mine in this way? The kandi is ready.' "

"Now, the poor pandit didn't even stop to pick up the kandi. Instead he ran for his life over to the edge of those fields where, trying to escape, he ended up trapped; and there he sat quivering, shaking, and pathetically saying that he was going to die."

"Then my uncles came up, and seeing what had happened they tried to calm my father down. But he was not yet finished with the insolent pandit; he wanted him to pay a fine for being so rude! In the end, however, the matter was dropped, and taking pity on the poor fellow, my relatives brought him back to the village, gave him his kandi, and sent him on his way."

"You see, that was a different era. We did have to give *bigar*, but this fellow was only a government servant, a clerk acting as though he had real authority."

* * *

"When my father was old and knew he was going to die, he called all five of us brothers up from Koldighat where we were looking after the buffaloes. He was up on the second floor of our old house and we all climbed up to where he was. As we sat there beside him, he told us that he was nearing death and that we should all live in harmony after he was gone."

"Now, my father was a drinking man, and he kept his liquor and his homebrew separate. He had a problem with his breathing, you see, and would cure an attack of asthma with a shot of liquor. He also ate meat. So, from his deathbed he told me to go and shoot him something to eat."

"I knew that my father was going to die, so I filled my pocket with cartridges and went up to the fields below Jabbarkhet near where those chans are now. As I got near the spring, I saw a kakar grazing on the opposite slope, down below Miss Campbell's house, but it was too far away for a good shot. I sat down and wondered what to do."

"While I was thinking, the kakar fell asleep in the shade of some bushes, so I began to work my way down the slope in order to get within range. However, I could not go down the ridge very far because the undergrowth was thick and made too much noise. I sat down to smoke another cigarette, and then another as I tried to figure out what to do. I could see the kakar's horns; it was a big male. Finally I decided to aim through the bushes and see what happened. I fired and the deer ran out. I fired again and it fell down. I ran over to where it had fallen, tied it up, and quickly made for home."

"I skinned and butchered it as fast as I could, and my mother quickly roasted the liver and gave some to my father; she gave him the liver to give him strength. He asked her to give him a bottle of liquor. She brought it. He drank half of it and ate two pieces of meat. That was all he wanted, he said. He didn't want anymore than that."

"As he finished eating we were all sitting around beside his bed. All five of us were sitting together and we took turns holding him in our arms. My mother was there, too. We were all together, and he died that night."

*   *   *

"My father almost settled over at Talanighat, you know. But he would have had to pay rent to the people there at a rate of one and a quarter rupees per month. And it was also hot at Talanighat, and he did not like it, so he stayed here instead. You see, we lack nothing here. We have food. We have water. We can wander through the jungle at will. That is why we are here. We have everything. Where else can you find this? But that was a different time."

"It was many years ago that my father died. And a year after he died, my mother passed away. It was while my elder sister was away in school at Roorkee. My mother, who was sick, told me to go and get her. So I went and explained to my sister that her mother was very sick. Then I brought her back to the village."

"Now, the stairs to our old house went up from the ground outside to the first floor. When we got back, I walked up the stairs in front of my sister and told my mother that I had brought her daughter back. Well, my mother must have seen my silhouette against the bright light outside, and hearing my voice thought that her husband had come back. She told me this, and I jokingly said that I was indeed her husband and had come back to get her and take her with me. I was joking, you see. Then I said that I was hungry. We ate, and then she died that night."

"When you have a mother and father it is good. When I would stay out late in the jungle, mine would worry and call for me. When they died, there was no one to call for me, and I wandered through the jungle at will. Those who would have called for me had died. One's parents are the most important people in the world, you see. What is god? He is close—yes, the truth is in the heart—but the greatest of all are those who have given birth to you. This is a very deep thing I am telling you."

*　*　*

"My work was going well back then, but if Steve and your father were not here, I too would be gone . . ."

"I have never been to Harsil, but we can go there. That is where my mother is from, so we will find friends there. And they will have liquor to share."

"Harsil is where my mamu is from, right? My father's younger brother is from up near Deodital. My brothers are up there. There is a road up beyond Uttarkashi that goes toward the village Kalsu. Agora is in the other direction. My real brothers live in Kalsu. There is a place where the Ganga turns and flows down the valley. Kalsu is on one side and Harsil on the other. All our friends will be there. There are places to stay and eat along the way. We wouldn't have to take anything but our clothes and bedding. We could even get there in one day. It wouldn't even be very expensive."

"Once your brother, Steve, and I almost died up there. We were hiking up to see a special cave. A schoolmaster of some sort, from England I think, had come along with us, and I ended up carrying his things. He told us that he was able to walk in the mountains, but then what did he do? He was behind us and got tired out, so he hired some women to carry his load! He hired some women from a village near the trail to be his coolies! Well, the sahib—your father that is—was on ahead and didn't see all of this, but I got angry and told the schoolmaster that I would carry his load. If he couldn't carry what I was unable to add to my load, he would just have to leave it behind! Why had he brought so much along if he could not carry it?"

"We climbed way up high into the mountains. Steve and I climbed way up while the others stayed below. It was very cold. We never did make it up to the cave, though, because we met some people coming down who said that an avalanche had blocked the road. They said that one person had died and another had just barely escaped with his life. I wanted to see this for myself, but we could only go up to a place where the valley forked. From there on there was just too much snow. There is probably still snow now in June, but when it begins to rain it will melt and the road will clear."

*   *   *

"I went up to the Kathling glacier with your brother, Steve, and your father once. It was cold and very windy, but we were lucky enough to find an abandoned Gujar's chan to camp in. There were coolies with us as well. We told them to come up into the high mountains with us but they were afraid. I told them to at least come and pay tribute to the mountains, but they did not have what it took. Out of fright they stayed back while we went on."

"I don't know what Steve had done, but when we went up into the high mountains he left his sweater and jacket behind. I don't know what sort of shirt he was wearing, but he was cold and tried to crawl under a bush to protect himself from the wind and the snow. I thought he would die and told him that the time had come to turn around. We had spent long enough up there. We came down quickly. And by the time we had descended the distance from Pathreni to Seraghat, only a kilometer or so, we realized that it had snowed up where we had been. We would have died had we decided to stay up there in the Gujar's chan for another night. It was a great chan, though, with straw spread out on the floor inside. One sahib had come from abroad. He was so cold that in rushing to get dressed he put his clothes on inside out before he realized what he was doing! He couldn't find his pockets! We had a good laugh. We drank a little rum and came home. It was only then that we got to rest and relax a little."

*   *   *

"In the old days Karori Mal was the 'chairman' of Landour, a wealthy merchant. He lived near the Khachar Khana and had two houses. But now that he is dead, his widow is left weeping. When I go into town I stop and talk with her and ask why she cries. I say to her, 'Mother, what is wrong?' She tells me long stories and says, 'Sit, come and sit.' You see, she is poor now and has nothing. You have to make money to eat, drink, and get around, but she does not even have that."

"What is the lesson learned from Karori Mal? It is that one must never leave gold buried in the ground, for there it is worthless. In the end it will be left in the ground, or else someone will come along to make a field and dig it up. People are born to work and to eat and to drink. That is just the way it is. Work must be done; one must have a plan, money, and work. Everything must be set. But to think that one will become a king simply by earning money, by saving—forget it! If you have money, then eat drink and be merry. You see, Karori Mal died. He left with nothing and left nothing behind. One must be happy while living. That is all. Death, in the end, comes to everyone."

"So what if we live in the jungle? Is there anyone who comes to ask what we are doing here? No, we are just here. It is we who are the real Karori Mals; the ones who have a good time."

*   *   *

"There was an old man who lived near to us at Koldighat. He was Sundar Singh's father's elder brother. I called his wife *chachi* [aunty]. Anyway, he was very sick and his wife asked me to go shoot a pheasant for him to eat. It would increase his strength. I told her I would."

"I had my muzzle loader then, and only had one shot, but I said I would try to shoot one for Seth sahib; that is what he was called. He was a *seth*, a wealthy man."

"My buffaloes were at Koldighat then and I milked them in the evening. The moon was bright, and as it got dark I noticed where the *kalij* pheasants were roosting. It was just like the other day at Singhadhar when you and I both noticed the pheasants going into the trees when no one else did. We will go back there someday, you and I, and shoot them."

"After I had finished the milking, I took my gun and slowly made my way toward the trees. Now there was some long grass on the hillside and two or three kalij pheasants were still in there. I was sitting in a shallow ravine and thought to myself that it would be good if I could get more than one in a single shot. That way I could keep one for myself and give the other to Seth sahib. I sat and waited until two were lined up, but I couldn't get the third to get into a position where I could fire."

"While I was waiting I heard my wife telling the others that food was ready. She didn't call out because she knew I was hunting but I could hear them all talking near the chans. I knew that I had to go because they would be waiting for me, so I shot the two which were close together. One died on the spot and the other fluttered down a little bit. Both were big cocks."

"When I got back to the chan my wife and the others were distilling liquor. I showed them the two pheasants. 'Cook one,' I said, 'the other I will take to Seth sahib tomorrow. He is sick, and may soon die."

"I got to Seth's in the morning. He was still sick and had only a little strength left. I told chachi to cook up the kalij pheasant and make some soup for the old man. That is how it is done, you see. He ate it, and I said, 'Good, good.' "

"But it was not long after this that his tongue stopped working and he could not talk. He still had the use of his hands, though, and he wrote out everything he had left undone: who owed him money and who he owed money to. He wrote all of this out. He died that evening. I was there and the *pradhan*'s elder brother was there as well. He died, but only after writing everything down. His tongue had stopped, but not his pen. Actually he wrote for three whole days—about village affairs and about the wholesale market in Dehra Dun—but then he lost his strength."

*   *   *

"The night lightning struck Chattarmani's chan there was some sort of festival going on. I had fallen asleep here in my chan right over there. Gura was there with me and my wife was asleep over there. Well, sir, I was very tired and a little drunk. After all, it was a festival night. In the night there was a flash of lightning and a clap of thunder so loud that my heart quivered. I woke the children up and my wife also woke up and asked what had happened. I said that it sounded like a bolt of lightning had struck very close. My heart was quivering as though I had been wounded. We went back to sleep, but just as dawn was breaking Rukam came down from Tibri and told us that lightning had struck Chattarmani's chan over at Kaphlani and both Daya Ram and Jibba had been killed. I was shocked. Well, even before it was light Chattarmani's mother, old Daya Ram's wife, who was in their house at Pathreni, went up to Kaphlani. Now Chattarmani's elder brother—by a different mother—was sitting next to the chan. Bhakat is his name. Well, we asked him what had happened but he could not tell us. He did not know how his brothers had died. He was a straight man, poor fellow; he just didn't know but there must have been a reason. People do not just die. I told Rukam to go into the chan and have a look around."

"We found where the lightning had struck the path right above the chan. The dirt was all charred, and a *kingor* bush had been burned. The lightning must have then cut down and turned toward the chan. It looked as though it had entered the chan at the corner of the roof from where it went down underground and then reemerged and went out by way of the roof again at the opposite end. Their hearth was situated slightly away from the wall, and Jibba and his wife were sleeping on one side while Daya Ram and his wife were on the other. It seems that the lightning came up through one brother and then went back down through the other. It then moved on, killing a bull and a cow that were tethered at the other end of the chan. When it left the chan it killed a prize buffalo that was giving a lot of milk. I went inside and checked things out for myself. I saw that there was a big hole in the wall where the buffalo had been tethered. Sundaru was very young then and was sleeping up above on a cot. When the lightning woke him up he didn't realize that his brothers were dead. He just thought they were unconscious. He kept shaking them and telling them to wake up. He kept calling out, "Brother, brother"—what brother? They were dead, you see, but still warm. The lightning had burned their skin black."

"It was raining hard and the question came up about what should be done with the bodies. When the other men came up with their milk they said that the bodies would have to be taken to Haridwar since they were pandits. I said, 'OK.' But that day there was much rain and it was hard to even get into Mussoorie since the road had been washed out. We did get as far as Mullangar and stopped at Prem babu's shop. At this point we found out that the police were coming to investigate. When they arrived I said, 'Listen, the brothers of these two men who have died are with us and we are their co-villagers who have come to accompany them. Nobody has killed these men.' We refused to let the police do an autopsy, to let them cut up the bodies. But the police did want to see the bodies, so we let them. I also told them to go on out to Kaphlani and look at the chan and see the dead animals. Then we sat there at Northern Stores, and Prem babu, the sardar who owns the small shop above the Gurdwara, Kishan Prasadi the pharmacist, Sita Ram, and I all wrote up a statement saying that the two men had been killed by lightning and that there was nothing suspicious about what happened. After that they took them off to Haridwar."

"I tell you, when I remember that day I get scared. And besides, it was very unfortunate. That very night Daya Ram had been invited down to Moti Dhar to celebrate the festival. But since it was raining, and he had probably had a little to drink, he had decided not to go. Had he gone down he would not have died. I guess his time had come, though, and the women survived."

"Among the pandits it is the custom that when a man's wife dies he may remarry, but if a wife's husband dies she may not. This is not right. It should be the same for both. How will a woman survive; how will she live? You see, Jibba's wife is young and all alone. She has nothing. At least Daya Ram's wife has children. They say that she will stay on in his name. But what is in a name? She is all alone."

*   *   *

"We had planted cholai in our fields on that day that you, me and Sham Rao from Rajpur went to Seokholi, Masrana, Loharighar, and Donk to survey and conduct a census for the development project. We had eaten our food near the spring at Loharighar, the pandit's village, and I had gone home to get water for Gura. On my way up, near Sungarghati, I met the night watchman from Oakville, who was carrying a note for you. I was planning to just take water to the chan for Gura to use and then come right back, but I figured it would be best to see what the note said."

"As you know, the note explained that my wife was very sick again. I wasn't able to come back, and I don't know where you stayed that night. I decided that it would be best if I went straight to the hospital and did not even stop at your house on the way. Later in the evening your parents, sahib and memsahib, came to see me there."

"What a problem! What difficulty! How was I to know that she was going to die. She could not even piss. There was poison inside her and that was why she was vomiting. That is what I learned in Delhi, afterward. It was after the operation that I asked the doctor."

"She was unconscious much of the way down to Delhi from Mussoorie, and when she was settled in the hospital she asked me how she had gotten there. I asked her if she did not remember that sahib, your father, had brought her in the car during the night. She said she only remembered getting there in the morning, but could not remember riding in the car. She was dying. She was full of poison."

"As soon as we got to Delhi, Dr. Talwar and memsahib, your mother, admitted my wife into the hospital. They gave her a number and came back in the evening to check on her. Later she said to me, 'You have brought me here to die, haven't you?' But I told her not to worry."

"We stayed there for a long time. After two days I knew my way around and could go to all the various places to pick up the things she needed. We played cards sometimes. There were also people in the recovery room who had no one to look after them. I would give them water, and if they wanted food, I would go and get that as well. That is what I did. I gave people food and water."

"The first night in Delhi I stayed at the Talwars' where Campbell sahib and your parents had made arrangements. I didn't realize that I should stay at the hospital with her. But the doctor there, Dr. Budhwa—or something like that, an Indian man anyway—said that I would have to spend the night there in the hospital with my wife so that I could look after her. I had not brought anything with me, so Dr. Talwar gave me a couple of rugs and a pillow on which to sleep. I went to the Talwars' house to eat though."

"Then! Again! Campbell sahib came; he came looking for me. He telephoned the Talwars where he knew I was staying. He told me that he would meet me at such and such a time at a certain place. And when he came, what did he do? He brought a whole trunk full of oranges and tangerines! He told my wife to eat them. Not to just drink the juice, but to eat the whole inside, pulp and all."

"Her treatment went on and on. After some time she was brought back out to the recovery room where patients rested when they were doing better. There was a garden outside where I would sit and walk around. People would wonder who I was and where I had come from. Whenever they asked I said that I was from Mussoorie, from the village of Path-reni. I told them everything; that I was taking my meals at the Talwars'."

"There were two others in the recovery room who, like me, were also from the hills. It was a blessing from god that I met them. Often we would have tea at four in the afternoon and then go for a walk."

"In the hospital recovery room we were not able to prepare food. But there was a boy from Katmandu whose leg was broken. He and his uncle, who was there to take care of him, had made arrangements to prepare food. Now, many of the people in the recovery room were from Madras and did not eat meat, but the two from Nepal did. One night they ordered liquor and told me to come and eat with them. So I went back to the Talwars' and told them I would be out for the evening. The boy and his uncle fixed meat and we ate and drank. I enjoyed myself. But then, later, my wife said to me, 'This is the first time I have seen you drink in three weeks. Something must be wrong.' I told her not to worry; that there was nothing wrong. 'You will not die,' I said. 'Think about living, not dying.' She was also worried about money, but I told her that if we did not have money on hand that I would earn it."

"There was a sardar there in the hospital too, a Sikh fellow whose mother was also sick with cancer. He was from Amritsar, and had taken her to Bombay and back for treatment. He told me he had been to Mussoorie, to the Savoy, and we became friends. He was a good man, poor fellow, and wanted to show me around Delhi. But I could not go because my wife was sick."

"Earlier, when we had left Mussoorie, I had written a letter to my wife's father telling him that his daughter was sick but doing all right. Later, when things got worse, I wrote him again to say that she was dying. I tried to telephone him and even told the principal of Woodstock to call and tell him to come. Finally we got through to him and he said he would come . . . but he never did."

"Sahib and memsahib, your father and mother, came to the hospital one day. They came and saw the doctor and took a look at the papers. It was Dr. Budhwa who told them that there was no hope for her. He said: 'Just . . . just . . . look after her as best you can and make her happy. That is all that can be done.' Your parents did not tell me this. It was Talwar memsahib who did. When your brother, Steve, came down from Mussoorie to pick us up I know he wanted to tell me, but then he thought that I would lose heart, so he did not; he kept it to himself. But I found out anyway."

"We left Delhi and came back up to Mussoorie where she spent one night in the hospital. That night I came on home. I tell you, it was very sad. My poor daughter saw me coming back alone along the path through Jain sahib's jungle and thought that her mother must have died. When I got to the village I told her not to worry, though. I told her that her mother was just staying in the hospital for a few days. But she was very upset; and not only that, she had cut her finger and was unable to cook or prepare food. So although I spent the night at home I ate nothing. I figured that I would just have tea at Panch Ram's shop on the way back to the hospital in the morning. It was very sad. Her finger was cut and she could not cook, so what were we to do. She couldn't make bread. Her finger did heal later, but it was a bad cut."

"When your brother came to pick us up at the Landour hospital my wife was feeling much better. Her illness was like that. It would come and go. We brought her along the road in the car and then carried her down from Tibri. When we got home she was all right, and sahib and memsahib, your mother and father, came to see her. She was all right for some time, but then again she became ill and we had to take her in to the hospital. This time we used Kapadia sahib's car, which your father drove, since his car was being repaired. We took her in to see the doctor and then brought her back the same way."

"It was raining that day, and my daughter made *subzi* from the flowers of the wild *kaudiya* plant. All of the women had gathered. My wife managed to eat some of the subzi and drink some tea, but she said she was feeling very sick. I told her not to worry, and then went out to shoot a wild chicken which would be cooked to give her strength."

"Later that evening she was lying on the bed and complained of pain and discomfort. 'Take these clothes off,' she demanded, 'and put these blankets on.' 'Sit by me,' she said whenever I had to get up and do something. I told her I was there and would not leave. She asked me for water, but did not have enough strength to drink. Then she died."

"My daughter was sleeping over there on the far side of the fire, and the old man was over there in that bed. I did not want to wake them up and tell them that she was gone. It would have upset them. I was upset. We had gone all the way to Delhi to cure her, but she had died anyway."

"Now, I had been lying beside her to make her feel better and she had put her arm over me. She had died that way, and I could not lift it off. What could I do? I thought to myself, look at all the trouble I have caused Alter sahib and memsahib, your mother and father."

"Although I could not move her arm, there was a bottle of liquor in the niche beside me that I could reach. I pulled it out and drank it down but still could not fall asleep! The whole thing was terrible. It was terrible. . . . But she is gone. That is done. Even so, it was your father who helped lift this sadness from my heart. I had no expenses."

*   *   *

"It was only a month after my wife died that the villagers from around here came and told me that something, some animal, was eating the grain in their fields. I told them to go away. I was still mourning and wanted them to leave me alone. But then the village women came and begged me to do something, and I began to think. What would they do if I didn't go to protect the fields? So I took my gun and went to investigate. I went to see what could be done."

"I went down into the fields where wheat had been planted and saw a barasingha grazing on the new shoots. I had my twelve-gauge and fired a slug. The slug hit it squarely, but it ran off down the slope. I figured that I had missed, but thought that I still might get a second chance if I was quick. The forest is mine! I know it! So I went down the slope after the barasingha. But I was in a hurry and did not look where I was going and my left foot slipped. Well, I went one direction and my gun went the other! It was very near the place where John sahib fell, Joe, just below the pandit's house on the other side of the ridge. I tell you, the hillside I fell down was so steep, and I fell with such force, that the bushes I grabbed on to came out in my hands!! I said to myself, 'Mother, today I have died!' "

"When it was all over I was lying unconscious. I used all my strength to stay alive, to remain conscious. This was a matter of my heart, of my resolve. Fortunately my legs had gotten stuck on a cactus, otherwise it would have been all over for me. Your brother, Steve, came to the rescue, and there were the villagers too, as well as the women. I was lying out there in the middle of the jungle and was given milk to drink and raw *haldi*, turmeric that is, for my wounds. It was Chattarmani the pandit's old mother who gave me these things, you know. They were all there, and I said, 'Do what you have to do quickly for I am dying.' I told Chattarmani and his family that I was as good as dead. They are my brothers, you know; we are of the same village. I told Chattarmani to bring me a paper and pen so that I could write. I wrote this down: 'No one has tried to kill me. I have no enemies. I went hunting and came to this grief on my own.' All this I wrote down so that no one would be held accountable; so that no one would get into trouble on my account. I have no enemies. Not my brother, his wives, or their children. I have no enemies in the whole village. But I wrote this down just so there would be no doubt, no question that it was anything but an accident."

"Anyway, Chattarmani and my brother Ratnu were there, and after I had written everything down, I told them to go and get your brother, Steve, so that he could get the car and drive me back to the hospital. But the car was in Dehra Dun being fixed, so they brought a dandi instead, a palanquin. They took me to the hospital where I stayed for some time. I recovered, but I still have a pain right here in my lower back."

"After my fall I was laid up for some time and was not able to go hunting. I had a craving for meat though and told the boys, Azad and Sundar, to go down the hill and shoot something. They had a couple of handmade cartridges with them, but they came back empty-handed. Well, I was still in pretty bad shape but decided to go down myself. I still had some strength, so I walked down the Bandar Chowki ridge. While I was sitting on the ridge, a kakar luckily came out right in front of me. Now, I couldn't use my left hand at all, but with great difficulty I managed to pick the gun up and wedge it between my toes. I finally had a chance to shoot and, 'Phaat!!' I fired and hit the kakar. Azad, who was on his way to Dhurmala, heard the shot and quickly turned around and ran back. Chacha—Tulasi, I mean—was sitting near the chans when I came back up. Since I could not go down to retrieve the kill I told him to do it. He went down and brought it back up. I skinned it, butchered it, and divided up the meat among everyone. It was a big sister-fucker; what horns!! I sent one leg and part of the neck to Austin sahib. I sent it so that he would know that I was not dead, that I was still alive!"

"I want to work, you know. I may be old, but I am still strong. I can still work. . . . Am I dead? No, I am still alive!"

* * *

"Ever since I was young, I have spent my life hunting. After I fell and nearly died I was lying down; I could hardly move, but when I saw the rifle I regained my strength and said to myself: 'I must get up. I must get up . . .'"

"The old lady went by this road, and sahib and I went hunting at Siyarunkhala. . . . My hunting was complete. That evening sahib, your father that is, and I went up to Tibri, to Chowdhri's orchard past the barbed wire. I told your father I could go even though I was still weak. I held a stick in my hand. You see, I am still alive! I could still wrestle you if I wanted to! This kind of strength comes to few men. It is a great thing. My broken bones have not rejoined though. . . ."

"I have only one question. Some say *khuda* (god), others say this or that, but I think *prebhu* (god) is the right name for god.* What do you think? . . ."

"I can tell you one thing at least. There is Coapman sahib, and there is this sahib and that sahib: Dr. Wysham, Dr. Garst, Dr. Smith, and Dr. Fleming. . . . But, in the end, I have come to Alter sahib. There are many sahibs who have taken me around—and John sahib has shown me things—but in the end it is Alter sahib who has lifted my troubles. . . ."

"Steve was very disturbed by all of this, you know; by my falling down the hillside, I mean. That is why he doesn't come hunting anymore. . . . So, it is like this, Joe. I must grow old with you. . . . But no, you are young! . . ."

"In my life I have done all kinds of work, but now I am just sitting around. I have been a thekedar, a contractor of milk. Yes, I have earned money. But what is the value of that? What is the point? What is important is that I have not lost anyone's respect. Ask anyone in Mussoorie and they will tell you. No one will say anything against me."

* * *

"One should always speak well of others; never speak ill of them. A good man will always be remembered after his death. On the other hand, when a bad person dies everyone will say, 'Good riddance.' You see, there are only two ways of talking: good and bad. There is nothing else."

"Now, if you say that something is yours then it is also mine; it is ours. Yours is yours and it is ours. Everyone must die, you see, but whether one is good or bad, that stays on; one's reputation is immortal. Look at your father. All of Mussoorie says that he is a good man. Why is that? It is because he *is* a good man; but not just because I say it, but because all of Mussoorie says it together."

* * *

"It is good that you own the estate now. Oakville is yours and now you can visit the village and travel freely. The world is like that. There are

---

* *Khuda* and *prebhu* are, in fact, synonyms. Both mean god. *Khuda* derives from Urdu and *prebhu* from Hindi, but it is unlikely that Dil Das was making a distinction between Islamic and Hindu denotations. My guess is that he was pointing out, with a degree of mirth, the inherent ambiguity in translation.

so many things; so much to say. But this is for certain: I am still strong, mind you, but it is my heart, my soul. Oh, what can I say; how can I tell you, friend! I wake up in the morning and then have to take a rest. I guess since I fell down and nearly died that I have gotten a little weak. But the things I have inside me no one else has. I have all the stories inside me. When and how much to work, and when to go. You see, if you don't do things at the right time then nothing will come of your work."

"Listen, I have seen that people in the plains drive around in cars and shoot animals from close range. That is easy. But here in the hills, even if you are a young hunter you will get only one chance to shoot. And if you don't take that chance, and aren't in the right place at the right time, then you will end up wandering around all day. Even if everything goes well, you get only one chance. And my strength is waning now. I have hunted here in the hills. What other hunting can I do? If I can't hunt, then what is left?"

*　*　*

"A man whose blood is different than yours can never take your life. Now he . . . Coapman sahib's life. . . . who knows what it is; it is in the heart . . ."

"Two people of the same blood will somehow find one another. I have told you, haven't I, that in the end it all comes back to John sahib and Campbell sahib and Alter sahib, your father. Who knows why this was; why it is? What was there about me? There must have been some sort of kinship between all of us. God only knows."

"I was a hunter; I still am. Remember, just the other week at Dhurmala when that leopard came right up to the door of the chan. They asked me to come and shoot it. 'Shoot it,' they said. . . . That dog lying right there was lucky to escape with its life. It was right there in the doorway when the leopard snuck up on it. But I guess all the noise we were making inside scared it off. Otherwise it would have caught the dog for sure. I guess the leopard got scared."

"My friend, the story of my life is that story: the story of hunting. I have worked all my life for the school. And some say that I have been a hunter. Forest guards have come after me to try and catch me and stop my hunting. The forest guard from Nali came and said he would catch me. I just laughed and said, 'How do you propose to do that?' By the time he got around to searching for me, I was long gone from the forest. I told him off. We are villagers who live here. Who did he think he was? Does he know what a cliff is? Did his father? These places:—Koldighat! Devi Dhang!—can he go anywhere near these places? He is only a mere government servant, a peon. I am a hunter and will walk on the cliffs where the forest guard cannot go."

"During my life the forest guard has been my coolie. He would carry the ghoral I shot while I would carry two! You see, what I am telling you is about the forest. You need strong men here. We are happy here and have fun."

"One day John sahib and I went to Sarona. We had no money with us. No food either, or anything. But when we got there they all invited us in and gave us food and a place to stay,"

"We stayed in a chan above the road that goes through the center of the village. It was Bisa's chan—Bishan Singh's. He went to his house and got us so much food we could not even eat it all. We drank and ate our fill. In the morning we shot a ghoral with John sahib's rifle. He was an *ustaad* of these things, a master. In the evening he shot a kakar. The whole village had meat to eat. This is why they are all his friends. There was no question of having a permit. In the villages there is no problem. Yes, honesty is a very important thing,"

"Truth is truth, and that is good, but a truthful and honest man cannot be caught."

"I have spent my life with Campbell sahib. It was his gun. He was my guru. I did not know what a gun was until he showed me. What is hunting; what is ammunition? I did not know these things. There was nobody who could catch us. Nobody. This is what John sahib would do. He did so much work over there in Nepal. He shot a tiger here when they said it couldn't be done. . . ."

"He said this to me. 'Yes,' he said. 'It is all right. It is all right,' he said. 'But there is only one hope for you,' John sahib told me. 'There is only one chance for your survival: stop this hunting business.' This is what John sahib said to me. And I said. . . . Well, what could I say but this: 'How can I do that?'"

"Is it I who have ruined John sahib, or has John sahib ruined me? Who has ruined whom through hunting? You tell me? Think of all the places he has taken me, one lone Pahari. Wherever he has gone, I have gone also. . . ."

"There is one thing, though. I wish he would come back one more time so that I could see him."

"Just think of all the men we have outhunted; all the men we have beaten. There is not an animal in the jungle that I cannot track and find. That is the kind of hunter I am. My eyesight is still better than a pair of binoculars. No one is better than me. . . ."

"John sahib is in America now. Smith sahib is in America too. Bobby is either in America or Katmandu, I don't know which. And then, there was Breni who was killed, and Dean who died in the war. . . ."

"I heard that Dr. Wysham was coming back from America to the school for a visit, but I do not know if he did or not. That is what I heard. . . . And Dick Smith!! Oh, friend! I met him at Oakville. At your house. I said, 'Dick!' and we hugged each other and remembered; we remembered. I keep meeting these friends of mine. That is the truth. I am still alive! I have not been beaten down, nor have I beaten any one else down. . . . Yes, there is one thing: my 'business' has been hunting, and the work I have done, I have done well."

"You see, the big hunters, the big rajas, have, in the end, all lost. Many stories could be told about them. They shot tigers, but in the end they were killed and eaten by them. Now listen. I am a Pahari. Will I who was born in the hills ever fall down the hillside? No, I am as sure-footed as a ghoral! . . . Will I fall? . . . Yes, it is just a matter of time before I fall, and when that time comes, it comes, and I, too, will die."

Dil Das died in Pathreni in 1986. I was studying for my Ph.D. oral exams in California when I got a telephone call from my parents, on furlough in Ohio, saying that they had received the news from Austin babu at Woodstock. Dil Das had apparently fallen sick sometime after my parents left in the early summer, and had gotten steadily worse. He could not digest anything he ate, and by the middle of July he began to get weaker and weaker. The weaker he got, the more certain he became that he was going to die, and after a while it was really only a matter of time. His brother Ratnu took him into the hospital a few times, and I think he was diagnosed as having worms. I do not know if he was given medicine. He did go back to the village, though, and died in his brother's chan. As worms will do, if left untreated, they moved out of the intestines and on up into his liver and lungs, right on into the heart, some people say, but that is a matter of conjecture—just hearsay.

It was not until 1988 that I went back to Mussoorie again, and then on out to Pathreni. Gura had been married off into a family in the village of Langarasu, down below Childers on the north slope below Landour, and all that remained of Dil Das's chan were the crumbled walls. Everything of value had been removed, and all that was left—the rotten thatch, the rocks, the earthen clay—had been left to find its way back into the landscape.

I was never one to pay much attention to the flora of the lower Himalayas, or to geography and other sciences of landscape. Unlike many of my Woodstock compatriots, I did not make a hobby of collecting leaves and lichen, but I do remember that sometime in the early 1970s there was a significant change—gradual, to be sure, but nevertheless profound—in the landscape around Pathreni.

No one could say for sure where it came from, but year by year a tall weed with large, flat, spade-shaped leaves, and a shiny, woody stock, moved further and further up into the valleys of the lower Himalayas. It is called *kala ghas*, or "black grass," on account of the color its leaves stain the skin, and some people say that it migrated down the mountain chain from Kashmir carried eastward in the wool of transhumant sheep. In any case, it has tremendous resiliency, and seems able to grow in any environment; and so, by the early 1980s it had taken over and grew almost everywhere, often displacing local flora like stinging nettle.

As its name might intimate, kala ghas is utterly useless. Nothing will eat it; it is not good for thatch; although you can burn it, it virtually explodes when lit, sending out a shower of dangerous sparks before quickly dying away; when dry it is too brittle to use for brooms, and, for the same reason, it cannot be woven. It is even dangerous to grab hold of while negotiating a steep climb up a mountainside, for its roots are shallow and pull right out. Yet when uprooted, it comes right back, relentlessly.

When I last visited Pathreni, toward the end of the monsoon season in the early 1990s, Dil Das's chan was nothing but a field of exceptionally large kala ghas, and there was nothing to remember him by except an alien weed.

I would like to be able to write a fitting end to Dil Das's heroic narrative and invent, or at least imagine, a more noble death. Given his own intimation, I would have him falling off a cliff, perhaps, or even being killed by a leopard. But that would be going too far; stretching the truth, even if remaining true to an imagined life. If the truth be known, he could not escape the world around him: the fertile ground of his chan-without-animals. In the end he drank too much, and so, although it was his liver which finally gave out, his jighuri, that is, I think it was really a matter of the heart.

In the end it is the *jighuri*; the heart which matters. The stories which are made are all made in the heart. All the stories which are told, their end is in the heart. Friends and brothers, keep it here in the heart. Tearing open his chest and showing his heart Lord Hanuman said, "Sir, god is here. Ram and Sita are in my heart." It is the heart which is everything. It is the heart. There has been no one like Hanuman. Whatever is said about anyone—man, lord, boss, or whatever—good must be said about him; something, anything good must be said on his behalf; on his behalf. Then, even when he dies he will stay alive. Do you understand? It is in the heart. It is hearts which should meet; which should come together.

Chapter 11
A Hybrid History of Encounter

As a primary mode of anthropological writing, ethnography has come increasingly under attack. For all its value as a means by which to challenge the pretense of Western civilization, it is a problematic genre that has tended to essentialize truth. The difficulty is, in essence, a question of representation. How can one convey the meaningfulness of difference without reifying the nature of that difference? In addressing this question my own perspective on Dil Das's life has been oriented most clearly by the work of Paul Rabinow, Vincent Crapanzano, and others who have taken a critical, reflexive, interpretive approach to the study of culture.[1] Unlike classical ethnography, narratives and critiques of this genre do not so much seek to uncover a truth about other people's lives, as seriously engage in the production of public knowledge; knowledge that is inherently dialogic to the extent that it is predicated on ethnographic multivocality.[2]

One of the problems anthropologists have encountered in this dialogic endeavor, however, is the seemingly inescapable fact that writing undermines the multivocality of oral experience. When all is said and done—which is to say, written down and published—one voice inevitably takes over and speaks for the other voices in the text regardless of how literal one's translations are, or how much "dialogue" has been introduced in order to decenter perspective and strategically confuse those points of reference that enable rational constructs of "culture" to take shape.[3]

As a conundrum, the problem—of representing through translation, and translating through representation—is unavoidable. In this sense, as Susan Stewart and others following Jacques Derrida have noted, writing is, essentially, a crime—an act of violence. Not a vicious or malicious crime necessarily, but an act of domination and subversion that is insidious by virtue of its proclaimed innocence. Authorship presumes authority and thereby defines a field of power. To try and circumvent this field, by saying, for example, that one has provided a literal, objective translation of what someone else has said, simply confounds the problem of representation. The act of writing words down effectively limits the inherent meaningfulness of language's ambiguity by bringing into play a fixed structure of syntax, grammar and style. To efface the authority of this structure, by claiming the studied innocence of a scribe, only obscures the nature of truth by nailing down, with a practiced slight of hand, every last slip of the tongue.

In struggling with the complex dynamic of power and truth, anthropologists have tried to unmask their own conceit in various ways by breaking down the barriers erected by ethnographic writing. However, the motivation for this kind of critical, dialogic reflexivity often seems to be ironically one sided: "our" attempts to give "them" an authentic voice by which means "we" can understand what "they" are all about. Alternatively, the perspective is changed, genres get blurred, and we discover ourselves in the process of representing them. The critical question, to my mind, is not so much whether this reflexive, modern, humanistic goal is reached, or whether they see themselves in our representations of them—a fact which, as I have said, writing elides—but whether or not there is some middle ground on which there can be a mutual discovery of difference, and whether or not this discovery can be made public in some way that fully acknowledges the power dynamics of representation.

In this regard it will seem ironic—since hunting and heroism are bombastically masculine domains—that my reflexive perspective on ethnographic authority and colonial encounter in the context of Dil Das's life is informed by feminist theory. As I read it, feminist theory both predates the reflexive turn in social science and has gone well beyond a simple critique of the epistemic paradigms of binary difference, the problems of disengaged interpretation, and the politics of writing culture.[4] Given its gendered locus, and concern with deeply embedded power structures, critical feminist theory of this kind is informed by a hypersensitivity to the dynamics of intersubjective experience and the reflexive politics of representation.[5] Representation of this kind is at once keyed to the subtle realities of cultural and national difference, yet speaks directly, if not exactly in one voice, to the transnational experience of feminist encounter. What this entails, as Lila Abu-Lughod has rightly pointed out, is to "write against culture" by positioning oneself in the marginal interstices of local history.[6]

In this regard Dil Das embodied a profound contradiction that points to the heart of a fundamental problem in anthropology, cultural studies, and, for that matter, the postcolonial world. This problem may be stated in any number of ways, but it is, ultimately, a question of identity and self-representation in a world no longer held together by comfortable truths; a search for meaning and purpose in an arena where history has fused and confused the structure of signification. Leave aside, for a moment, the issue of making sense—by means of paradigms, analyses, or even language—it is hard enough to know how to define the terms of empathy when the foundations of encounter are at once predetermined by an ideology of segregation and undermined by the narrow contingency of a shared past on the edge of the empire. Perhaps the only recourse is to poetics and veiled sentiments that portend neither fact nor fiction but an emotional state of suspended animation between the "I" and "Other" of now-and-then. But for all its potential as an alternative frame of reference, poetics defines a dangerous space where nostalgia threatens to trivialize that which memory cannot capture. It is a tangled, disoriented space where the fact and fiction of structurally incongruous biographies intersect producing hybrid identities as pregnant with meaning as they are contextually confused—which brings to mind an image.

There is an old Kodachrome slide that my father has of Dil Das taken around the time when I was born in 1958. It is tinted red, and there are spots of mold where moisture has worked its way in between the cardboard frames. It is mixed in with a bunch of other old slides which, despite annual resolutions, never get sorted into their proper categories: pictures of my grandparents on furlough in Kansas; pictures of me and my two brothers among friends in Etah, a small town in western Uttar Pradesh; pictures of us building a snowman in Ithaca, a small town in upstate New York; pictures of my parents' wedding in Mussoorie—my mother being carried in a white satin sedan chair hoisted on the shoulders of four uniformed coolies—and pictures of countless treks and expeditions to Kashmir, Kulu, Kedarnath, Corbett Park, and other places. It is here, I imagine, where Dil Das's photo would fit. It was taken on a hiking trip back into the higher Himalayas on the ridge above Deodital, a lake near Bandarpunch in the highest range of the mountains. It is taken from behind, a posed shot, with Dil Das standing casually on a patch of snow in woolen pants, hiking boots and flannel shirt, looking out over the ridges toward Gangotri and the source of the Ganga. He was a young man then, about thirty-five, about my father's age. For some reason—perhaps the faded red tint of the weathered Kodachrome, or the flannel shirt—the photo always makes me think of other pictures I have seen of hunters in Montana: heroic, rugged men standing on the edge of mountains looking out and far away, as though the distance they could see was somehow a measure of their stature. The picture of Dil Das always appealed to me—larger than life on the wrinkled screen standing in the corner of the living room—in part because it provided a glimpse of what he had been like before I could possibly have known him, and, in part, because it fit an image of the man which seemed in keeping with his self-perception.

Anthropological literature is full of enigmatic characters who stand, wittingly or unwittingly, on the cusp of experience and perception. Some of these characters are stranger than others, but all of them are more or less on the fringe of at least two worlds, neither of which is really their own. There are hundreds of biographies, autobiographies and translated memoirs that depict these local, very personal histories of change and transformation.[7] I have not undertaken a review of this literature here except to note that Dil Das's story is not at all unique. For example it bares some affinity with Paul Radin's *Crashing Thunder*, Leo Simmons's *Sun Chief*, John (Fire) Lame Deer and Richard Erdoes's *Lame Deer: Seeker of Visions,* and even more with Theodora Kroeber's *Ishi.*[8] And to be symmetrical, if not exactly fair, it is not unlike some of the epic memoirs of colonial heros we were required to read in high school—Lewis and Clark on the frontier of one empire, T. E. Lawrence in the backwaters of another, and Mahatma Gandhi at the heart of an epic colonial encounter. But to my mind Dil Das and others like him do not so much provide a perspective on what used to be called "culture contact," as they do a clear vantage point on the working of power. The harsh reality of encounter relentlessly undermines rational myths of continuity by chipping away at insulated categories: the predicates of difference. Beneath the epic binarism of Rudyard Kipling's famous opposition—or Louis Dumont's, for that matter—there are, in fact, countless examples of places where East and West do meet and of people who embody what might be termed a mongrel perspective on power; a perspective that is radically decentered and self-consciously "abnormal." It is not enough to simply recognize this fact, however. The phenomenology of such discontinuity, no matter how empathetic or reflexive, only leads back to a pure relativity of us and them—by way of centering and normalizing tendencies—unless it fragments the binary constructs of representation and deals directly with power as an undifferentiating whole. Some attempt must be made, therefore, to write a hybrid history of encounter.

In her book entitled *The Rhetoric of English India*, Sara Suleri makes an argument that is germane to the project of hybridity. She points out that colonialism "precludes the concept of 'exchange' by granting to the idea of power a greater literalism than it deserves." Her argument is that a discourse of "otherness," despite—and in some cases as a result of—being granted a privileged status in the production of "alternative histories," still remains ". . . embedded in a theoretical duality of margin to center." What she proposes, in the context of literary analysis, is to examine "the story of colonial encounter [as a] decentering narrative that is impelled to realign with violence any static binarism between colonizer and colonized."[9]

The challenge, therefore, in writing Dil Das's life-story-fused-with-mine is to avoid the reflex tendency to incarnate marginality and centeredness; to avoid reifying power. This, I believe, is what Lila Abu-Lughod is getting at—theoretically in order to "recapture anthropology" —when she positions herself, precariously and experientially, outside culture and into the historical space defined, among other things, by mixed marriage.[10]

Like a mixed marriage in many ways, the narrative Dil Das and I produced strains against duality at almost every turn, and provides, therefore, a dramatic case of how encounter can efface ideology. There is nothing sentimental—and certainly no self-aggrandizement—implied in this fraternal project of conjoint paternity. To be sure I have had to struggle against, and perhaps over-compensated for, a dogged sense of nostalgia for otherness; nostalgia born from the powerful conjunction of missionary practices, Christian faith and liberal humanism. As Suleri writes, "[t]o tell the history of another is to be pressed against the limits of one's own—thus culture learns that terror has a local habitation and a name."[11] Terror replaces sympathetic nostalgia in the decentered space of encounter, and horror—rather than, say, guilt—is attendant in the effacement of power which results.

By what right, however, can one speak of this—this telling of stories— as an act of horrific disclosure; as a kind of terror, according to Suleri, "that must serve as . . . the interpretive model" of colonial encounter in a postcolonial world of really, truly crude violence?[12] My answer to this is framed in terms of time and space, the passage of which and distance between tends to obscure the eye-for-an-eye relations of cause and effect in a tit-for-tat world of escalating face-to-face violence. Time and distance seem to trivialize, banalize and tranquilize some kinds of violence, while rendering other forms pruriently horrific, and the work of writing is here directly implicated. Epic history and large scales of distance sometimes efface the pointed language of blame and reprisal and make it difficult to fully appreciate the logistics of violence in seemingly impersonal acts that take a great deal of time to commit and are not directly comprehensible in terms of who is terrorized by what. These acts are social facts, like poverty, being outcaste and being marginalized in modernized India. But there is also the more gradual, protracted, and thereby insidious—if not so bloody—violence of disorientation that occurs when the local, first-person pronominal history of caste prejudice, economic exploitation and colonial nostalgia does not conform to the will of a third-person master narrative. This, as the eleventh-century epigraph from Alberuni suggests, is the forced together but antithetical relationship between eyewitness and hearsay.

But the central point is that writing, as an act of cultural articulation, as a "species of hearsay," is a necessary form of distortion. And there is a degree of horror entailed in drawing together the past, the present and the future and thereby making the mutuality of power and power-lessness visible. I say this not to render all forms of violence the same, or say that one cannot distinguish between forms, scales and levels of violence. I say this only in order to work toward an effacement of time and distance so as to get some understanding of violence as an intimate, very personal, but not always visible fact; an understanding that hope-fully makes this fact visible without turning it into an object of prurient concern. The point then is to reveal power and thus make the pro-tracted violence of everyday life apparent in a transparent account of encounter that seems to be all fun and games, but is not; seems to be about the triumph of friendship, but is not. I say this only because, as a native son, I have watched, from a distance far too great, but as a par-ticipant observer all the same—as a prodigal bastard, that is, if I may follow Roland Barthes's epigraphic advice—the sequential, unnatural, premature deaths of Dil Das, Sheri Das, Rukam Das, Ratan Das, Jankhi Das, Tulasi Das, and Abal Das. Or perhaps I should simply say, to press this history squarely against my own, what we used to say in grade school when forcing an issue of disbelief by way of an oath that invoked a kind of intimate class of horror—really truly, kiss a coolie.

To be quite honest, one of the main reasons why I decided to record Dil Das's stories was so that I could find the time and money to visit family and friends back home. From the very start I got interested in an-thropology because it provided a means by which I could kill two birds with one stone: pursue an academic career in the United States and yet maintain close ties with my Indian roots. Although my initial attraction to the discipline was innocent enough—the English literature course I wanted to take was booked up—I have deliberately played off of anthro-pology's emphasis on doing field work in faraway places in order to beat a path back to my front door—which, I suppose, is the long way around either to a kind of mutated armchair anthropology or, depending on your point of view, a deconstructive mode of "going native" by already "being there." In any case, I have been able to use my relatively unique position in order to claim—to get grants for research—a degree of famil-iarity with the Other in my backyard. Consequently, it seemed so simple to turn old friends into new informants so as to translate intimate experi-ence into alien knowledge. And yet it was not simple or innocent at all.

I remember once, while doing fieldwork for my master's thesis, sitting in Dil Das's home recording and playing back on my tape recorder song fragments which the children from the village were singing. I was irritated. My batteries were running down and I wanted to record something of substance. But everybody wanted to have a turn and it was, under the circumstances, impossible to say no. Dil Das was running the show while his nephew Azad was the one who pushed the buttons on the machine. Gradually interest faded, along with the strength of my batteries, and the voices on the tape slowed down and slurred until they sounded ghostly and contorted. We all laughed, and I resolved to get nothing of value done. But then Dil Das's wife, who had repeatedly claimed that she could not and would not sing, gave voice to a song that I cannot for the life of me remember, but will never be able to forget. It was a beautiful, lilting song full of melancholy and pathos telling of a bride's departure from her natal village; and she, knowing that the poison of cervical cancer was eating away her insides, sang it with what I can only describe as a kind of haunting, dispassionate reserve. She was able to evoke a mood of powerful, intimate feeling while remaining completely detached, and it was somewhere between passion, pain and profound detachment that her song hit upon what I imagine to be a fundamental truth which cannot be translated out of experience.

And yet, what troubles me, is that I wish I had been able to record the song. I wish I had been able to capture it, take it home, and play it over and over again in order to get at its truth by extracting its meaning word by word, phrase by phrase, rhyme by rhyme. What troubles me, in other words, is that I remember her song as a piece of information that slipped through the cracks, and that I cannot, simply by virtue of who I am, remember it as anything else. But I think it was the haunting tension in her voice—there but not there—which makes me realize now that her song defined, for me at least, not only the limits of anthropological knowledge but its insipid, alienating power as well. The reflexivity of fieldwork's intersubjectivity—rapport, as they say—is predicated, not on being there, and being there for ever longer periods of time, but on being able to leave and remember. Rapport, in other words, is predicated on difference, and the necessity of reproducing difference. Which brings to mind a caveat.

In his book on being and becoming Tamil, E. Valentine Daniel concludes his introduction by giving the reader "some significant biographical data" that is framed in terms of language.[13] He points out that his father was a native speaker of Tamil "whose English was poor," married to an Anglican whose "mother tongue was English," living in the Sinhalese speaking south of Sri Lanka. On account of general linguistic confusion, brought on by the contingency of transnational identity, Daniel writes, "[f]or me, at least, anthropologizing began early." My concern is with the vexing question which this sardonic "biography" suggests: where does that anthropologizing lead when self and other merge?

What is presented here as a problem of "mobius identity" may also be read, precisely, as an opportunity to get past rapport and rethink the question of how anthropology makes its subject. And this, at least in large part, is exactly what Daniel has done in a subsequent book, an anthropograpy of violence in Sri Lanka.[14] Recently a number of other scholars have also taken the reflexive critique of anthropology in this direction and ask, pointedly, where do "native" anthropologists stand in relation to the production of knowledge about difference, and, more significantly, where do people "without pedigree" stand in relation to the pure-bred categories of race, ethnicity and citizenship. As Arjun Appadurai has indicated, categories such as "native" that clearly demarcate the appropriate boundaries of time and space, are complex intellectual myths that are becoming increasingly hard to believe in.[15] The transnational nature of culture demands to be taken seriously, and poses important political and theoretical questions about anthropology, what anthropologists do and who anthropologists are. Unlike earlier critiques that simply challenged the authority of anthropology to poach knowledge on dark continents, the work of Arjun Appadurai along with Ruth Behar, Smadar Levi, Kamala Visweswaran, Kirin Narayan, and Lila Abu-Lughod makes it clear that border-crossing, both intimate and international, local and global, has profound implications precisely because it reorients the whole object of the discipline away from the categorization of people, places, and things, and even away from the project of writing culture anew.[16] It relocates the subject of anthropology in a matrix of hybridity that remains permanently enmeshed—politically and emotionally—in the fact of exile. I am, perhaps, somewhat more skeptical, and nervous, than others about the production and reproduction of hybrid texts, and maintain, following Barthes, that sarcasm rather than, say, sympathy, rage, love or what have you, is the condition of truth in the domain of chronic exile. Regardless, it is in this light that self-reflection, far from being solipsistic, narcissistic, and nihilistically decadent, can become a powerful critique of pure-bred dualism and the numerous monuments built on that foundation.

*   *   *

It would be nice to be able to write Dil Das's story in terms of a narrative of resistance, to turn encounter into a strategic weapon of the weak. Moreover, there would be a degree of heroic symmetry to Dil Das's story if I could say that he bravely pitted himself against the massive oppression of everyday life. There are clear examples from Dil Das's life of institutionalized power being resisted in particular ways—by poaching, by illegally cutting trees and fodder, by brewing illicit liquor, and by diluting milk with water. Each of these subversive tactics could be called a weapon of the weak. Over the years I have been incited by my own liberal Christian past to see in these local tactics an epic drama of quiet rebellion; a call to arms by a "soul of revolt" incarnated in the imperative, utopian inevitability that sooner or later the meek shall inherit the earth. But the fact remains that far from being clear articulations of a kind of blind faith in self-confidence, these modes of resistance simply underscore the multiplex nature of power, and implicate Dil Das and his peasant "co-conspirators" in a broader, more diffused set of what Foucault calls "force relationships."[17]

As Lila Abu-Lughod has pointed out, a critical focus on modes and strategies of resistance in terms of these force relationships allows one to diagnose the forms and consequences of power without jumping to the romantic, humanistic conclusion that anyone, given half a chance, can set him or herself free.[18] Therefore, resistance stands in a complex relationship to power, and what one is able to see going on in Pathreni and other villages is not the "radical rupture" of impending revolution, but rather what Foucault calls a "plurality of resistances" which are imbedded within force relationships; force relationships that can be either innocuous and naive, or violent and strategic, among other things.[19]

In Dil Das's narrative there are many clear examples of reified, binary power relations. But on account of his position between two worlds, and his dramatic and painful effort to come to grips with the elegiac dystopia of encounter, it is equally important to focus on the dynamics of a less clearly defined configuration of force relations. Dil Das drank heavily, and a consideration of intoxication helps diagnose the workings of a kind of power that cut to the very heart of his being. If he was obsessed with hunting, he was addicted—in a metaphoric rather than strictly "medical" sense—to alcohol.

In the sociological literature on alcohol and alcoholism it is virtually a commonplace to say that intoxication is an escape mechanism from social oppression, economic exploitation, and political repression, as well as depression and other psychological problems. Perhaps less common, but still widely accepted, is the view that alcohol consumption and public drunkenness can be a form of protest against various mores, rules, and laws. However, both of these perspectives seem to be rather one-dimensional since their understanding of intoxication is both static and binary with reference to power relations. In any case, neither argument helps get beyond a purely objective, and inherently paradoxical discourse on cause and effect. This discourse talks a great deal about drunkenness but does not take intoxication seriously as a condition that can speak for itself. While intoxication may well be biochemically determined, I think it would be wrong to assume that drunkenness is therefore an insipid category whose significance is predetermined by objective factors. One tends to think of drunks as those who have lost control of their faculties, as people who do not make sense. However, it seems to me that the nonsensical, or irrational nature of intoxication—in spite of whatever its own discursive history as a category might be—allows for a critique of binary meaning and rationality, while at the same time being a condition of affected dependency and powerless addiction. It is, therefore, precisely because drunkenness cannot be simply construed as a one-dimensional critique of power that one is able to look at the complex mechanics of drinking, and what people say when they are drunk, in order to decode the subtle working of a pervasive, discursive field of force relations.

Unlike a significant number of other dudwallas—the man I found dead under a lamppost early one January morning above our house, the man who walked off the cliff below Ashton Court, the men I often saw, straddling their milk cans, hunched over unconscious as their horses took them home—and unlike Ratnu, Rukam, Sheri, Abloo, and Jankhi, who periodically drank so much they could not stand up, much less walk and talk, I am certain that Dil Das did not drink in order to drown his sorrow and escape the world around him. He drank, as he put it, in order to give himself courage in the face of various kinds of danger, to give himself strength, and also as an antidote to pain. But as his stories clearly indicate, mostly he drank for the pure and simple pleasure of getting drunk with friends. In this respect he was not in the least unique. Liquor is consumed in Garhwal, as in many other places, simply in order to build and rebuild bonds of friendship. But given the nature of his unique friendships, intoxication enabled Dil Das to focus sharply on a rather confusing aspect of his life. That is, he drank strategically— at least much of the time—in order to evoke the mood of a life that was already disoriented and blurred in certain crucial respects. In other words, intoxication provided an appropriate state of mind in which to construct, and to some extent live, his fused narrative; a state of mind which allowed the sober categories of clear distinction to dissolve into a meaningful fiction of mutuality. Intoxication makes this meaningful fiction possible, but visionary drunkenness is predicated on the dangerous praxis of seeing things as you want them to be, or as you hope they are—a kind of slurred imaginary communitas. And it is here where the pure pleasure of friendship can lead, if not to the bottom of a lamppost, the bottom of a cliff, or simply into the gutter, then into a world where borders are unmarked and the road home takes you into exile.

We were sitting outside of Dil Das's younger brother's home on the ridge above Pathreni, just below the old Tehri road. I had brought a bottle of "English" rum, known as *pakki*, and Dil Das had a bottle of *kacchi* (raw homebrew) with him. Earlier in the afternoon, Rukam Das and I had drunk half the bottle of rum, and before coming up from the village, Dil Das had drunk half of his bottle of kacchi. There were four or five of us there, and since rum is, on the whole, regarded as more potent than kacchi, we began to talk about the problem of fairly distributing what was left. Making what I thought was an offhand, and rather weak joke, I said that we should just mix the two together since they were of the same *jat* in any case.

The word *jat* can mean several things. On the one hand it signifies the sharp and hierarchical differences between caste groups. This meaning of the term has particular poignancy for those who, like Dil Das and his family, are classified as so different as to be "outcast." In effect, jat-based distinctions of this sort preclude the mixing of substances between high and low, pure and impure. On a more innocuous level, however, the term *jat* can simply mean a subtype or variety of some otherwise more uniform, inclusive category such as buffaloes, melons, or grass. Thus, depending on the level of discourse, kacchi and pakki are either very much alike or else radically different and "unmixable." In any event, the joke brought down the house and became a conversational trope for what remained of the afternoon. It was funnier than I had expected, I now think, because it played off of the ambiguities of power and difference which our encounter, and other such encounters before—the us and them of caste, class and nation—had already effaced. We mixed the rum and kacchi together that afternoon—in an old hot-water bottle which Dil Das used as a decanter—and agreed that it was half again as potent as rum on its own.

Over the years, Dil Das drank too deeply of the raw homebrew he distilled. He drank himself to death, in fact—if what the doctor said is true—just as he was trying to imagine and talk himself to life. Dil Das was obsessed with hunting and addicted to liquor, but it was talking—the endless process of telling and retelling stories—that kept him alive. What may well have killed him, finally, was that his friends the missionary boys—his complicit interlocutors—bid farewell and abruptly truncated a dialogue by bringing it all back home and unpacking it as nostalgia, data, and critical self-reflection. We sobered up. We stopped listening. And Dil Das, left speaking a story that no one was able to hear, ended up re-creating a past whose mythic structure progressively undermined his present. He talked himself to death, as it were, by telling stories whose significance could convey only the painful truth of an imagination constantly besieged by harsh reality.

Glossary

Terms

Auji (Baijgi): caste of drummer-musicians and basket-weavers.

babu: accountant; clerk.

barasingha: swamp deer; "twelve-horned deer." Dil Das used this term rather loosely to signify deer which may, in fact, have been of various other species.

bhajan: devotional songs.

chachi: aunty.

chakor: partridge.

chamar: leather worker.

chan: hamlet; cow shed.

chapati: flat, baked whole-wheat bread.

charpai: "four-legged" rope cot.

chela: disciple.

cholai: a type of grain.

cholu: small sour plum.

chowki: post; station; checkpoint.

chowkidar: watchman; guard.

dairywalla: an indigenous designation derived in part from English and used by local resident dudwallas when referring to seasonal milk contractors who rent in the Mussoorie milk-shed area during the peak market season.

dandi: palanquin.

das: enslaved; a state of complete, passionate, enraptured acquiescence used most often in the context of devotional Hinduism.

dehi: yogurt.

dhoti: loincloth.

dhudi: elephant grass.

dil: heart.

doab: two streams; the fertile land between the Jammuna and Ganga in the gangetic plain.

doon: an area of fertile land and lush forest between the Himalayan foot-hills and the Siwalik hills.

dudwalla: milkman.

garib: poor.

ghara: a large brass, clay, or aluminum water-carrying pot with a wide base and narrow mouth.

ghoral: mountain goat.

Gujar: nomadic Muslim buffalo herders.

gul gulla: a round confection.

gur: hard, unrefined molasses.

guru: preceptor; master teacher.

haldi: turmeric.

halwai: confectioner.

Hanuman: the monkey god of the Ramayana epic who is devoted to Lord Ram.

harijan: ex-untouchables; "children of god."

hiran: black buck.

jalebi: pretzel-shaped confection made from deep-fried flour paste and sugar syrup.

jat: caste; type; kind.

jid: cocksure attitude; bravado; pride.

jighuri: an ambiguous part of the anatomy that can mean either heart or liver.

kacchi: "raw" home-brewed liquor distilled from gur and blackberry roots.

kakar: barking deer.

kala ghas: "black grass;" a plant that is not indigenous to the Garhwal Himalayas. Although "black grass" is most likely the best translation, the proper term may be or have been "khala" and not "kala," thus changing the meaning to "ravine grass."

kandi: a large, loosely woven basket used for carrying things.

kankar: any small stone or pebble.

kastura: musk deer.

khichari: a mixture of rice and lentils cooked together.

khikot: a long, drawn-out yodel laugh used to punctuate songs.

khuda: god.

khukari: a distinctive machetelike knife used in Nepal.

kirtan: devotional songs.

kurta: a commonly worn, long, loose-fitting shirt in North Indian dress.

langur: a large, black-faced, long-tailed gray monkey that lives in troops.

L.G.: large-game shotgun shell filled with six to eight lead slugs.

lingam: the phallic form of Lord Shiva.

machan: a hunting blind, or seat, built in the branches of a tree.

maidan: flat plain; playing field.

malik: master; lord.

memsahib: madam.

mochi/moochi: cobbler; shoemaker.

nawab: aristocrat; landed gentry.

pahari: a general term that refers to the people who live in the lower Himalayas.

pakka makan: a solid cement, stone, or brick house; primary residence.

pakki: commercial "English" liquor like rum, gin, or whiskey.

pakori: batter-fried vegetables.

pan: a betel-leaf, betel-nut, lime paste, and spice concoction which is chewed for pleasure.

pandit: a Brahmin priest; used commonly as a title for all Brahmin men.

pinda: food; feed.

pradhan: headman.

prebhu: god.

sabzi: vegetables.

sahib: sir; mister.

sal: a straight-growing, broad-leaved, hardwood tree that grows in the terai.

saletu: a long, thick, pointed staff used for carrying bundles of fodder.

sardar: chief; a Sikh man.

serow: a small, short-horned goat.

seth: a wealthy man.

shaitan: demon.

shikar: hunting.

shripanch: literally means "honored five," but is used commonly to refer to a headman, leader, or government representative.

sur: a kind of beer fermented from a mixture of cooked grains and sour bread.

tangnor: ibex.

terai: a band of forest, scrub, and swampland between the Himalayan foothills and the cultivated plains of North India.

thekedar: contractor.

theki: milk container.

ustaad: master.

Place-Names

Aglar: A small river which runs from near Dhanaulti in the east down to the Jummuna in the west through a big valley which separates the first and second range of the Himalayas.

Agora: A small village above Uttarkashi on the way to Deodital.

Amritsar: A city in Punjab.

Bandar Chowki: Monkey's Post. A short, steep ridge extending directly below Pathreni to the west.

Bari Dhang: Big Cliff. A cliff of black granite on the ridge above Koldi-ghat which runs south from the pine forest below Moti Dhar village, more or less parallel to Donk, down as far as Loharighar, about four kilometers to the southeast of Pathreni.

Bhataghat: A small cluster of shops, storage rooms, and residences on the Tehri road two kilometers above Pathreni where toll tax is collected from all motor traffic.

Birganj: A town on the border between India and Nepal.

Chamasari: A village on Pari Tibba about four kilometers south of Path-reni. Chamasari refers both to the larger village *gram* (administrative unit), of which Pathreni is one of thirteen small settlements, and also the main village in the *gram*, which has a population of about two hundred.

Dehra Dun: A large urban center at the foot of the hills below Mussoorie.

Deodital: God's Lake. A small high-altitude lake located in a valley above Uttarkashi and below Bandarpunch. Stocked with trout by the British and appointed with a small forest bungalow, it is a popular site for fishing, trekking, and camping.

Devi Dhang: The Goddesses' Cliff. A spectacular scrub- and cactus-covered cliff off the end of the Donk ridge and opposite Chamasari. A sheer drop of almost four hundred meters from top to bottom, it is a place where ghoral can often be found.

Dhanaulti: A village about eighteen kilometers east on the road to Tehri near to which is a large *deodar* pine forest. It is a popular place for weekend treks.

Dhobighat: A village of washermen built on a stream at the extreme lower end of the cantonment at the base of Pari Tibba. The village was built by the colonial cantonment board to provide laundry facilities for military personnel. The Dhobis who live there now do laundry for schools, hotels, and individual clients.

Dhurmala: A cluster of chans out the Tehri road about twelve kilometers where Dil Das has close relatives.

Donk: A long, sparsely populated ridge which extends south from Pathreni for about two kilometers. It ends abruptly at Devi Dhang, where the ridge falls away four hundred meters straight down to a stream below the village of Chamasari.

Hackman's: One of Mussoorie's primary old colonial hotels located on the Mall.

Hamer and Company: One of the old colonial-era retail shops on the Mall.

Haridwar: One of the primary holy cities in the sacred geography of Hinduism. It is located at the point where the Ganga flows out of the mountains.

Jabbarkhet: A small cluster of shops where Dil Das and others from Pathreni get their supplies. It is located on the Tehri road below Landour. This is also where Mr. Jain the landlord lives.

Kathling: A glacier at the source of one of the primary tributaries of the Ganga.

Kimoi: A village to the northeast of Landour and about five kilometers north of Pathreni over the ridge near Bhataghat and down toward the Aglar River.

Koldighat: A cluster of three or four chans belonging to Dil Das and his neighbor Chattarmani, located along a stream in the valley two kilometers to the southeast of Pathreni at the bottom of Bari Dhang.

Kulu: A popular tourist spot and picturesque mountain valley in the Himachal Himalayas.

Kulukhet: The toll gate on the road up to Mussoorie from Dehra Dun.

Kumaun: The hill district to the east of Garhwal.

Landour: The eastern part of Mussoorie comprised of a large market, the cantonment extending above Mullangar Hill and, at the far end, the missionary community and Woodstock School.

Library Bazaar: A high-class shopping area on the western end of Mussoorie near the Savoy Hotel and the summer residences of various rajahs and maharajahs.

Loharighar: A small Brahmin village of twelve or fifteen homes located opposite Chamasari on the ridge running down from Moti Dhar just above the confluence of the Koldighat stream and the Dhobighat stream at the cremation grounds.

Ludhiana: A primary city in the state of Punjab, the site of one of the largest and best-equipped missionary-run medical facilities in North India.

Manali: A town in the Kulu valley.

Meerut: A major city between Dehra Dun and Delhi and the site of a large military cantonment.

Moti Dhar: A small village whose name means "thick ridge" located to the east of Pathreni just above Bari Dhang. It consists of five or six chans built on either side of the old pack trail which runs up from Rajpur and Sahasradhara in the doon to the south.

Mullangar: The easternmost part of the Landour bazaar. Mullangar refers to the shops, hotels, and residences located on a steep slope that marks the initial incline of the Landour hillside and the cantonment property.

Nagal: A village between the mountains and the plains. It has a bad reputation among the Chamasari villagers as a place that harbors thieves.

Nagdwan gaon: A village across the valley from Pathreni and to the east of Chamasari where Dil Das has some relatives.

Nag Tibba: The tallest mountain in the second range of the foothills about fifty kilometers to the north of Mussoorie across the Aglar.

Nainital: A hill station to the east of Mussoorie located on a lake.

Nali: A village located two ridge systems and ten kilometers to the east of Pathreni.

Northern Stores: The last retail shop on Mullangar Hill at the east end of Mussoorie. Prem babu, the Brahmin proprietor, was one of Dil Das's good friends.

Oakville: The Alter family home. It is a large, plains-style bungalow with nearly thirty rooms surrounded by gardens which my parents bought in 1980 after leaving Woodstock in 1978.

Palisades: A duplex house owned by Woodstock School where staff and faculty are housed.

Pari Tibba: Witch's or Fairy's Hill. A twelve-kilometer-long sloping ridge running from a high point in the west down to Sahasradhara to the east. Chamasari and Nagdwan gaon are on the ridge's northeast face and Dhobighat is in a shallow saddle below the western peak on one side and the east end of the Landour cantonment and Woodstock School on the other. Looking south and west from Pathreni, Pari Tibba blocks the view of the plains.

Pathreni: Dil Das's village; a small cluster of hamlets located on the south face of a long ridge within the larger boundary of Chamasari village on the first range of the Himalayas.

Pinerock: A duplex house near Woodstock School which was owned by the Presbyterian church. It is used to house faculty, staff, and missionary families.

Raipur: A town in the doon to the east of Dehra Dun.

Rhotang: A high-altitude pass at the top of the Kulu valley which leads back into the high Himalayas.

Rishikesh: A town twenty kilometers upriver from Haridwar.

Salarni: A chan in the valley between Pathreni and Dhobighat on the hillside facing Pari Tibba.

Savoy Hotel: Along with Hackman's, one of the most upscale colonial-era hotels in Mussoorie. Located near Library Bazaar at the west end of the Mall.

Seraghat: A cluster of three chans that belong to the Chamasari pradhan's family, located in the valley below Pathreni about two kilometers to the south.

Siwaliks: An old, worn-down mountain chain at the base of the Himalayas which marks off the southern edge of the doon.

Sungarghati: A saddle on the Donk ridge about a kilometer south of Pathreni.

Taftan: A house near Woodstock School for faculty, staff, and missionary families.

Tehri: An old city on the banks of the Ganga where the maharajah of Tehri Garhwal had his capital. Located to the east of Mussoorie about forty-five kilometers along a narrow, winding road.

Uttarkashi: Northern City of Lights. A small city of some religious significance, and one of the primary urban areas of Garhwal, located to the north of Pathreni on the banks of the Ganga on the road to Gangotari. Although it is only about 140 kilometers away from Mussoorie by motor-road, it takes most of a day to get there by driving east to Tehri and then back to the northwest along a road that cuts up the winding river valley.

Uttarkhand: The Himalayan region, roughly the mountainous area of Uttar Pradesh. If you split the word, drop a consonant, and lengthen the "a" (Uttar Kand) it means "The Epilogue."

Wynberg-Allen School: One of the older boarding schools in Mussoorie located on the ridge opposite Woodstock.

Notes

Chapter 7. Dairying: An Untold Story

1. Marshall Sahlins, "The Original Affluent Society," in *Stone Age Economics* (New York: Aldine, 1972).

Chapter 11. A Hybrid History of Encounter

1. Paul Rabinow, *Reflections on Fieldwork in Morocco* (Berkeley: University of California Press, 1977); Vincent Crapanzano, *Tuhami: Portrait of a Moroccan* (Chicago: University of Chicago Press, 1980). See also Kevin Dwyer, *Moroccan Dialogues: Anthropology in Question* (Baltimore: Johns Hopkins University Press, 1982).

2. In particular it is worth noting here James Clifford and George Marcus, eds., *Writing Culture: The Poetics and Politics of Ethnography* (Berkeley: University of California Press, 1985); George E. Marcus and Michael M. J. Fischer, eds., *Anthropology as Cultural Critique: An Experimental Moment in the Human Sciences* (Chicago: University of Chicago Press, 1986); James Clifford, "On Ethnographic Authority," *Representations* 1, no. 2 (1983): 118–46, and Vincent Crapanzano, "The Writing of Ethnography," *Dialectical Anthropology* 2 (1977): 69–73.

3. Clifford Geertz, *Works and Lives: The Anthropologist as Author* (Stanford: Stanford University Press, 1988).

4. See, for example, Claudia Salazar, "A Third World Woman's Text: Between the Politics of Criticism and Cultural Politics," in Sherna Berger Gluck and Daphne Patai, eds., *Women's Words* (New York: Routledge, 1991), 93–106; Doris Sommer, " 'Not Just a Personal Story': Women's *Testimonios* and the Plural Self," in Bella Brodzki and Celeste Schenck, eds., *Life/Lines: Theorizing Women's Autobiography* (Ithaca: Cornell University Press, 1988), 107–30; Inderpal Grewal and Caren Kaplan, eds., *Scattered Hegemonies: Postmodernity and Transnational Feminist Practices* (Minneapolis: University of Minnesota Press, 1994); Soheir Morsy, "Fieldwork in My Egyptian Homeland: Toward the Demise of Anthropology's Distinctive-other Hegemonic Tradition," in S. Altorki and C. El-Solh, eds., *Arab Women in the Field: Studying Your Own Society.* (Syracuse: Syracuse University Press, 1988). See also, Jose E. Limon, "Representation, Ethnicity, and the Precursory Ethnography: Notes of a Native Anthropologist," in Richard G. Fox, ed., *Recapturing Anthropology: Working in the Present* (Santa Fe: School of American Research, 1991).

5. Judith Stacey, "Can There Be a Feminist Ethnography?" *Women's Studies*

International Forum 11, no. 2 (1988), republished in Gluck and Patai, eds., *Women's Words*, 111–120; Lila Abu-Lughod, "Can There be Feminist Ethnography?" *Women and Performance: A Journal of Feminist Theory* 5 (1990): 7–27; Marilyn Strathern, "An Awkward Relationship: The Case of Feminism and Anthropology," *Signs* 15, no. 1 (1989): 7–33; Ann Oakley, "Interviewing Women: A Contradiction in Terms," in Helen Roberts, ed., *Doing Feminist Research* (Boston: Routledge and Kegan Paul, 1981), 30–61; Daphne Patai, "U.S. Academics and Third World Women: Is Ethical Research Possible?" in Gluck and Patai, eds., *Women's Words*, 137–53.

6. Lila Abu-Lughod, "Writing Against Culture," in Fox, ed., *Recapturing Anthropology*, 137–62.

7. See, for example, H. David Brumble, *An Annotated Bibliography of American Indian and Eskimo Autobiographies* (Lincoln: University of Nebraska Press, 1981).

8. John (Fire) Lame Deer and Richard Erdoes, *Lame Deer: Seeker of Visions* (New York: Washington Square Press, 1972); Paul Radin, *The Autobiography of a Winnebago Indian* (New York: Dover Press, 1963); Leo W. Simmons, *Sun Chief: The Autobiography of a Hopi Indian*, (New Haven: Yale University Press, 1974); Theodora Kroeber, *Ishi in Two Worlds: A Biography of the Last Wild Indian in North America* (Berkeley: University of California Press, 1961).

9. Sara Suleri, *The Rhetoric of English India* (Chicago: University of Chicago Press, 1992), pp. 1–2.

10. Abu-Lughod, "Writing Against Culture."

11. Suleri, *Rhetoric of English India*, 2.

12. Ibid.

13. E. Valentine Daniel, *Fluid Signs: Being a Person the Tamil Way* (Berkeley: University of California Press, 1984), 57.

14. E. Valentine Daniel, *Charred Lullabies: Chapters in an Anthropography of Violence* (Berkeley: University of California Press, 1997).

15. Arjun Appadurai, "Putting Hierarchy in Its Place," in George E. Marcus, ed., *Rereading Cultural Anthropology* (Durham: Duke University Press, 1992).

16. Ruth Behar, *The Vulnerable Observer: Anthropology that Breaks Your Heart* (Boston: Beacon Press, 1996); Smadar Levi, "Border Poets: Translating by Dialogues," in Ruth Behar and Deborah Gordon, eds., *Women Writing Culture* (Berkeley: University of California Press, 1995), 414–27; Kirin Narayan, "How Native Is a 'Native' Anthropologist?" *American Anthropologist* 95, no. 3 (1993): 671–86; Kamala Visweswaran, *Fictions of Feminist Ethnography* (Minneapolis: University of Minnesota Press, 1994); Lila Abu-Lughod, *Writing Women's Worlds: Bedouin Stories* (Berkeley: University of California Press, 1993).

17. Michel Foucault, *The History of Sexuality*, vol. I (New York: Vintage Books, 1990), 96–98.

18. Lila Abu-Lughod, "The Romance of Resistance: Tracing Transformations of Power Through Bedouin Women," *American Ethnologist* 17, no. 1 (1990): 42.

19. Foucault, *History of Sexuality*, 96.

Acknowledgments

A significant portion of this book was written between 3 and 6 A.M. from 1992 to 1994 in Kalamazoo, Michigan, and Landour, Uttar Pradesh, India, during a time when I was trying to do various other, more practical and pragmatic things, both personal and professional. I must, therefore, with somewhat bleary eyes, express my most heartfelt appreciation to Peter and Nathaniel, who have awakened me to many things, but who, at a critical point in time, were fast asleep.

Not only because it was written at odd hours of darkness but also because of how I like to work, nobody saw the manuscript until I thought it was completely done. It is not directly part of my other work, and therefore I have not engaged others in it directly. Nevertheless, I am indebted to a number of people who have, perhaps in ways they are not aware of—and may well disavow—contributed to my thinking on the subject at hand. Most significantly Nicole Constable, caught in the dangerous space between colleague and spouse, has, in addition to helping me get the kids to bed, awakened me to many, many things. She also was employed while I was not able to find work, and thereby has paid, in some sense, for the enforced leisure of writing I was able to impose upon myself. For a debt of many dimensions, many, many thanks. My brother, Steve Alter, read a draft of the manuscript, and provided useful comments and encouragement.

The others who have read and commented on the manuscript are, for the most part, I am afraid, anonymous. Nevertheless, I am eternally grateful to two readers who provided extremely useful critiques that have immeasurably improved the final product. For locating these anonymous readers, and providing good counsel and encouragement along the way, I would like to thank Marlie Wasserman, Peter Agree, and, most directly, Patricia Smith. Over the years the manuscript has bounced around a bit, but I am delighted that it has come to rest at the University of Pennsylvania Press. Patricia Smith's enthusiasm for the project is greatly appreciated. Noreen O'Connor's hard work has made this a better book. My sincere thanks to Paul Stoller, whose praise for the manuscript couldn't have come at a better time.

When reading acknowledgments in other books that are replete with name after name of individuals who made significant contributions in one context or another, I am always amazed, with a sense of admiration tinged with exhaustion, of how public and intellectually didactic most peoples' scholarship is. For better or worse, I am afraid, I tend to work behind closed doors and encounter books more than people. Consequently, in a very important way, the number of individuals I should acknowledge is nearly uncountable. Books tend to pile up, with long, entangled pedigrees, ideas upon ideas upon ideas that countless people have had a hand in shaping. But to name names here would, I am afraid, be interminable and not entirely fair. Nonetheless, I am indebted to a number of scholars who have shaped my thinking and have had a hand in shaping how I read books and untangle ideas: Johannes Fabian and Betsy Traube, on one register, and Linc Keiser on another, while I was at Wesleyan; Paul Rabinow and James Clifford on one register, and Gerry Berreman on another, while I was at Berkeley. I dedicate this book to Gerry for what he has taught me about anthropology and the politics of caste, and for his uncompromising support over the years. I dedicate it also to Betsy, who introduced me to anthropology and the study of myths, to the various pleasures of French social theory, and to the fundamental importance of writing clearly in order to think critically. With any luck this book is both a mythology and a politics of truth.

Index